Okanagan Trips & Trails

A guide to backroads and hiking trails in BC's Okanagan-Similkameen region.

by
Judie Steeves
&
Murphy Shewchuk

Sonotek® Publishing Ltd.
P.O. Box 1752
Merritt, BC Canada V1K 1B8

www.sonotek.com

Canadian Cataloguing in Publication Data

Steeves, Judie.
  Okanagan trips & trails

  Includes bibliographical references and index.
  ISBN 0-929069-12-9

1. Outdoor recreation--British Columbia--Okanagan-Similkameen--
Guidebooks.
2. Trails--British Columbia--Okanagan-Similkameen--Guidebooks.
3. Okanagan-Similkameen (B.C.)--Guidebooks. I. Shewchuk, Murphy. II.
Title.
FC3845.O4A3 1999   917.11'5044   C98-911072-9   F1089.O5S73 1999

Sonotek® Publishing Ltd.
P.O. Box 1752,
Merritt, BC
Canada V1K 1B8

Telephone and facsimile: (250) 378-5930
E-mail: publisher@sonotek.com — URL http://www.sonotek.com

Photographs by the authors unless otherwise credited. All illustrations are protected by copyright and may not be reproduced in any form without prior written consent of the publisher.

Cover Photo: Gillian, left, and Emily Vergnano hike the upper trail in Kalamoir Regional Park with Kelowna and Okanagan Lake in the background. Photo © Judie Steeves.

Printed in Canada.

Map 1
The Okanagan - Similkameen region of southwestern British Columbia.

Table of Contents

Acknowledgments

The seed for a book on hiking trails and backroads in and around the Okanagan Valley was planted in the summer of 1997. Judie Steeves had embarked on a series on hiking trails in her weekly *Trail Mix* outdoor column for the Kelowna Capital News and Murphy Shewchuk's *Okanagan Country* backroads book was nearly out of print and in need of an update.

A chance meeting brought the two together early in 1998, when Murphy was touring the Okanagan, promoting the recently-released second edition of his *Coquihalla Country* guidebook.

Both seemed headed toward an Okanagan outdoors book featuring trails and backroads, so it seemed natural to work together on such a project. Nancy Wise of Sandhill Book Marketing in Kelowna helped nurture the seed. It is still growing, but the time has come to sample the crop.

A number of groups and individuals deserve thanks for their invaluable assistance. They include members of the Central Okanagan Naturalists' Club; the Western Canada Wilderness Committee; Canadian EarthCare Society; Jeanette Bosch and other staff in the Central Okanagan Regional District Parks Department; Roger Venables and other staff at the Ministry of Forests; BC Parks staff; City of Kelowna Parks Department; the Lakeview Irrigation District; Ursula Surtees, curator of the Kelowna Museum; authors and historians such as Bill Barlee, Harley Hatfield, and curator Randy Manuel of the Penticton Museum; naturalist Joan Burbridge; photographer Gordon Bazzana; Mary Bailey, Scott Boswell and many others.

Dedications

Special thanks go to hiking partners Sharon Coleman, Carol Ulm, daughters Gillian and Emily and their friends, and my husband Dennis Vergnano.

I would especially like to acknowledge the late Chess Lyons. He certainly had a profound effect on my interest in identifying plant life, beginning when I was a child and my Mom gave me an autographed hardcover copy of his freshly-reprinted *Trees, Shrubs and Flowers to know in British Columbia.*

—Judie

I would like to add my heartfelt thanks to my wife Katharine. Without her note-taking skills and knowledge of the flora and fauna of the region, my portion of this book would not have been possible.

—Murphy

•••

Introduction

British Columbia is the custodian of some of the most spectacular wilderness remaining in the world, including the unique ecosystems of the Okanagan basin.

However, there has been and continues to be degradation of these precious wild areas even by those who revere them.

As more and more of us discover the wonders of our natural environment, it becomes increasingly important that each of us ensures it is protected and preserved so our children may also know its wonders.

Keep this in mind as you head out on the backroads and byways. Educate yourself to protect and preserve our natural areas, even as you enjoy them.

Remember to protect yourself as well, by learning about the nature of the area your trip or trail will take you into before you leave. Arm yourself with up-to-date maps, a compass (and the skill to use it), water, some sustenance, and suitable clothing.

Always let someone know where you plan to go and when you'll be back, and don't travel alone.

Water and waste.

Although it's essential to life, water can harm that life instead. No open body of water should be considered safe to drink without first treating it for invisible parasites and microorganisms which can otherwise cause mild to acute illness.

One of the most common causes of illness is the *Giardia lamblia* cyst, which multiplies in the intestinal tract of warm-blooded animals such as humans, and causes an illness often called beaver fever. The cysts are spread in water contaminated by the feces of infected animals or people and are present in more than 70 per cent of our watersheds.

To be safe, either boil your water for one minute before cooling and drinking it; treat it with four drops of iodine tincture per litre or four drops of pure household bleach per four litres of water, up to double that if cloudy; or filter it with a special system available in outdoor stores.

If using the iodine or bleach method, make sure you stir it in and let it sit for at least half an hour before drinking.

Cryptosporidium is resistant to chlorine, but boiling takes care of it.

We can help prevent the spread of such internal infections by being responsible about disposal of our waste in the outdoors.

Never use streams and lakes as a bath, toilet or sink.

Use the proper facilities provided whenever possible, but otherwise when hiking or camping in the back country, the ideal solution is to carry out all human waste.

If that goes further than your commitment to preserving the natural environment, do ensure you never urinate or defecate within 100 metres (110 yards) of open water. Instead, dig a small hole and replace the sod after you're through.

When camping, wash water should be disposed of in a hole, 25-30 centimetres (one foot) deep, at least 100 metres from any body of water.

Create as little waste as possible. Always pack out what you pack in.

In wilderness areas, tread lightly in both the figurative and the literal sense, leaving no trace of your presence behind you. That way, both you and those who follow will enjoy fields of wild flowers, trees alive with birds and forests full of wildlife.

Leaving no trace begins with good planning before you depart, eliminating leftovers and reducing the garbage produced while on your trip.

Wild ways.

Wherever possible, use existing trails. Do not detour around muddy sections since the added traffic will break down the trail edge and widen it, or cause multiple trails which scar the natural areas that are the reason you go hiking.

Where trails don't already exist, select a route over the most durable terrain such as gravel creek beds, sandy or rocky areas. Whenever possible, avoid steep, loose slopes and wet areas.

Many plants die if they're stepped on and some soils will erode even after being trampled lightly.

When camping in a wilderness area, select a site that would be least damaged by your stay. Choose either high use sites already damaged or pristine sites in durable areas such as on rocky terrain or a gravel bar rather than the forest floor or sites with low growing shrubs.

Do not cut trees for firewood, furniture or boughs for beds. If you must have a fire, use an existing fire ring if possible, built on rocky or sandy soil away from trees, dry vegetation or roots. Use only as much dry dead wood as you need.

Burn your fire down to ash before pouring water on it until it is cold enough for you to lay your bare hand on it. Leave no sign of your fire.

Remember that you are entering wild animals' homes when you're in the wilderness. Respect their space and minimize your intrusion on their lives. View them from enough distance that they are unaware of your presence.

Leave your pets at home.

Trail etiquette.

Trails are often used by hooves, feet and wheels, but by using common sense, communication and courtesy, conflict, danger and damage can be avoided.

Trail protocol suggests that the most mobile yields the right-of-way, but there are exceptions to the rule. Ideally, cyclists yield to everyone and hikers yield to horses. A loaded string of horses going uphill always has the right of way, and a cyclist climbing steeply will appreciate the same courtesy.

Hikers: If you encounter horse riders, your group should step off to the same side of the trail, the lower side if possible, allowing two to three metres for them to pass. If you come up on horses from behind, greet the riders before you pass so they're aware you're there before you startle either the animal or rider.

Mountain Bikers: Always anticipate a horse or hiker around a blind curve. Prevent the sudden, unexpected encounter possible from a bike's quick and silent approach. Yield to hikers and equestrians. Get off the bike and move to the lower side of the trail to let horses pass. When approaching from behind, speak so they know you're there. Learn to minimize damage to trails with techniques such as riding and not sliding, and cycle on designated trails. Meadows are easily damaged by bicycle tires. Stay off trails when they're wet and muddy since they'll become pathways for water erosion.

Horse Riders: Use an experienced, steady mount, and give clear directions to other trail users on how you would like them to stand clear. In steep, rough country, downhill traffic yields to uphill travellers, but use common sense. Whoever can pull off easiest should. Avoid soft and muddy trails.

Warn others of wire, potholes and boggy areas.

Above all, respect private property, 'No Trespassing' signs, and leave gates as you found them.

•••

Fig 1:
Hiking the ridges.
(Photo HIK-025 © Murphy Shewchuk)

Symbols used in this book.

	Photography Opportunities.
	Wildlife Viewing.
	Birdwatching.
	Wildflowers.
	Interpretive Trail.
	Point of Interest.
	Viewpoint.
	Picnic Site.
	Open Picnic Shelter.
	Enclosed Picnic Shelter.
	Sleeping Shelter.
	Wilderness Campsite.
	RV Park.
	Campground.
	Campfire Ring.
	RV Sani-Station.
	Public Washrooms.
	Amphitheatre.

	Accommodations.
	Meal Service.
	Fuel.
	Public Telephone.
	First Aid Station.
	Hospital.
	Museum.
	Airport.
	Information Centre.
	Marina.
	Swimming Beach.
	Angling.
	Boat Launch.
	Canoeing & Kayaking.
	Sailing.
	Motor boating.
	Windsurfing.
	Hiking Trail.

Rock Climbing Route.

 Golf Course.

 Rockhounding.

 Shooting Sports.

 Horse Riding.

 Bicycle Trail.

 Mountain Bicycle Trail.

 Motorcycle Trail.

 Four-Wheel-Drive Road.

 Canoe Portage.

 Winter Sports.

 Ice Fishing.

 Alpine Ski Hill.

 Nordic Ski Trail.

 Snowshoe Trail.

 Sledding Hill.

 Ice Skating.

 Snowmobile Trail.

 Chairlift.

 Gondola Lift.

 Cave.

 Tunnel.

Important Notice!

Although every effort has been made to provide accurate information, backroad and trail conditions in the Okanagan Valley and surrounding mountains are constantly changing. Consequently, neither the authors nor the publisher can guarantee the continuing accuracy of this information.

We will, however, attempt to post any changes or corrections to our World Wide Web site at http://www.sonotek.com between printings.

We look forward to corrections and comments on ways that you think this book may be improved. Please write to the publisher at the address listed in the front of the book. You can also e-mail us at <publisher@sonotek.com>.

•••

1

North Okanagan & Shuswap

Vernon and Area

The North Okanagan forms a transition zone between the hot, dry southern reaches of the Okanagan Valley and the wetter, more moderate Shuswap region. The physical division between the two drainage basins, however, is barely perceptible. If it were not for a geographical marker alongside Highway 97A north of Armstrong, most travellers would not notice the change.

The North Okanagan region offers many unique recreational opportunities. Silver Star Ski Resort ranks among the best in the province and western North America. The skiing and snowmobiling trails here become hiking, biking and horse riding trails in mid-summer, presenting an opportunity to explore sub-alpine forests and alpine meadows. South of Vernon, less than an hour from Silver Star, the semi-desert rocky ridges and emerald green bays of Kalamalka Provincial Park present a sharp contrast to the forested alpine. With sheltered, sandy beaches and 10 kilometres of trails through the grasslands, it is an attractive recreation destination.

Somewhere between the two climatic extremes lay several other parks. Ellison Provincial Park, southwest of Vernon on Okanagan Lake, also has rocky bluffs, sheltered bays and sandy beaches, but it has a few more trees to keep it a touch cooler in mid-summer. Mabel Lake Provincial Park, higher and farther into the Monashee Mountains, north of Lumby, has sandy beaches and clear water in the heart of the forest.

When you've had your fill of strenuous activity the historic O'Keefe Ranch, northwest of Vernon, is open all year around for a glimpse of the area's colorful past. The museum in Vernon, the Armstrong Fair and a host of other diversions will also keep you enjoyably occupied.

While researching and writing this book, it quickly became apparent that the region could easily fill a book of its own, thus what we offer here is only a brief glimpse at what lies off the beaten track. May it whet your appetite enough to keep you exploring until that book is written.

May we meet along the way.

•••

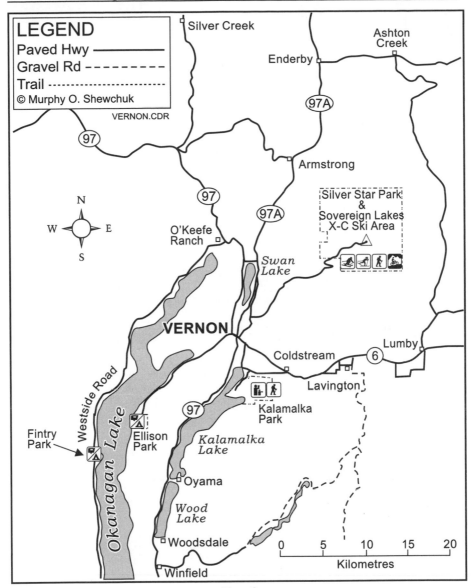

LEGEND
Paved Hwy ————
Gravel Rd - - - - - - -
Trail ....
© Murphy O. Shewchuk

VERNON.CDR

Map 2

Vernon and the North Okanagan area.

2

Ellison Provincial Park

By Murphy Shewchuk

Statistics:	For map, see page 13.

Distance:	16 km, from the junction of Hwy 97 and 6.
Travel Time:	One half hour.
Elev. Diff:	Minimal.
Condition:	Paved throughout.
Season:	Year around.
Topo Maps:	Vernon, BC 82 L/SW (1:100,000).
Forest Maps:	Vernon Forest District.
Communities:	Vernon and Okanagan Landing.

Located just 16 kilometres from downtown Vernon, on the northeastern shore of Okanagan Lake, 200-hectare (500 acre) Ellison Provincial Park is a land of rocky, forested headlands and sheltered, sandy bays. The diverse terrain, combined with the North Okanagan's relatively dry climate (less than 40 cm of precipitation per year) and abundant sunshine, makes it a favorite for a wide range of recreational activities.

Okanagan Landing Road.

To get there, take 25th Avenue west from the junction of Highway 97 and Highway 6 on the south side of downtown Vernon. Follow 25th Avenue as it becomes Okanagan Landing Road, and continue south along the east shore of Okanagan Lake to the end of the road at the park.

Fifty-four private, yet spacious campsites, suitable for most types of camping units, are tucked into an attractive natural forest setting with toilets and firewood nearby. A children's playground is located in the large grassed playing field near the amphitheatre. For additional security there is a resident park contractor. A campground host is also on site from May through September to answer questions.

Easy walking trails provide access to the lakeshore where rocky headlands separate two beautiful bays, with coarse sandy beaches. Here, scattered under the shade of the forest canopy, are more than 50 picnic tables with fire pits.

Drinking water and firewood are nearby and the large change house includes flush toilets and showers. The various trails across the rocky headlands provide some boulder-climbing excitement for young explorers and an opportunity to bird watch or photograph the scenery and wildflowers.

The gradually sloping bottom and the warm water make the three main beaches very popular during the summer months. For safety reasons, swim buoys at South Beach closely follow the edge of an underwater shelf. Watch for steep drop-offs outside the buoys and anywhere along the rocky cliff edges. Please remember that there are no lifeguards on duty. Don't swim alone and watch your children whenever they are near or in the water.

Diving and snorkeling.

Scuba diving/snorkeling buoys in Otter Bay mark the boundaries of western Canada's first freshwater dive park, sponsored by the Vernon Scuba Club and BC Parks. Sunken artifacts add to the variety of fascinating plant and animal life that thrive in the bay's warm waters.

Abundant fish life, including carp, burbot, kokanee and trout, is attracted to the rocky outcroppings and vegetation along the lake front. The best fishing is in the deeper waters offshore anywhere along the north arm of Okanagan Lake. A BC angling license is required.

While there isn't a boat launch at the park (the closest is six kilometres to the north), water skiing, cruising, and fishing are popular park activities. Mooring buoys offshore in South Bay and Otter Bay are part of a marine park system sponsored by the Okanagan's yacht clubs. Houseboats can pull ashore at Sandy Beach. The standard park camping fee is charged for overnight use by boaters. If staying in the campground you can leave your boat pulled up on the beach, but please remove all life jackets and other equipment for safe keeping.

Printed guides are available for more than six kilometres of walking trails that provide access to many of the park's natural features and scenic view-points. A one-hour return walk on the nature trail will take you up and down the undulating benches typical of this portion of the Thompson Plateau. Most of the park is dominated by ponderosa pine and Douglas fir stands with grassy open areas and rocky outcroppings along the headlands. Porcupine and Columbian ground squirrels are commonly seen near the nature trail.

A park interpreter is in attendance from mid-June through Labor Day to pro-vide a variety of entertaining and informative programs on the area's human and natural heritage. Highlights during the season are the children's programs and special visits from the McMillan Planetarium. Because of the distance from the city lights, Ellison's clear night sky provides some of the best star viewing in the Okanagan.

Excellent base.

Ellison Provincial Park can also be an excellent base from which to explore the North Okanagan. The region's climate has supported its position as a prime fruit growing and ranching area since the mid 1800s. Cycling the rolling hills past orchards, farms and ranches can be an excellent family activity. Historic O'Keefe Ranch, northwest of Vernon, is open all year and it is well worth exploring. (See *Westside Road*, page 44, for more information.)

Kalamalka Provincial Park, just east of Vernon, (see page 17) has broad, sandy beaches and 10 kilometres of trails through the grasslands. Mabel Lake Provincial Park, 23 kilometres north of Lumby, (see page 28) has beautiful sandy beaches, open grassy playing fields and great fishing. The 81-unit Mabel Lake campground is not quite as busy mid-week during July and August.

Fig 2:
The rock bluffs at Ellison Prov. Park.
(Photo ELP-008 © Murphy Shewchuk)

Echo Lake Provincial Park, off Highway 6, 47 kilometres east of Vernon, has picnicking and fishing with boat launch facilities, a store and fishing equipment rentals. Echo Lake Resort in Echo Lake Provincial Park has housekeeping cabins and a campground. Reservations are preferred.

Silver Star Park, 22 kilometres northeast of Vernon, has chairlift operations for summer mountain biking and hiking alpine meadows, with alpine and Nordic skiing in winter. (See *Silver Star Park* on page 20 for details.)

•••

3

Kalamalka Park

By Murphy Shewchuk

Statistics:	For maps, see pages 13 & 18.

Distance:	7.6 km, Highway 97 in Coldstream to parking lot.
Travel Time:	Less than 10 minutes, on paved streets.
Season:	Year around.
Topo Maps:	Vernon, BC 82 E/SW (1:100,000).
Forest Maps:	Vernon Forest District.
Communities:	Vernon and Coldstream.

Located on the northeast side of beautiful Kalamalka Lake, Kalamalka Provincial Park encompasses an 890-hectare (2,200-acre) remnant of the natural grasslands that once stretched from Vernon to Osoyoos. Access is easy. If you are travelling from the south on Highway 97, you can turn right on College Way in Coldstream and follow it and then Kickwillie Loop down to Kalamalka Lake. Swing left and follow Westkal Road to Kalamalka Road, keep right past the public beach to Kidston Road (3.8 kilometres from Hwy 97). Turn right on Kidston Road and follow it another 3.8 kilometres to the parking lot. Access from Highway 6 is via Kalamalka Road and Kidston Road.

Kalamalka Provincial Park has all-season appeal. Easy walking and horse riding trails wind through the grassland slopes and along forest ridges. Many scenic viewpoints overlook a shoreline indented with bays and tiny coves. The spring wildflowers are truly spectacular. In summer, the beaches attract boaters and swimmers wanting relative seclusion. The golden hues of autumn have their own appeal. In winter, cross-country skiers enjoy the park's wild beauty and rolling hills.

As shown on maps posted at the parking lot and trailheads, BC Parks has established three distinct color-coded management zones: These color-coded zones indicate the facilities provided and the restrictions imposed to reflect the special needs of each area. Red (Jade and Juniper Bays, Cosens Bay Beaches), Yellow (Turtle's Head Point) and Green (Rattlesnake Hill, Bear Valley, Cosens Valley, grasslands) zones have been established to ensure a balance between recreational requirements and the need to protect the park's unique environment.

Wide range of activities.

The range of park activities at Kalamalka Park is unusually wide. Some of the old roads and hiking trails are being upgraded to provide easy walking to the main ecological features and view points. Horse riding is permitted in portions of the park and access to routes through the grasslands and over Rattlesnake Hill are provided at the Red, Watertower, Hydro and Cosens Bay gates. Horses are

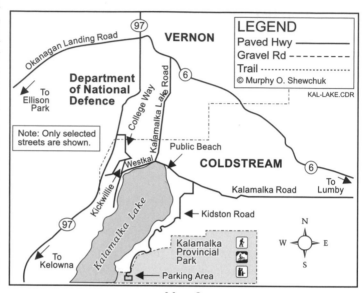

Map 3
Vernon and Kalamalka Lake Park area.

permitted in the Cosens Bay Beach area, but only from October 31 to March 31.

Bicycle riding is allowed on routes in the grasslands and Rattlesnake Hill. However, it is worth noting that these routes are shared with hikers and horse riders. Juniper Bay has a picnic site just above the beach with tables and grassy play area. A display explaining the park's natural history is located nearby. Swim buoys mark off swimming areas in Jade, Juniper and Cosens Bays. Boaters are encouraged to use Cosens Beach and Jade Beach as well as the many tiny coves between Rattlesnake Point and Cosens Bay. Kekuli Bay Provincial Park, across Kalamalka Lake, has boat-launching facilities.

Dryland plants and animals.

Kalamalka Park and the surrounding area has a diversity of wildlife although none is particularly abundant. You may see coyote, deer, or black bear but are more likely to observe Columbian ground squirrels and yellow-bellied marmots. Pacific rattlesnakes, shy creatures that only wish to be left alone, are an important part of this fascinating ecosystem. For botanists, there are four distinct plant associations — arid grasslands, woodland, forest and wet areas — with more than 430 species of vascular plants so far identified in the park (10 of these are rare in British Columbia).

Please be aware that this is a natural environment protecting one of the few remaining habitats for Pacific rattlesnakes. Practice safe hiking procedures when in rattlesnake country — stay on the trails and watch where you are putting your hands, feet and seat. These animals usually strike only when threatened with no chance to escape. If a bite does occur, try to stay calm and seek medical aid at the Vernon Hospital.

Fig 3:
Rock bluffs at Kalamalka Provincial Park. (Photo 437-D-18A © Murphy Shewchuk)

Stay on the trails.

There is another reason to be aware of where you sit. This area was used as a military target range during World War II and unexploded bombs are still working their way to the surface.

Of special note to drivers is that Cosens Bay Road is open only to authorized vehicle traffic. Properly licensed motorcycles, trail bikes and mini bikes operated by licensed drivers are permitted in the parking areas, but nowhere else in the park. From a safety perspective, please keep close watch on children: there are no lifeguards in attendance. Deep drop-offs exist outside the buoyed swim areas and along the lakeshore. Cliff jumping can be extremely hazardous because of projecting rock shelves and debris just below the surface. Other regulations concerning pets, parking and noise are posted in the park.

•••

4

Silver Star Park

By Murphy Shewchuk

Statistics: For map, see page 13.

Distance:	22 km, from Highway 97 in Vernon.
Travel Time:	One half hour.
Condition:	Paved throughout.
Season:	The year around.
Topo Maps:	Vernon, BC 82 L/SW (1:100,000).
Forest Maps:	Vernon Forest District Recreation Map.
Communities:	Vernon.

There are a few who think that mountains have no personalities — that they are mere piles of rock held together by the moss and trees that cover their slopes. These nonbelievers have obviously never skied the mountains of British Columbia's Okanagan region.

Take Silver Star, for example. This peak has a warm, western personality garnered, in part, from the resort staff and the friendly residents of nearby Vernon. First impressions are lasting impressions. And should you arrive in the evening, the first impression at the start of your Silver Star ski vacation is of an 1890s Old Canadian West village.

Former silver mine.

Silver Star comes by its Old West theme quite honestly. Some sources suggested the mountain, originally named Aberdeen Mountain, received its present name from the starlike appearance of the peak on a moonlit winter night and the silver deposits that were discovered near the 1915 metre (6,280 foot) summit in the 1890s. Silver Star was a mining hotspot in 1896 when a quartz vein containing silver, lead and gold was discovered. A forestry lookout was built near the top in 1914 and skiing began in the early 1920s. An access road was built into the area in 1939, setting off the chain of events that led to today's modern development.

Ski to your door.

Today, the scene on your evening arrival from Vernon is of well-lit ski slopes, a cozy hotel complex and the mellow lighting of the pedestrian square. Everything is true ski-to-your-door at Silver Star. Night skiing on the lower slopes and a lighted five-kilometre cross-country loop trail are only a few steps from any of the hotels. Daylight broadens the picture. The hotels look bigger — big enough to accommodate more than 1850 people. The mountain looks bigger — in fact, with the Putnam Creek addition, it's twice as big as it was a few years ago. And the service is even friendlier.

Silver Star offers a blend of skiing under near-perfect conditions. Fine slope grooming often means an earlier start and a longer spring skiing season than other ski resorts. The original Vance Creek area of Silver Star Mountain offered plenty of variety. But the recent opening of the adjacent Putnam Creek development has doubled the skiing terrain to 260 hectares (700 acres), adding considerable intermediate and expert terrain. The addition also makes Silver Star the second largest ski area in British Columbia. For those interested in specs, the mountain now has a vertical difference of 760 metres (2,500 feet) and an average snowpack of 250 centimetres (100 inches). It also had, at last count, more than 60 runs served by three quad chairlifts, two double chairs, two T-bars and one handle tow.

Fig 4:
Silver Star Ski School. © Murphy Shewchuk

If you brought your skinny skis, you will be particularly pleased with the range of cross-country ski trails on Silver Star Mountain. A low-cost lift ride takes you to the top of the Summit Chair and the beginning of a well-groomed 15-kilometre loop that brings you back to the hotel complex — with plenty of diversions. The diversions include some 50 kilometres of trails that are part of the Sovereign Lake network in Silver Star Provincial Park and 20 kilometres of groomed trails adjacent to the ski village.

Fig 5:
Bridget and Harriet try out the Sovereign Lake trails on Silver Star Mountain.
(Photo SSS-053 © Murphy Shewchuk)

The Sovereign Lake ski trails are operated by the North Okanagan Cross Country Ski Club. The club assists with the construction and planning of the ski trails, parking lots and warm-up shelters under a park use permit. A fee is charged for trail usage to help offset maintenance costs. The Vernon Snowmobile Club has also been involved with trails in the park.

Mountain bike in summer.

Silver Star doesn't shut down in summer. From late June until Labor Day, you can join the Silver Star Mile High Descent Tour that takes you from the summit, through alpine meadows, lush forests, grasslands and orchards to the city of Vernon. You and your mountain bike will ride the chairlift to the top and be guided back down via the ski trails and road to a waiting bus which will then take you back up to the ski village. Rental bikes are available. If you find guided tours too restrictive, you can take your time and your camera and explore the mountain trails on foot, bicycle or horseback.

To get to Silver Star, turn east off Highway 97 on 48th Avenue (Silver Star Road) in north Vernon and follow the signs for 22 kilometres to the ski village. Good snow tires are necessary in winter.

•••

5

Three Valley to Enderby via Mabel Lake

By Murphy Shewchuk

Statistics:	For maps, see pages 13 and 29.

Distance:	Approx. 90 km, Three Valley Lake to Enderby.
Travel Time:	Two to four hours.
Condition:	Some rough gravel, may be closed in winter.
Season:	July through October.
Topo Maps:	Shuswap Lake, BC 82 L/NW (1:100,000).
	Revelstoke, BC 82 L/NE (1:100,000).
Forest Maps:	Salmon Arm Forest District Recreation Map.
	Vernon Forest District Recreation Map.
Communities:	Revelstoke, Sicamous and Enderby.

If you are looking for an excuse to get off the pavement while on your way from the Rockies to the Okanagan, this British Columbia backcountry road is a few kilometres shorter than the regular route via Sicamous. But as is the case with most backroad shortcuts, the Mabel Lake Shortcut will probably take you twice as long as Highway 1 and Highway 97A.

There are, however, two major reasons to make a mid-summer meander through the heart of the Monashee Mountains. The first reason is to get away from the hell-bent-for-destruction crowds that seem to be intent on turning the Trans-Canada Highway into a training ground for crash-test dummies. The second reason is actually much more positive than negative — unless you just happen to be a fish — and it is the relatively easy access to quiet recreation sites on Wap Lake, Mabel Lake and several other off-the-road lakes.

Take note of my mention of mid-summer. The north end of this route passes through the heart of the Monashee rain forest and ease of access depends on logging activity and the prerequisite road maintenance. Washouts and late-season snow drifts are common on the section between Three Valley Lake

23

and Wap Lake, so a full fuel tank, a shovel and lots of time are definite requirements before heading south. These items, plus a chainsaw or a good swede saw and an axe should be part of any backroad explorer's kit anyway.

The Mabel Lake Shortcut hasn't gone unnoticed by others. There were rumors more than two decades ago that the government was considering routing a brand-new four-lane highway through here in a direct link from Revelstoke to the Okanagan Valley and then the Coast via the Okanagan/Coquihalla Connector. The arguments then — and now — are that this route, if continued down the west side of Okanagan Lake, would bypass most of the congestion and development of the Shuswap, Okanagan and Thompson valleys. I have no idea if this option is still being considered and I don't intend to ask anyone. It's much more fun to speculate based on true ignorance than on inside knowledge.

We've made the trip several times during the past dozen years. The first was in mid-August, 1986, and washouts and questionable bridges were the rule, rather than exception. By August, 1988, a rotting bridge across the Wap River had been replaced by a steel structure and most of the washouts had been re-routed or rebuilt with larger culverts. In late August, 1998, the road, though narrow and rough in spots, was easily passable by cars or light trucks with fair clearance. Logging was active south of Wap Lake and logging trucks could be expected at any time. Although logging activity changes from year to year, it is probably safest to travel this route on weekends or evenings. Better yet, contact the British Columbia Forest Service office at Salmon Arm (250 833-3400) for up-to-date information.

A logging railway.

For the purpose of this backroad trip, kilometre "0" is the junction of the Trans-Canada Highway and Three Valley-Mabel Lake Forest Service Road, 20 kilometres west of Revelstoke near the west end of Three Valley Lake. The grade is easy here, with smooth wide corners that hint that this is not your average logging road. A bridge at km 1.3 that looks remarkably like a railway bridge confirms the suspicion that other methods of transportation may have been used here before rubber-tired vehicles became king of the backroad.

David Stewart, himself a semi-retired king of the backroads, has a plausible explanation in *Okanagan Backroads Volume 2*, published by Saltaire in 1975 and long out of print:

"The valley of the Wap has an interesting past," writes Dave Stewart. "Around the turn of the century, an English firm with headquarters in London built a logging railroad from Three Valley, on the CP main line, in past Wap Lake. Until two or three decades ago, traces of the old railway could be seen, along with a steam donkey engine and the big old stumps left by the loggers of that far-away time. In 1948 I stumbled on several racks of steel rails not far west of Wap Lake (we called it Frog Lake those days). Presumably this steel is still hidden in the dense underbrush: the logging railway it had been intended to extend having disappeared over the intervening four decades."

Gordon Bell, owner of the Three Valley Gap Motor Inn at the east end of Three Valley Lake, had the good fortune of meeting one of the descendants of the original operators. According to his information, the logging railway once extended

Fig 6:
Forest Service Recreation site at Wap Lake.
(Photo SHG-484 © Murphy Shewchuk.)

as far south as Mabel Lake, with spur lines up many of the side valleys. The company operated one of the largest sawmills in western Canada at the west end of Three Valley Lake with, says Gordon, three planers, a post office and a hotel. The Bell House hotel (no relation) was later dismantled and moved to the top of Mount Revelstoke where it became the Mount Revelstoke Chalet until Parks Canada tore it down around 1970.

Giant cedars.

Giant cedar stumps, some with the spring-board notches still clearly visible from the hand logging of a previous era, surround the Frog Falls F.S. Rec Site at km 4.4. Nearby Wap River starts in the southeast on the slopes of Mount Begbie, and after a northward rush, swings south here as it twists and tumbles down to Mabel Lake. A wide trail leads from the rec site to the crest of the 25 metre high two-step Frog Falls.

The trail to the falls passes, buried in the mountain side, what was, until recently, one of the largest private hydroelectric plants in BC. Faced with an estimated $450,000 tab from BC Hydro to run lines from Revelstoke or Malakwa to his resort at Three Valley Gap, Gordon Bell set out to build his own power plant using the 30 metre head developed at Frog Falls and two additional run-of-the river dams farther upstream. After obtaining the necessary permits from seven different bureaucracies, Bell went ahead with construction.

The Three Valley Gap system is unusual in two ways. First, it uses water pumps operating as turbines to drive the 150,000-watt electric generator instead of the more expensive specially-designed turbines. And secondly, it is a constant load system, using an electronically-controlled load distribution system to maintain a steady AC supply while heating and lighting the complete resort. Bell's system cost almost what Hydro would have charged, but his real saving is in the elimination of an enormous monthly energy bill.

Wap Lake Forest Service recreation site.

The road south of the recreation site and the Wap River bridge follows the old railbed near the valley floor. Several side roads lead to the left into the high country and some maps hint that there may be a route to Sugar Lake through here, but I haven't yet confirmed that rumor. Water lily marshes near km 10.5 are the first hint of Wap Lake, but it is almost two kilometres farther along the old railbed before you reach the small Forest Service Recreation Site at the west end of the lake.

South of the lake, the road swings away from the river for several kilometres, skirting a knoll before crossing under a 500,000 volt power line near km 16 and again crossing the river half a kilometre farther along. The BC Hydro power line links the Revelstoke hydro plant with the rest of the system at the Ashton Creek substation near Enderby.

A junction near km 19.5 marks the beginning of a climb away from the valley floor. On one trip through, a small sign on the road to the right signaled the start of the Kingfisher Forest Service Road. On our latest trip, this road appears to be a continuation of the Three Valley-Mabel Lake Forest Service Road.

The road to the right leads to Enderby, while the road to the left (Mabel Lake Forest Service Road) again crosses Wap River, and with a little luck and good planning could take you all the way to Lumby.

Noisy Creek Forest Service recreation site.

Three Valley-Mabel Lake Road climbs steadily, reaching an elevation of about 850 metres (2,800 feet) before it crosses into the Noisy Creek drainage. Side roads lead into several old log cuts (and a few newer ones) where wild blueberries, raspberries, huckleberries and moose are plentiful. The roadside markers begin a countdown as you continue south. Another junction just south of the 21K marker (36 kilometres from Three Valley Lake) marks the route down to Noisy Creek F.S. Recreation Site at Mabel Lake. It's a five kilometre drive down to the lake, but the large recreation site and excellent beach are well worth the trip. In fact, the site is actually two quite different campgrounds split by Noisy Creek and its delta. The south campground looks down the lake with a few waterfront campsites and a larger number sheltered in the trees. The campground north of the delta gets the morning sun and could be better protected in the case of a storm. Although the road was somewhat rough, it was passable to truck campers and a variety of other vehicles in the summer of 1998. According to some of the campers we talked to, this has been a popular site for at least 30 years. Firewood is usually in short supply, so plan on collecting wood on the ground from the old logged areas on your way down.

Mabel Lake Road.

Beyond the Noisy Creek junction, Three Valley-Mabel Lake Road crosses into the Danforth Creek drainage. Rough side roads lead west into Mount Mara and the Hunters Range and east into Stony, Holiday and Noreen lakes. Then the backroad parallels Kingfisher Creek valley before making a long, winding descent to Mabel Lake Road and the Shuswap River, approximately 56.5 kilometres from Three Valley Lake.

Fig 7:
Mabel Lake, looking south from Noisy Creek. (Photo SHG-343 © Murphy Shewchuk.)

Kingfisher, at the western outlet of Mabel Lake, is a small resort community that comes alive during the summer. Located at the end of the pavement 37 km east of Enderby and about five kilometres east of the junction with the Three Valley-Mabel Lake F.S. Road, it may be your last chance for supplies if you are following the Wap Lake route north.

Shuswap River canoe route.

The 36-kilometre route west to Enderby passes through a peaceful pastoral valley with several acccss points to the Shuswap River. Canoeists favor the river, and except for the Skookumchuck Rapids near the outlet of Mabel Lake, it is considered "rather tranquil and a large breeding ground for Canada Geese." The Kingfisher Environmental Interpretive Centre, approximately 10 kilometres west of the Three Valley-Mabel Lake Road junction, may be a good spot to spend an afternoon.

A junction near the Ashton Creek General Store, 10 km east of Enderby, presents another backroad detour south through the Trinity Valley to Lumby. But if Enderby and Highway 97A is your present destination, continue west through the broad Shuswap River Valley and you'll soon be back at civilization.

•••

6

Mabel Lake Road (East Side)

By Murphy Shewchuk

Statistics: **For maps, see pages 13 and 29.**

Distance:	110 km, Lumby to Highway 1 at Three Valley Lake.
Travel Time:	Four to five hours minimum.
Conditions:	Partly paved, some rough gravel sections.
Season:	Dry weather. North portion may be closed in winter.
Topo Maps:	Sugar Lake, BC 82 L/SE (1:100,000)
	Revelstoke, BC 82 L/NE (1:100,000)
Forest Maps:	Salmon Arm Forest District Recreation Map.
	Vernon Forest District Recreation Map.
Communities:	Lumby, Vernon and Revelstoke.

The Mabel Lake area has held a special attraction to me ever since I flew over the area in a helicopter almost two decades ago. The long, narrow lake looked particularly inviting, partly because of its beauty but more importantly because of its apparent isolation. Time often has a way of passing without allowing us to follow our dreams, but fortunately we have been able to explore the area on several occasions. Initially, topographic maps presented conflicting information and our usually reliable sources weren't much better. Except for the warning about frequent wash-outs north of Wap Lake and the hint of a beautiful waterfall on Cascade Creek, we were on our own.

After several trips, we have concluded that a south to north traverse seems to be the best way to explore this backroad. Should bad roads force us to turn back at Wap Lake, we would have at least experienced the beautiful Mabel Lake area — and, weather permitting, we could return to the Enderby area via the road on the west side of Mabel Lake.

We have had to negotiate rotten bridges and skirt some ridiculous washouts, yet we always made it through. However, next year could be different. Before you set out to explore this route, check with the Forest Service office in Salmon

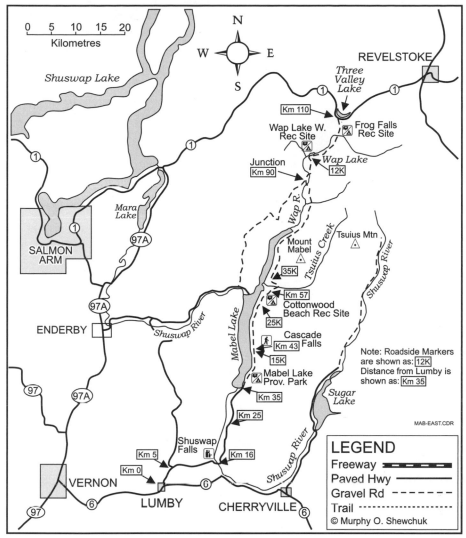

Map 4
North Okanagan and Shuswap area -- Vernon to Revelstoke.

Arm (250 833-3400) AND be sure to have enough fuel and supplies to travel double the 110 km distance.

Lumby Starting Point.

Reset your odometer to zero at the corner of Highway 6 (Vernon Street) and Shuswap Avenue in Lumby. Then, as you head north on Shuswap Avenue, the Trinity Valley Road, near km 5, becomes the first point of diversion. This road to the left follows Vance Creek and Trinity Creek northwest through Trinity

Valley to Ashton Creek. Then it is a short drive on to Enderby, providing a scenic route to the heart of the south Shuswap. The road to Mabel Lake continues east down Bessette Creek to Shuswap Falls, passing through bottomland rich with hay, corn and livestock. If you live in an Interior community, you may see Silver Hills Bakery products (at km 9) on your store shelves. Rawlings Lake Road, near km 11.5, provides an alternate route to Highway 6, east of Lumby.

This backroad route crosses the Shuswap River near km 16. The river rises in the heart of the rugged Monashee Mountains, north of Sugar Lake, before looping south to Cherryville. Dams at Brenda Falls at the foot of Sugar Lake and at Shuswap Falls, near km 16.8, harness the flow of the river to generate electricity. Here at Wilsey Dam, BC Hydro has created a recreation area with trails to the falls and canyon. Paddlers on the Shuswap River use the wide trails to portage around the falls and rapids.

Mabel Lake.

The paved road swings north near Shuswap Falls, climbing away from the river. Near km 35, an opening in the timber provides the first glimpse of the south end of Mabel Lake (and the last glimpse of pavement).

A trail to the water's edge provides access to launch a car-top boat and fish the area around the river outlet. In the mid-1970s, the landowner attempted to sell much of the land near here to the government for use in Mabel Lake Park. The government declined the offer, however, because of the swampy land and because they saw no need to expand the park.

Mabel Lake Provincial Park, at km 37.8, can be a welcome sight in a summer afternoon. On more than one occasion, we have had our choice of sites and camped near the beach and playground. The beach gets the afternoon sun, and with the lake's long, undulating shoreline, never seems particularly crowded.

A Pioneer Store keeper and a Pioneer Lumberman.

On one particularly beautiful afternoon, after a swim and supper, I settled down to read *Grassroots of Lumby: 1877-1927*, a hard-cover book I acquired earlier at the Lumby information centre. From it, I learned that the surrounding land first belonged to Reginald Sadler, a young Englishman who came to Canada at the turn of the century. T.A. Norris, Lumby's first school teacher, later bought the lake shore property and lived here for some time before selling it in the 1930s. Will Shields, who spent much of his life as a store keeper in Lumby, and Henry Sigalet, a pioneer lumberman, bought the property, building comfortable summer homes near the lake.

Born in Ontario in 1884, Shields came to Lumby about 1910 and retired to the Vernon area in 1956. Henry Sigalet was born in Alberta in 1899 and came to the Okanagan Valley two years later. In the midst of the depression, Henry Sigalet built a lumber mill in nearby Squaw Valley, and in 1940 he opened a mill in Lumby. Both Shields and Sigalet died in 1972, not long after completing negotiations on the sale of the property for the Mabel Lake Park site.

Fig 8:
Cascade Falls, north of Mabel Lake Provincial Park.
(Photo SHG-469 © Murphy Shewchuk.)

The majority of park development work took place from 1978-80, but there have been recent additions to the facilities. The 85-unit campground has an attractive 2100-metre-long shoreline with an excellent beach. Hemlock, red cedar and birch shade the property, indicative of the cooler, wetter climate compared to the dry Okanagan Valley.

Cascade Falls Trail.

The gravel road, now known as Mabel Lake Forest Service Road, winds along the mountainside well above the lake as it continues north of the park. Logging roads offer the occasional diversion as do roaring creeks. A small roadside sign near km 43.0 (about 5.7 km north of the park entrance and just beyond the 15K marker) indicates the start of the trail to Cascade Falls. The falls lives up to its name. It resembles an ever-broadening veil as it tumbles down the steep rocky slope. The 300-metre switch-back trail to the foot of the waterfall will require some caution but otherwise is not difficult. If you enjoy photography, a tripod and wide-angle lens will help when photographing the falls. A close-up or macro lens will also prove useful for the many fungi, berries and wildflowers along the trail.

Cottonwood Beach Recreation Site.

As you continue northward, Torrent Creek, a boulder-strewn waterway near km 51 marks the first return to Mabel Lake since leaving the provincial park. The occasional logging road climbs to the right, away from the main track, but otherwise Mabel Lake Road follows the timbered benches. If the provincial park campground is full, you might want to consider exploring the Cottonwood Beach Forest Service Recreation Site near km 56.8. In general, this backroad continues north, except for a loop east to avoid the canyon of Tsuius Creek. If Three Valley Lake is your destination, keep left at the major junctions.

The road climbs high above the lake, presenting some spectacular views as it winds through the timber. Then it begins to descend, presenting a last brief glimpse of Mabel Lake through the trees at km 77. Some maps suggest that the old road once crossed Wap River near the north end of the lake. However, the present route to the west side of the lake is still another 10 km to the north.

Fig 9:
Crossing the Wap River bridge. (Photo SHG-473 © Murphy Shewchuk.)

From the north end of Mabel Lake to the Wap River crossing near km 89, the route varies from a good gravel logging road to a somewhat narrow, lumpy backroad. The creeks reveal the terrific force of flash floods that can occur almost any time of the year. The forest roads that veer east off the main road often appear better and more used. This can be deceiving — a point brought home when one ends up in a log landing.

Alternate Route to Enderby.
The junction near km 90, a short distance north of the Wap River bridge, is the first left turn to ignore in your relentless search for Three Valley Lake. Three Valley-Mabel Lake Road to the left (west) climbs steadily to a high valley paralleling the west side of Mabel Lake and then continues south to the Shuswap River outflow of Mabel Lake. (See page 23 for details.)

The road straight ahead again crosses the Wap River near km 93, after traversing a few sandy sections. The road passes under a 500 kilovolt power line a short distance beyond the bridge and swings left through the timber.

It may not be apparent at first, but the gravel road and the Wap Lake West Recreation Site, at km 97, sit on what was once a railway bed. A logging railway, built near the turn of the century, carried timber north to the CPR at Three Valley Lake. (See page 24 for additional information.)

Wap Lake is unusual in that the railway bed allows good casting from the shoreline as well as providing several places to launch a canoe or car-top boat. Camping is limited, with a few spaces at the Forest Service recreation site and a wide spot or two along the road. On one trip, while I tried casting from the shore, the rest of the motley crew picked huckleberries and blueberries for dessert. A tasty frying-pan upside-down cake compensated for my usual lack of trout for that very same frying pan.

Beyond Wap Lake, the backroad skirts the colourful lily-dotted marshes and the river, bouncing over several rough sections that could be difficult in the spring or after wet weather. This is the section that has been almost impassable in the past and is most likely to present a problem in the future. The steel-framed bridge across the Wap River, near km 105, is a sign that you have survived the worst and that the rest of the road to the Trans-Canada Highway SHOULD be a cinch.

Frog Falls.

An old sign in a tree just north of the bridge points to an overgrown trail leading upstream to Frog Falls. Giant cedar stumps stand like guards at the hidden trail entrance. However, a few hundred metres beyond the bridge, a side road leads into an excellent Forest Service Recreation Site and a wider trail to the crest of the falls.

Beyond the Frog Falls recreation site the much-improved road begins a steady descent to Three Valley Lake and Highway 1. After following South Pass Creek and the old logging railway bed, it reaches pavement approximately 110 km from the heart of Lumby. If you are attempting to travel this route southward, look for the "Three Valley-Mabel Lake Forest Service Road" sign on the south side of Highway 1, (the Trans-Canada Highway) approximately 21 kilometres west of Revelstoke.

Three Valley Gap.

If you've had enough of camping and your own cooking, you just might want to stop in at the Three Valley Gap resort at the east end of the lake. With hard work and ingenuity, Gordon Bell has turned an old railway whistle-stop into a fine hotel and unique heritage destination. In addition to the hotel, restaurant and gift shop, there are numerous restored pioneer buildings and railway cars.

•••

33

7

Grizzly Hill / Dee Lakes

By Murphy Shewchuk

Statistics:	For map, see page 35.

Distance:	Approximately 100 km from Highway 97 in Rutland to Highway 97 in Winfield.
Travel Time:	Allow one day minimum.
Conditions:	Mostly gravel. Portions closed in winter.
Season:	Best in dry weather — June to October.
Topo Maps:	Kelowna, BC 82 E/NW (1:100,000).
	Vernon, BC 82 L/SW (1:100,000).
Forest Maps:	Vernon Forest District Recreation Map.
Communities:	Kelowna, Lavington and Winfield.

If you are looking for an opportunity to explore the Okanagan Highlands and try some serious fishing, there are more than two dozen lakes on the plateau surrounding Grizzly Hill, northeast of Kelowna, that just might fill the bill. If you are planning an overnight jaunt, there are two fishing resorts and more than a dozen Forest Service recreation sites that can accommodate you.

Some of the lakes have roadside access while others may require you to pack your canoe or belly-boat a short distance. Not all lakes or access roads are well-marked. A little bush-sense will be necessary, but if you are willing to explore, you may just find your own private hide-away, even on a busy summer weekend.

A couple of important points to note. First, if you are looking for pristine wilderness, this isn't it. Much of the area has been logged — some of it so long ago that they seem to be back for a second time. Secondly, many of the lakes are dammed. They serve as domestic water reservoirs for communities in the Okanagan Valley. With this in mind, there are often special fishing restrictions including bans against gasoline motors.

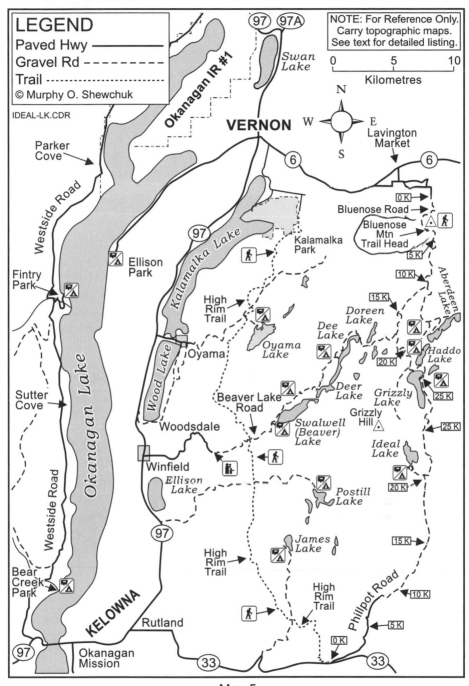

Map 5
Okanagan Highlands: Kelowna, Vernon, Lavington area.

Rutland starting point.

In dry weather, two-wheel-drive access is possible from the Rutland area of Kelowna, or from Winfield or Lavington. During the "wet" season, which some Okanagan residents suggest hardly ever happens, a four-by-four may be required to safely negotiate some of the steeper hills.

While there are at least three ways in, the route from Rutland (a community within Kelowna) via Highway 33, appears to have the fewest steep grades on the gravel sections. With the junction of Highway 97 and Highway 33 as your reference, follow Highway 33 eastward as it climbs across the foot of Black Knight Mountain and then follows Mission Creek upstream. Look for Phillpot Road, approximately 20.5 kilometres from Highway 97.

High Rim Trail.

A sign at the junction of Highway 33 and Phillpot Road marks the first of many possible diversions. If you are interested in some serious hiking, you may want to take a close look at the Okanagan Highlands High Rim Trail (see page 40 for details). The trail starts here at Phillpot Road at an elevation of about 860 metres and climbs steadily to about 1145 metres elevation at Cardinal Creek. It generally stays near the 1250-metre elevation zone as it meanders some 50 kilometres north across the mountainside before descending to Kalamalka Provincial Park, near Vernon.

It is important to note that this is a wilderness hiking trail not suited for bicycles or horses. It will require skill, endurance and proper equipment.

Ideal Lake.

If you are going to leave the hiking for another trip, reset your odometer and take Phillpot Road north up the Belgo Creek valley. The pavement ends in a gravel pit about 6.5 km from Highway 33. Then you are on Phillpot Forest Service Road as you climb up onto the Okanagan Highlands. The road levels off near the 18K marker at an elevation of about 1220 metres (4,000 ft). The junction near the 19K marker signals your departure from Phillpot F.S. Road. Take Ideal Lake F.S. Road to the left and stay on it for another three kilometres to the Belgo Dam (Ideal Lake) Forest Service Recreation Site.

Belgo Dam is really three dams on the south end of this 146-hectare (360-acre) lake. Ideal Lake is an excellent family lake that can provide budding anglers with their limit of smaller rainbow trout. The large 30-vehicle recreation site is spread throughout the trees with cartop boat launching available at two of the dams.

Older maps show the road continuing north around the west side of the lake, but when we last tried it, this route was blocked by windfalls.

Grizzly Swamp.

If you are interested in continuing north to explore more of the highland lakes surrounding Grizzly Hill, backtrack about 1.5 kilometres to the junction near the 20K marker. The road is marked "Hilda Creek" and cuts off at right angles from Ideal Lake F.S. Road. It climbs eastward for about half a kilometre before swinging north on what is labeled Phillpot Main on the signposts.

If you reset your odometer at the "Hilda Creek" junction, watch for access roads to

Fig 10:
Wollaston Lake.
(Photo KEL-164 © Murphy Shewchuk)

"Grizzly Swamp" near km 9 and a road across one leg of it at km 10. While the 1984 topographic map (Vernon 82 L/SW) shows this area as a swamp, this is certainly not the case now. Although this 190 hectare (469 acre) lake still has the tell-tale marks of a new reservoir, including dead trees on the fringe, it also has an excellent fishery for rainbow trout to 45 cm (18 inches).

According to one source, Grizzly Swamp was an excellent source of rainbow trout before it was turned into a reservoir in 1978. In the following years the fishery declined until the lake was completely drained in 1987. Subsequent stocking of Pennask/Beaver rainbows has resulted in a renewed fishery for large trout.

There are no formal recreation sites at Grizzly Swamp, but there are several places where self-contained campers can set up to try the fishing. There is also a recreation site at Specs Lake, about one kilometre north of the crossing.

Beyond Specs Lake, the road crosses the upland valley at the foot of the Grizzly Swamp dam. A major junction about 2.3 km from Specs Lake (km 13.2) provides another opportunity to explore the uplands. Wollaston and Treen lakes lie in separate hollows four to five kilometres to the south. In the past they were both best considered walk-in lakes as the mud holes in the final few hundred metres would swallow most vehicles — even in dry weather.

Haddo Lake.

Fortunately the road to Haddo Lake (km 13.4) doesn't fit into the same category. Although narrow in places, it does have a solid bottom and should not pose any serious difficulty for a vehicle with decent clearance. Beyond the turn-off to Haddo Lake, the road winds down to Duteau Creek and then climbs up the west side of the valley. Junctions at km 18.1 and km 18.9 will take you west to Dee Lake and then south past Swalwell (Beaver) Lake to Winfield.

Bluenose Mountain and Lavington.

However, before we give you the blow-by-blow description of that route, let's continue 22 kilometres north. If you have been watching the roadside markers, you may have noticed that they are counting down. A junction to the right near the 11K marker presents the opportunity to explore Aberdeen and Nicklen lakes. At 254 hectares (627 acres) Aberdeen is one of the larger lakes on the up-lands. It is reported to produce wild rainbow trout to one kilogram (2.5 pounds).

The road (now marked Aberdeen Lake F.S. Road) begins a steady descent at the 9K marker. Watch for signs marking the Blue-nose Mountain Trail near the 5K

Fig 11:
On the Bluenose Mountain Trail.
(Photo © Murphy Shewchuk)

marker. If you are interested in a spectacular view of the Lavington area, take a hike up the Bluenose trail. It will take one to two hours return to navigate the switchback trail to the north peak. Keep left at a junction near the saddle be-tween the peaks and watch your step at the top.

Beyond the Bluenose Mountain Trail parking area, it's about 9.5 km to Henry's Café and the Shell Station at the junction of Highway 6 and School Road in Lavington. If you are planning to return to the Highlands, this would be a good place to re-stock your larder and fuel tank.

Dee Lake.

Meanwhile, back at the Dee Lake junction, if you choose to wind your way southwest to Winfield, you'll have plenty of opportunity to explore more lakes and Forest Service recreation sites. Doreen Lake, about four kilometres from the junction (near the 20K marker) is just off the road with good access. Fishing regulations list it as "artificial fly only" so double-check before you drag out the "Ford Fender" or the worms.

Beyond Doreen Lake, the road swings northward around the end of Dee Lake before continuing southwest. If you aren't ready for another night at a Forest Service recreation site, Dee Lake Wilderness Resort (a.k.a. Dee Lake Lodge) will offer you a few more comforts. Approximately 1.7 km farther south, a side road leads a short distance to the Island Lake recreation site. Another 5.5 kilometres and you should be close to the Beaver Lake recreation site. While there may have been five (or more) distinct bodies of water in this chain before man started messing around, the reservoir dams have changed all that. In high water, you can paddle and portage your canoe from the north end of Dee Lake to the south end of Swalwell (Beaver) Lake.

Beaver Lake.

Canada must be full of Beaver lakes. The name must be used darn near as often as Loon, Round and Green. Fortunately the map makers seem to have given this lake a more distinctive name. Unfortunately Swalwell does not seem to have met with the approval of the local gentry and Beaver is the recognized name everywhere except on the map.

The Bussmann family (Tony, Lucie, Sara and Alex) have been operating Beaver Lake Mountain Resort (a.k.a. Beaver Lake Lodge) since 1994. Their operation can be best described as a fishing camp with a difference. The well-built cabins and the colorful playground filled with rambunctious kids are a sharp contrast from the pre-World War II beginnings of this camp. In addition to the "fishing experience", they offer canoeing, cycling and hiking in the summer. There is also winter access to the area from Winfield and from Christmas to March, you can add snowmobiling, cross-country skiing and snowshoeing to the ice fishing possibilities.

Beaver Lake Road.

The road begins a steady descent to Winfield shortly after passing Beaver Lake Lodge. If you look closely, you may notice the "High Rim Trail" markers about three kilometres from the lodge. This is one of several points where the trail crosses regular access roads, making it possible to hike smaller sections of the trail using a two-car system.

After another 12 km of brake-burning descent, you should be rolling through the heart of Winfield and approaching Highway 97.

Now, wasn't that more fun than the direct route from Rutland to Winfield — even if it will be difficult to explain to your "significant other" why you spent an extra day and drove an extra 80 kilometres to travel the 16 kilometres?

•••

8

High Rim Trail

By Judie Steeves

Statistics: **For map, see page 41.**

Distance: 50 kilometres, Kelowna to Vernon.
Travel Time: Several days, in all. Less to hike a section.
Condition: Seasonal. High altitude wilderness hiking trail.
Season: Spring, summer and fall without snowshoes.
Topo Maps: Kelowna 82E/14 (1:50,000).
                 Oyama 82L/3 (1:50,000).
Forest Maps: Vernon Forest District Recreation Map.
Communities: Kelowna, Vernon.

Although the steepest parts of this highland wilderness hiking trail are at both ends, some sections are recommended for experienced hikers only. It is not suitable for horses, trail bikes or mountain bikes. There are no formal campsites, garbage cans or toilets along the trail.

This is a very wild trail cut through dense forest in places, and traversing wet areas in others. However, it also includes wide open spaces with excellent panoramic views of the central Okanagan Valley. For the bird watcher or nature photographer, the trail passes through some excellent wildlife habitat representative of the various elevations in BC's southern interior. It is a cool, green, clean alternative to spending a hot summer day baking on a beach in the Okanagan Valley bottom. The High Rim Trail was conceived and constructed by local volunteer members (mostly seniors) of the Western Canada Wilderness Committee. It is part of the Okanagan Highlands Trail that, as this was written, is a vision still in the process of becoming reality.

Easy access.

The northern trailhead access is from Vernon off Cosens Bay Road through Kalamalka Provincial Park. Access to the southern terminal is from Kelowna by turning east off Highway 97 on Highway 33. Drive through the Rutland area to Phillpot Road, 20.5 kilometres east of the junction of Highway 97 and 33.

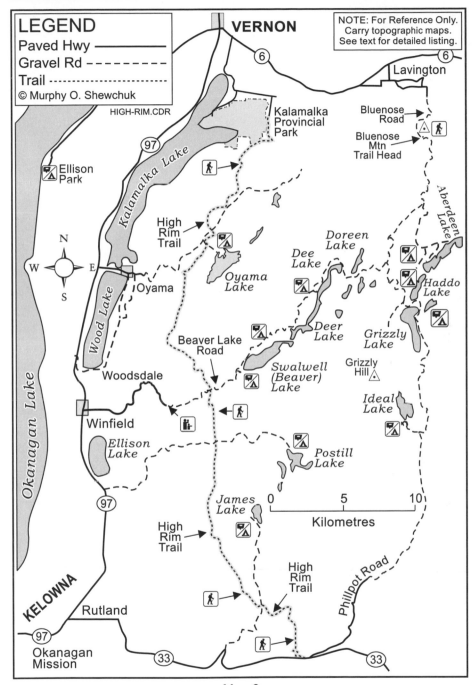

LEGEND
Paved Hwy ———————
Gravel Rd ― ― ― ― ―
Trail ·····················
© Murphy O. Shewchuk

HIGH-RIM.CDR

NOTE: For Reference Only.
Carry topographic maps.
See text for detailed listing.

VERNON

Lavington

Kalamalka Provincial Park

Bluenose Road

Bluenose Mtn Trail Head

Kalamalka Lake

Ellison Park

Aberdeen Lake

High Rim Trail

Doreen Lake

Dee Lake

Oyama Lake

Haddo Lake

Oyama

Wood Lake

Deer Lake

Grizzly Lake

Beaver Lake Road

Swalwell (Beaver) Lake

Grizzly Hill

Woodsdale

Ideal Lake

Okanagan Lake

Winfield

Ellison Lake

Postill Lake

James Lake

Kilometres

0   5   10

High Rim Trail

High Rim Trail

Phillpot Road

KELOWNA

Rutland

Okanagan Mission

Map 6
High Rim Trail — Kelowna, Vernon, Lavington area.

This is also the route out of the valley to the Big White Ski Resort, McCulloch Lake and Beaverdell.

There are also eight other points where the trail can be accessed, mainly from secondary gravel roads. This allows you to hike individual sections of the trail if you're not prepared to do the whole 50 kilometres at once. By leaving your vehicle at one of these points, you can hike to the next access point and arrange to be picked up there. That way you don't have to retrace your steps along the trail.

James Lake Road.

On a south-to-north basis, another access, 6.7 kilometres north along the James Lake Road, avoids the steep initial climb up the trail from Phillpot Road. James Lake Road branches off Highway 33 about 13 kilometres east of Highway 97. Next access north along the trail is 12.1 kilometres along the Postill Lake Road from Highway 97. The Beaver Lake Road out of Winfield presents another access possibility, 12.9 kilometres from Highway 97.

You could also reach it 12.6 kilometres along the Oyama Lake Road from Oyama. There have been reports that the trail is difficult to follow in the clear cuts on the Goudie Plateau, but with a compass and care observant hikers can make their way through. From the Postill Lake Road to the Beaver Lake Road the trail is more clearly visible.

Diverse country.

The Okanagan High Rim Trail is an opportunity to see the valley from a different angle — above. You will cross canyons and creeks over bridges that consist of a large log, with matching handrails. You'll walk between fallen logs with only 50 centimetres removed for you to pass by with your shoulders unscratched — intentionally left this way to discourage ATVs and dirt bikes. You'll feel your way through waist-high fields of fireweed in clearcut areas and meadows.

At the Phillpot Road trailhead on Mission Creek, your starting point is about 860 metres in altitude. There are six stations along the trail, with postings of measurements such as the altitude, kilometres and name of the station. The first station is Cardinal Creek, and it is about 1145 metres in altitude. Here a 25-metre-long tree was felled to span the canyon about four metres above the creek. The Cardinal Canyon Bridge is the tree, with a 26-centimetre-wide de-barked walking space, and a handrail attached to one side. It is simple and unsophisticated, but it works.

Kalamalka Provincial Park.

Most of the trail north is at the 1250-metre elevation, until you approach Kalamalka Provincial Park at Vernon, and descend into the valley.

Fig 12:
Hikers from Oyama and Vernon crossing a log bridge — June, 1994.
(Photo © Mary Bailey, Armstrong, BC.)

The trail traverses Crown-owned forestland along the rim of the valley, on the eastern fringe of the Thompson Plateau. Some important features of the trail include viewpoints, lakes, Wrinkly Face Cliff, and The Monolith.

On the 50 kilometres from Phillpot Road to Kalamalka Park, you pass through widely diverse habitat, ranging from sagebrush and grasslands to marshes and from ponderosa pine to lodgepole pine and Engelmann spruce. Bear and deer, cougar and smaller mammals abound, along with the full range of wildflowers, birds and bushes commonly seen in the interior, and a few that are more rare.

Go prepared.

Before embarking on the High Rim Trail be sure you are properly equipped with suitable boots and hiking clothes, including a hat. Take water, food and emergency supplies. Take and understand how to use your map and compass. And for those dire emergencies, a cellular telephone, with a spare fully-charged battery, could be a real asset. Most important of all, never hike alone.

•••

9

Westside Road

By Murphy Shewchuk

Statistics: For map, see page 45.

Distance:	64 km, Highway 97 at O'Keefe to 97 at Westbank.
Travel Time:	One to two hours.
Condition:	Mostly paved, with narrow, winding sections.
Season:	Year around. May be slippery in winter.
Topo Maps:	Vernon, BC 82 L/SW (1:100,000).
	Kelowna, BC 82 E/NW (1:100,000).
Forest Maps:	Vernon Forest District Recreation Map.
Communities:	Vernon, Kelowna and Westbank.

If you are looking for a scenic drive that will not rattle the fenders off the old auto, you might want to take a close look at Westside Road. It has plenty of reasons to recommend it — and a few reasons to consider an alternative route. If you have lots of time, the pluses, such as historic O'Keefe Ranch, Fintry Provincial Park, Okanagan Lake Resort, Bear Creek Provincial Park and numerous side roads and lakeside viewpoints, are well worth it. However, if you are in a hurry, consider staying on Highway 97. Westside Road really is not conducive to hurrying at any time of the year.

Access is from Highway 97, between Westbank and Kelowna, or Spallumcheen, northwest of Vernon. I have chosen to describe Westside Road in a north-south direction, beginning at Highway 97 near the O'Keefe Ranch.

Historic O'Keefe Ranch.

O'Keefe Ranch had its beginning in 1867 when Cornelius O'Keefe and Thomas Greenhow drove a herd of cattle from Oregon to the North Okanagan. A year later, O'Keefe homesteaded 65 hectares (160 acres) nearby, and within 40 years his cattle were grazing over 6,000 hectares (15,000 acres) of the North Okanagan's prime grasslands. O'Keefe gradually built up one of the largest cattle empires in the Okanagan Valley, establishing his own community to

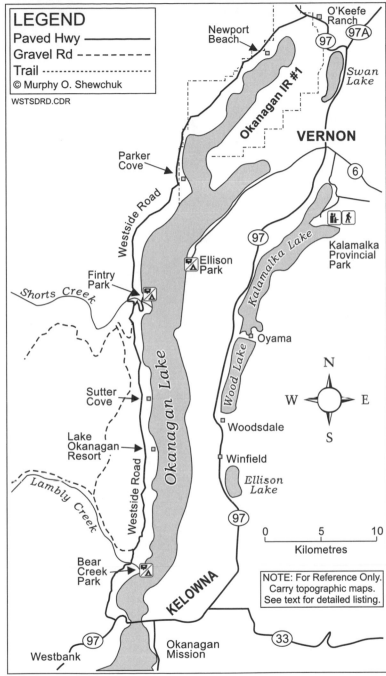

LEGEND
Paved Hwy ———————
Gravel Rd - - - - - - -
Trail ....
© Murphy O. Shewchuk
WSTSDRD.CDR

Newport Beach

O'Keefe Ranch

97 97A

Swan Lake

Okanagan IR #1

VERNON

Parker Cove

6

Westside Road

97

Kalamalka Lake

Kalamalka Provincial Park

Ellison Park

Fintry Park

Shorts Creek

Oyama

Wood Lake

Okanagan Lake

Sutter Cove

N
W   E
S

Woodsdale

Lake Okanagan Resort

Winfield

Ellison Lake

Lambly Creek

Westside Road

97

0   5   10
Kilometres

Bear Creek Park

KELOWNA

NOTE: For Reference Only.
Carry topographic maps.
See text for detailed listing.

97

Westbank

Okanagan Mission

33

Map 7
Westside Road — Vernon - Kelowna Area.

serve the ranch and its employees. It had a store, post office, blacksmith shop and church.

The living ranch museum has preserved many of the original buildings and much of the period farm equipment. To complement the ranch setting, the historic O'Keefe Ranch has a restaurant and other attractions and is usually open from mid-May to Thanksgiving. For a small entry fee, you can explore the old buildings, many of which contain their original furnishings. In the summer months, you can also ride around the ranch aboard a horse-drawn hay wagon.

Fig 13:
St. Ann's Church at O'Keefe Ranch.
(Photo VER-056 © Murphy Shewchuk.)

St. Ann's Church, a notable landmark alongside Highway 97, stands on its original site near the ranch house. The oldest Catholic Church in the BC Interior, it was built in 1889 and is still in excellent condition.

Okanagan Indian Reserve.

With the junction of Highway 97 as km 0.0, follow Westside Road south through the Okanagan Indian Reserve. The dry hills alongside the road appear quite barren in late summer, but in April and May they are a mass of color as a wide variety of wildflowers compete for the spring rains.

The sunny, dry climate has also attracted a growing number of hobby farms, retirement communities and beach resorts. Newport Beach Recreational Park, near km 5.3, offers a full campground and marina facilities. Newport Beach is also one of the northernmost accesses to 110-kilometre-long Okanagan Lake. Newport Beach marina could be your launching point for an extended boat trip to Penticton.

The Native community at Six-Mile Creek (km 13.3) is home to the Sn-qt-pas-xn-c'utn, the Six-Mile Creek Education Centre, complete with a state-of-the-art, multimedia computer network and an extensive reference library. Westside Road leaves the reserve near km 21.5, just south of the Parker Cove community.

The Killiney Beach area, near km 27, also offers access to the lake. There are some excellent viewpoints south of Killiney. Be careful when you pull off the narrow road.

Fintry Delta Road.

Fintry Delta Road, near km 34, marks the access to the mouth of Shorts Creek and one of the oldest communities on the west side of the lake — and one of BC's newest provincial parks. See page 48 for more information on the history of the delta and Fintry Provincial Park.

Lake Okanagan Resort.

Lake Okanagan Resort, near km 47, is a first-class facility that is attracting attention — and guests — world-wide. If "roughing it" at Fintry Provincial Park doesn't turn your crank, you could consider the luxurious three-bedroom chalets and one-bedroom suites, complete with kitchenettes, as a replacement for your tent. Add a half-dozen tennis courts and an executive par 3 nine-hole golf course, and you have a suitable get-away from the rat-race.

If you decide not to stop at the resort, you can pull over at an excellent viewpoint near km 52 or detour down to Okanagan Lake at Traders Cove Marine Park near km 56. The park entrance is opposite Bear Forest Service Road (a.k.a. Bear Main Road or Bear Road). If you are looking for a little more excitement, you could follow Bear Road southwest into the high country and join the Okanagan Connector just west of the Pennask summit. See the *Bear Road* section on page 102 for more information.

Bear Creek Park.

Bear Creek Provincial Park, near km 57, is also well worth a stop. Westside Road acts as the boundary between two quite different natural environments that create a wide-ranging diversity in the park. To the west, Lambly (Bear) Creek has cut a spectacular steep-walled canyon in its final descent from the rugged 1800-metre-high Pennask Plateau. To the east the fan-shaped delta in Okanagan Lake has been developed into a fine camping and picnic area with excellent beaches. See *Bear Creek Provincial Park* on page 51 for more details.

As you continue south from Bear Creek Provincial Park, watch the lakeshore nearer Westside for remnants of the docks that once served the Okanagan Lake ferry, prior to construction of the floating bridge. The junction of Westside Road and Highway 97 (km 64), a few minutes southwest of downtown Kelowna, is the southern terminal of this scenic backroad.

Do you turn left and cross the floating bridge to Kelowna or turn right to Westbank and points south? The decision is yours!

•••

10

Fintry Provincial Park

By Judie Steeves

Statistics:	For map, see page 45.

Distance:	32 kilometres from Kelowna.
Travel Time:	A 45-minute drive from Kelowna.
Condition:	Paved and well-maintained.
Season:	All.
Forest Maps:	Vernon Forest District Recreation Map.
Communities:	Kelowna, Vernon, Westbank.

Fintry Delta Road, off Westside Road, 34 kilometres south of Highway 97 near Vernon, marks the access to the mouth of Shorts Creek and one of the earliest settlements on the west side of Okanagan Lake.

It's also home to the Okanagan Valley's newest provincial park, a 360-hectare (889-acre) historic estate, valued as well for its representation of rare Okanagan eco-systems, and an invaluable shoreline extending more than 1800 metres (6,000 feet) along Okanagan Lake. The province purchased the Fintry estate in December 1995, for $7.48 million including a $2 million contribution from the Central Okanagan Regional District. Fintry Provincial Park was officially designated on April 30, 1996. By mid-June, it was open to campers with 50 campsites, drinking water, flush and pit toilets and showers. The remainder of the park is undeveloped except for the historic buildings on site, and a new, solidly-built 300-step stairway that leads to some excellent views of the waterfall in Shorts Creek Canyon.

The waterfall on Shorts Creek creates a humid micro-climate that is home for ferns, cedar trees and other plants not usual in the arid Okanagan. While the ecosystem surrounding the falls represent some of the unusual in the Okanagan Valley's natural heritage, the dry hillsides, deep canyon and the alluvial fan at the mouth of the creek present excellent examples of what is common in this valley.

Preservation of the wilderness corridor along the creek is also part of the park's value. It is essential to ensure a link for wildlife, including the remnants of the Shorts Creek California bighorn sheep herd, to migrate from the lakeshore to the rocky bluffs with minimal interference from man. Deer winter on these south-facing slopes and bears den up amongst the rocks above. Kokanee and rainbow trout spawn in the creek.

Members of the Central Okanagan Naturalists' Club report sighting 57 species of birds in just a few hours. They expect there are more than 100 species here year around. At least three rare plants on the delta were reported by the group.

Okanagan History in a Capsule at Fintry.

Fig 14:
Waterfall at Fintry Provincial Park.
(Photo FIN-007 © Murphy Shewchuk.)

The history of the Okanagan, its water transportation links, its orchards, its eccentric inhabitants, and its natural beauty is illustrated in miniature at Fintry.

Captain T.D. Shorts, the first settler on the delta, was co-owner and master of the first powered freighter to ply Okanagan Lake. In partnership with Thomas Greenhow, Thomas Dorling Shorts launched the *Mary Victoria Greenhow* on April 21, 1886. Unfortunately, the coal-oil burning two-horsepower engine was much too small for the 32-foot-long ship. The craft's maiden voyage to Penticton turned out to be a comedy of errors that cleaned out the valley's supply of lamp coal-oil.

Shorts later retired to Hope, BC where he died in 1921 at the age of 83. After Shorts, the delta land was owned, in succession, by The Honorable John Scott Montague, Viscount Ennismore, Sir John Poynder Dickson and The Honorable James Dunsmuir.

David Erskine Gellatly became the first farmer there when he leased the property in 1895. He moved to Westbank with his wife Eliza and their nine children in 1899.

According to David Falconer, "Capt. J.C. Dun-Waters arrived in the Okanagan in 1909 and purchased the first parcel of land that was later to grow into Fintry Estate from a Major Audain. Dun-Waters named his new property after Fintry, Stirlingshire, Scotland, where he grew up on his family's estate."

"Originally, the growing of the finest Okanagan apples possible was Dun-Waters' chief interest. One hundred acres was planted to apples alone, and an extensive web of irrigation fluming was installed. The two suspension bridges [across Shorts Creek] were built in that pre-war period to support the wooden irrigation pipe."

J.C. Dun-Waters became known as the Laird of Fintry and Art Bailey recalled: "When the passenger sternwheeler came into Fintry Landing he would often ask people what their religion was, and if it was to his liking, they received a bottle of his own scotch and were asked to join him ashore. Others were refused entry."

The Laird had the nine-bedroom manor house constructed of local granite in 1911, and although it was gutted by fire in 1924, the addition was saved and the interior was rebuilt that year. It still remains standing adjacent to the campground. That year Dun-Waters embarked on an ambitious foray into the realm of raising Scottish Ayrshire dairy cattle. He constructed an unusual octagonal dairy barn designed by Vancouver architect John J. Honeyman. It can still be seen in the park, although it is off-limits to visitors. Honeyman also designed the White House, now called the Stuart House, which is currently leased out.

Fairbridge Farm School.

In July, 1938, Captain Dun-Waters, then in his 70's, donated this self-contained estate to the Fairbridge Farm School, then part of a philanthropic scheme aimed at strengthening the British Empire and improving conditions for underprivileged British children. The scheme was conceived by Kingsley Ogilvie Fairbridge (1885-1924), a South African-born reformer who was raised in Southern Rhodesia. There were other Fairbridge Farm Schools in BC, including one at Duncan, that operated until 1950.

Arthur W. Bailey arrived in the Okanagan Valley in 1961, with the intention of developing Fintry into a California-style resort community. He concedes that he was "a little bit premature," but he did build a hotel complex at Fintry Estates. As part of his efforts, Bailey also outfitted the *Fintry Queen* to carry his clients to the resort before Westside Road was paved. According to Bill Chubb of the Westbank Yacht Club, "The *Fintry Queen* was originally built as a ferry, a sister ship to the *Pendozi*, powered by two diesel engines with two propellors on each end. It was retired from service when the Okanagan Lake bridge was opened in 1958. A third is still in service between Crofton and Vesuvius Bay."

Arthur Bailey sold out in 1981.

•••

11

Bear Creek Provincial Park

By Murphy Shewchuk

Statistics:	For map, see page 45.

Distance:	Nine kilometres from Kelowna.
Travel Time:	A 15-minute drive from Kelowna.
Condition:	Paved and well-maintained.
Season:	All.
Forest Maps:	Vernon Forest District Recreation Map.
Communities:	Kelowna and Westbank.

One of the busiest camping destinations in the Okanagan Valley is Bear Creek Provincial Park, located across from Kelowna on the west shore of Okanagan Lake. This 178-hectare (440-acre) park is open from April to October with camping fees in effect throughout the season. To reach Bear Creek Provincial Park, turn west off Highway 97, two kilometres south of the Okanagan Lake floating bridge, and follow Westside Road north for seven kilometres. To get to the park from Highway 97 near O'Keefe Ranch, northwest of Vernon, follow Westside Road south for 57 kilometres.

Wild Canyons to Waterfront.

Westside Road acts as the boundary between two quite different natural environments that create a diversity worth exploring. To the west, Lambly (Bear) Creek has cut a spectacular steep-walled canyon in its final descent from the rugged 1800-metre-high Pennask Plateau. In the process, the rushing water has created a fan-shaped delta in Okanagan Lake, to the east of Westside Road.

Above and on either side of the canyon, ponderosa pine and Douglas fir dominate the dry, rocky hills. Juniper, bunchgrass, Indian paintbrush, arrow-leaved balsamroot, Oregon grape and prickly-pear cactus compete for the area's meagre rainfall. Below, in the shady confines of the canyon, moistened by the mist rising off the waterfalls, is yet another world. It is one of maple and birch, of Saskatoon and chokecherry, of wild rose, horsetail and moss.

Swallows glide gracefully through the canyon, red-tailed hawks ride warm afternoon updrafts high above, and owls hoot the night away. Tree-frogs are noisiest in the spring; the crickets click in the summer; and the coyote's song occasionally drifts down from the hills.

A network of trails encircles the lower canyon, with parking available near the Lambly Creek bridge, west of Westside Road. Note that there are some

Fig 15:
Beach scene at Bear Creek Provincial Park.
(Photo BCP-015 © Murphy Shewchuk.)

very steep cliffs along the canyon walls. For safety reasons, stay on the trails when hiking. A loop hike on the mid-canyon trail to the canyon rim and then upstream to the footbridge presents an excellent example of typical north-slope environment in desert country. The walk back down the north side of the canyon is much drier. Watch for the remnants of an old irrigation ditch near viewpoint #5. Because of the west-east flow of Lambly Creek, early to mid-morning could be the best time to photograph the waterfalls on the canyon floor.

Once a working ranch.

The park campground, day-use picnic area and boat launch facilities are on the delta of Lambly (Bear) Creek. Once an integral part of Bear Creek Ranch, the S.M. Simpson Sawmill Company purchased the site from the ranch for its logging activities, and later sold it to Crown Zellerbach Canada Limited. In 1981, the British Columbia government purchased the land from Crown Zellerbach for a provincial park. As a condition of sale, Crown Zellerbach maintained the rights to continue its booming activities north and south of the main beaches.

When Bear Creek Park originally opened in the early 1980s, it contained 80 campsites, but a recent expansion added another 42 campsites plus associated facilities. There are now 122 campsites, plus showers and washrooms with flush toilets. In addition to the canyon trails, there are lakeshore trails and over 400 metres of sandy beach. At the amphitheatre, a park interpreter provides interesting programs from mid-June to early September.

•••

12

Central Okanagan

Kelowna and Surrounding Area

Kelowna has grown at such a rapid pace in recent years that a newcomer may initially be impressed with its urban sprawl rather than the quiet places to be found with further exploring. Kelowna and the surrounding area offers many outdoor recreation opportunities if you take the time to look beyond (and sometimes between) its hotels, shopping centres and housing developments.

Knox Mountain Park, for example, can be quiet early in the morning before the sounds of the city start to drift upward. Woodhaven Nature Conservancy, at the end of Raymer Road in Okanagan Mission can be quiet — or noisy — any day of the week. It depends on whether or not you consider the frantic chatter of a squirrel part of the quiet or part of the noise. The pathways in Mission Creek Regional Park are seldom devoid of people, but it is easy to let the burble of the water flowing through the kokanee spawning channel carry you away from your surroundings.

The trails into the north slopes of Okanagan Mountain Provincial Park can also be quiet and devoid of people — even in mid-summer. Access to the park is off Lakeshore Road from Kelowna, by boat across Okanagan Lake or via the Chute Lake Road, north of Naramata. In keeping with the wilderness nature of the park, facilities are minimal throughout.

Bear Creek Provincial Park, on the west shore of Okanagan Lake, has full facilities, but the spectacular canyon and waterfalls encourage wild birds and animals — and satisfy the need for free space that is part of the wild animal within all of us. Hardy Falls Regional Park in Peachland has a canyon and waterfall, although on a much smaller scale. It is also much more accessible for those with limited mobility.

If you have that urge to get mobile, backroads lead up into the hills from Peachland, Westbank and Kelowna where you will find places to golf, trek, cycle, fish or camp in summer — or ski, snowmobile or ice-fish in winter. These backroads can also provide alternate routes to other parts of the Okanagan Wonderland.

•••

13

Public Gardens in Kelowna

By Judie Steeves

Statistics:	For map, see page 55.

Distance:	All within the City of Kelowna core.
Travel Time:	Allow half a day to wander around.
Condition:	Wheelchair accessible; level paths.
Season:	Year-round.

These rambles in four public gardens in Kelowna will take you from the formality of the beds of colorful Dutch tulips at Veendam Garden to the controlled serenity of Kasugai, a Japanese walled garden. A short drive away you may stop and wander around the Edwardian garden surrounding historic Guisachan House, then complete your garden tour with a visit to the new xeriscape demonstration garden at Benvoulin Heritage Park.

Dutch color dots the green.

Veendam Way in Kelowna's City Park is lined with gardens that are brilliant with color in spring from the masses of tulip bulbs planted to honor Kelowna's sister city in the Netherlands. That color continues through spring, summer and fall with both annuals and perennials maintained by Kelowna's park staff. They are sheltered by mature trees which shade those who wander on the grass or along the lakeshore. However, in 1997, brutal winds decimated the big trees in City Park, ripping out the old cottonwoods by the roots and damaging a number of other specimen trees. Although new trees have been planted, it's a more open park than it was before that sudden, devastating storm. An adjacent rose garden is another feature of City Park. There's also a children's water park, a restaurant and concession, a sports oval with a running track, and a lawn bowling green. City Park is bounded by the lake, the Okanagan Lake Floating Bridge, Highway 97, Abbott Street, and the foot of Bernard Avenue where the Sails sculpture by R. Dow Reid stands. The entrance to Veendam Way is 0.3 km from Highway 97 on Abbott Street.

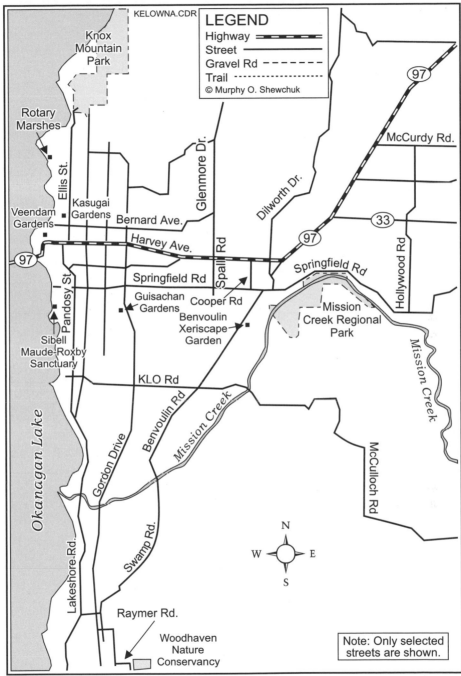

KELOWNA.CDR

LEGEND

Highway	═══════
Street	──────
Gravel Rd	─ ─ ─ ─
Trail	··············

© Murphy O. Shewchuk

Knox Mountain Park

Rotary Marshes

Ellis St.

Glenmore Dr.

Dilworth Dr.

McCurdy Rd.

97

97

33

Hollywood Rd

Kasugai Gardens

Veendam Gardens

Bernard Ave.

Harvey Ave.

Spall Rd

Springfield Rd

Springfield Rd

Pandosy St.

Guisachan Gardens

Cooper Rd

Benvoulin Xeriscape Garden

Mission Creek Regional Park

Mission Creek

Sibell Maude-Roxby Sanctuary

KLO Rd

Benvoulin Rd

Mission Creek

Gordon Drive

McCulloch Rd

Okanagan Lake

N

W ⊕ E

S

Swamp Rd.

Lakeshore Rd.

Raymer Rd.

Woodhaven Nature Conservancy

Note: Only selected streets are shown.

Map 8
Kelowna public gardens and bird-watching parks.

A peaceful enclave in a bustling downtown.

Kasugai Gardens was opened in 1987, a tribute to Kelowna's other sister city, Kasugai, Japan. Entering this carefully-manicured walled garden is like entering a different world from the bustling transit mall and busy city core outside. Even the noise is muted by the thick walls and green growth and by the

Fig 16:
Kasugai Gardens. (Photo © Judie Steeves.)

restful sound of trickling water from the stream that flows through this well-maintained garden. Ducks perch on the rocks, staring at the large carp which inhabit the waterfall-fed pond. A bridge arches over the water to take strollers from one path to another. Sculptured pines, Japanese statuary, topiary and patches of colorful flowers greet the eye in little vignettes all around this tranquil retreat. It's a perfect setting for family photos, a quiet contemplative stroll or a discreet discussion. Unlike the brash boldness of the Bennett clock sculpture outside the walls, inside is all peace and serenity. Outside, the clock sculpture towers over the low garden walls, set in a fountain of constantly-flowing water. It was built by the public to honor the years of service to his community by former BC premier W.A.C. Bennett, a Kelowna resident who governed the province from 1952 to 1972. He died in February, 1979. The entrance to this garden is 0.4 kilometre north of Highway 97 (Harvey Avenue), at the foot of Pandosy Street on Queensway, just behind Kelowna City Hall.

Step back in time.

Guisachan House was built in 1891 for the Earl and Countess of Aberdeen, and many of the trees and gardens surrounding it date from as much as 100 years ago. The Edwardian gardens were established by Elaine Cameron, who, with her husband Paddy, purchased the property in 1903. They lived there for 81 years. The property was purchased by the City of Kelowna in 1986 as a city park and the gardens have been restored to their 1920's splendor by the people of Kelowna. You won't be the first if you hear the mysterious sound of horses' hooves and buggy wheels along the avenue of 100-year-old cedars on a night bright with a full moon. Guisachan House was designed in the Indian colonial bungalow style, and became the focal point of a 480-acre ranch. It was named after Lady Aberdeen's childhood home in Inverness-shire, Scotland. Lord

Fig 17:
Guisachan Gardens.
(Photo © Judie Steeves.)

Aberdeen was Governor-General of Canada from 1893 to 1896. The gardens feature a rose arbor and rose garden with more than 100 varieties arranged in formal beds, each labelled. They begin to bloom in late May, and continue through to the first heavy frosts in November. Many are fragrant, and they include a new rose bed with the winter-hardy Prairie Series developed at the Morden Manitoba federal agricultural research facility. A rhododendron and a shade garden are special features of the perennial and annual beds which are defined by the walkways through Guisachan Gardens. McDougall House, built by John McDougall in 1886, The Milk Shed gift shop, a remnant of the era when this was a dairy farm, and an elegant restaurant in Guisachan House, operated under the eye of gold medal-winning Master Chef Georg Rieder are other features in the park. Guisachan Heritage Park is managed by the Central Okanagan Heritage Society. To reach this garden, drive 1.8 kilometres south of Highway 97 (Harvey Avenue) on Gordon Drive and turn right onto Cameron Avenue just past the traffic lights at Guisachan.

A heritage of native plants.

Benvoulin Xeriscape Garden opened in 1998 between McIver House, which was built in the early 1890s, and the Benvoulin Church, which was constructed in 1892. It was restored by the Central Okanagan Heritage Society, beginning in 1984 and is now a unique community facility used for public,

Fig 18:
Benvoulin Xeriscape Garden and McIver House. (Photo © Judie Steeves.)

cultural and family events such as weddings. The society decided it would be in keeping with the heritage of the Kelowna pioneers who inhabited these buildings and with today's acceptance of the need for environmentally-responsible landscaping, to establish a garden with the heritage plants which would have survived in this arid valley with little if any irrigation. From the early-blooming, native spring sunflowers and Saskatoon bushes, to summer's golden gaillardia flowers, hardy roses and purple echinacea, to the red sumac leaves and silver and yellow rabbit brush of autumn, it illustrates that there's lots of color in drought-resistant plants. At this colorful little garden, you will learn that planning and design, soil analysis, plant selection, practical turf areas, efficient irrigation, the use of mulches and proper maintenance all make up a xeriscape garden. Xeriscape is a new word coined to mean "letting the outdoor environment we create echo the nature of the natural world, saving water, time and money." This demonstration garden is located 1.1 kilometre from Highway 97, south on Cooper Road, then right at its end onto Benvoulin Road. Follow the Heritage signs. The address is 2279 Benvoulin Road.

•••

14

Birding Walks in Kelowna

By Judie Steeves

Statistics: **For maps, see pages 55 & 62.**

Travel Time:	Allow an hour or so for each.
Condition:	Well-maintained.
Season:	Year Around.
Topo Maps:	Kelowna, BC 82 E/14 (1:50,000).
Communities:	Kelowna.

From the dramatic towering osprey snag in Rotary Marshes in downtown Kelowna, to the relative serenity of the Sibell Maude-Roxby Bird Sanctuary south along the lakeshore, and the well-hidden Woodhaven Nature Conservancy, bird watchers could spend the better part of a day behind their binoculars right in the city.

Each of these little spots of wilderness inside the city boundaries has been either saved from or restored after man's efforts to alter the natural landscape.

Build it and they'll find it.

Restoration of the two or three-hectare marshland only began in 1995, but Rotary Marshes has already been discovered and adopted by the birds it was intended to attract.

Located adjacent to a high-rise condominium development and Kelowna's more-formal Waterfront Park, this rebuilt wetland is already home to a family of ospreys who were quick to make use of the high-rise tree trunk provided by the community for them to perch on and nest atop.

Re-creation of this little marsh was a joint effort of local Rotarians, the city, senior governments, local foundations, corporations, industries and volunteer citizens after years of serving as recipient of dirt and other fill from a variety of sources.

A wooden walkway on stilts now allows human families to see into the living-rooms of winged families with a minimum of disruption to the wild things.

This marsh restoration is a work in progress, but if the amount of use by birds is any indication it is progressing well.

Decades ago, this was the wetland where Brandt's Creek was filtered through the bulrushes before entering Okanagan Lake.

To reach Rotary Marshes, turn north off Highway 97 (Harvey Avenue) onto Water Street, a block from the Okanagan Lake Floating Bridge. Follow Water Street across downtown Kelowna's main street, Bernard Avenue, past the city hall, community theatre, courthouse, art gallery, a resort hotel and Waterfront Park, to Sunset Drive.

Turn left onto Sunset and almost immediately you'll see the entrance to the marsh on your left, 1.7 kilometres in total from the highway.

Don't park on this side of the road, however there is parking on the other side.

Kelowna's Riverside Forest Products mill can be seen at the end of the street.

A flourishing memorial.

The Sibell Maude-Roxby Bird Sanctuary is a more-established wetland preserve, named for a woman who lobbied unsuccessfully for the protection of this marshy area in the 1940s.

It wasn't until 1988, two years after her death, that restoration actually began in a joint project of the Central Okanagan Heritage Society and the Central Okanagan Naturalists' Club.

Fig 19:
A boardwalk in the Sibell Maude-Roxby Bird Sanctuary. (Photo © Judie Steeves.)

In the meantime the marsh had been filled in with garbage, grass clippings and dirt, and the water had been drained and diverted.

It had to be dredged, a groundwater pump system installed and islands re-created to restore the vital wildlife habitat that Sibell and her husband Victor had recognized decades earlier.

This sanctuary is the last remaining foreshore marsh in the central Okanagan.

Fig 20:
Female Redwing Blackbird.
(Photo BBR-097 © Murphy Shewchuk.)

It too features a series of raised wooden walkways so human feet can tramp through the marsh without destroying the fragile plant life and disturbing the delicate balance that keeps this little ecosystem working.

Waterfowl, shorebirds, insects, fish such as carp, aquatic mammals and reptiles now make their home here amongst the two-metre-high cattails, towering cottonwoods and dense willow thickets.

The sound of traffic swarming over the Okanagan Lake Floating Bridge is in the background as you walk through this misty marshland. However, the foreground is full of the seasonal sounds of the marsh, whether it's the mating noises of mallards, the call of the red-winged blackbird, or migrating waterfowl taking off from the water on their way south after a rest.

The sanctuary is found at the foot of Francis Avenue, near Kelowna General Hospital.

Turn south off Highway 97 onto Abbott Street near the east end of the Okanagan Lake Floating Bridge, and follow it for 1.7 kilometres as it twists and turns. Turn right onto Francis Avenue and park. You're at the lake. Just walk down to the sandy beach and turn right into the marsh.

Kinsmen Park, which includes a playground, beach and grassy area, is to your left.

Woodhaven - A secret in the city.

Surrounded by a chain link fence, Woodhaven Nature Conservancy is an island of wildland smack in the middle of an area of blacktop and concrete in the Mission area of Kelowna.

Within this nine-hectare (21.6-acre) haven of wilderness are three distinct biogeoclimatic zones which you can explore along several kilometres of trails that loop through this Central Okanagan Regional Park.

It features not only the dry grasslands and ponderosa pine that is typical of the Okanagan's Dry Interior Zone, but also a sharply contrasting mature stand of cedars more typical of the Wet Interior Zone.

Take a self-guided tour with the aid of interpretive map brochures, available near the little parking lot inside the entrance to Woodhaven. Please respect the

privacy of the care-
takers, whose rustic
home nestles inside
the park among the
trees.

In 1973 this un-
usual wooded area
was threatened by
development, with
the first two acres
bought and tree
clearing begun be-
fore the efforts of
naturalists Jim and
Joan Burbridge to
protect these ma-
ture and diverse
woods.

They convinced
civic politicians
this plot of wilder-

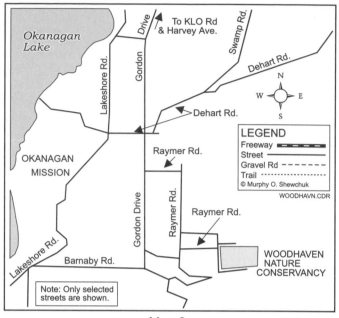

Map 9:
Woodhaven and area.

ness warranted preservation for future generations to learn from and enjoy.
They raised funds from the Nature Trust of BC and the Nature Conservancy of
Canada to purchase the land.

It's now home to dozens of species of birds, from the colorful western tana-
ger and yellow warbler to the familiar American robin and Oregon junco, the
noisy Steller's jay and magpie.

Trail features range from the old black cottonwoods clustered along the
creek trail, to the fragrant western red cedars that allow only shafts of sun to
reach the ground through their thick canopy along the cedar trail, and the distinctive ponderosa pine dotting the hillside along the flume trail.

Watch the open hillsides for patches of prickly pear cactus which can attach
themselves to your leg as you go by.

Reach this peaceful little oasis by turning south off Highway 97 (Harvey
Avenue) onto Gordon Drive at the Capri Centre Mall. Follow Gordon Drive for
7.2 kilometres, then turn east on Raymer Road. Follow Raymer Road for 1.8
kilometres to the gate of Woodhaven Nature Conservancy.

•••

15

Knox Mountain Park Trails

By Judie Steeves

Statistics: **For map, see page 55.**

Distance:	Three-kilometre drive up access road.
Travel Time:	Trail lengths vary.
Condition:	Variable.
Season:	Access road closed to vehicles in winter.
Topo Maps:	Kelowna, BC 82 E/14 (1:50,000).
Forest Maps:	Penticton Forest District Recreation Map.
Communities:	Kelowna.

Knox Mountain Park is a near wilderness area smack in the middle of the City of Kelowna with panoramic views out over the city, Okanagan Lake and the Okanagan Valley. Within its 235 hectares there are hiking and cycling trails, two lookouts, a pond and mountaintop, grasslands and forest, lakeshore and sage-dotted hills. Access is by a three-kilometre paved road to a lookout with picnic facilities and the Simpson Pavilion.

The pavilion was named after Kelowna pioneer S.M. Simpson who started Kelowna's first sawmill as a one-man operation in 1913. The sawmill is now owned by Riverside Forest Products Ltd., and is situated at the base of the mountain on the shore of Okanagan Lake.

A trail system that criss-crosses the park begins at the pavilion, making a series of loops in all directions. They vary from well-developed and maintained trails to intermediate ones and rough foot paths. Some are used by mountain bikers, while others would be unsuitable for bikes. Portions of the park are too steep for anything but billy goats and beard's tongue penstemon. Other portions are very fragile, with just a thin layer of soil over bedrock, which is easily disturbed and destroyed. Patches of delicate bitterroot, rock rose, or *Lewisia rediviva* flower briefly on the exposed hillside in summer.

Short trails include a 1.2-kilometre hike from the Apex Lookout to the parking lot near the city reservoir, part-way up the mountainside; a 0.5-kilometre hike from the lookout to a meadow, and a 0.8-kilometre trail from there down to the road near the Crown Lookout.

Several trails wind up the mountain to the Simpson Pavilion, where you can carry on a bit farther to the summit. From there you could strike off on a 1-kilometre trail to Magic Estates, a residential subdivision.

From there, walkers can continue on into a network of trails that wind their way through the North Glenmore area of Kelowna. Those trails can also be accessed through neighborhood parks such as Millard Glen Park. They include a walk along Brandt's Creek in Glenmore.

Fig 21:
Bridget on the Knox Mountain Trails.
(Photo OKO-394 © Murphy Shewchuk.)

Paul's Tomb.

There's an easy 2.6-kilometre walk to Paul's Tomb along the lakeshore. The roadway (blocked to cars) begins just past Poplar Point, or you can access it via a difficult, twisting pathway down the mountainside from the trail between Magic Estates and the summit.

Paul's Tomb is the tomb of an early Kelowna settler, Rembler Paul, who is remembered as a colorful eccentric, but one who was fairly well-off. He and his wife are still entombed on the site. He owned the property and had the tomb built about 1910 for 12 coffins, but the rest of the family declined to have their caskets laid there. In recent years it was closed up because of vandalism. However, the couple remain buried there in what is probably the only tomb in the whole Okanagan Valley.

Reach Knox Mountain Park's access road by turning north off Highway 97 (Harvey Avenue) onto Ellis Street, and driving 2.4 kilometres through the downtown area of Kelowna.

•••

16
Mission Creek Greenway

By Judie Steeves

Statistics:	For map, see page 55.
Distance:	7-kilometre greenway, with plans for more. 12 kilometres of hiking trails.
Travel Time:	Depends on your mode of travel.
Condition:	Excellent. Greenway is hard-packed gravel, on the level. Trails are easy.
Season:	Year around.
Topo Maps:	Kelowna, BC 82 E/14 (1:50,000).
Forest Maps:	Penticton Forest District Recreation Map.
Communities:	Kelowna.

Designated one of BC's Heritage Rivers in 1998, Mission Creek begins at the junction of the Shuswap/Kettle and the Okanagan watersheds, dropping from an elevation of 1829 metres (6,000 feet) to the floor of the Okanagan Valley as it winds its way over 43 kilometres. On its way down, it boils through narrow canyons, whooshes over waterfalls, gurgles through forested glades, and spreads out over flatter land before spilling into Okanagan Lake.

This little creek contributes a third of the total amount of water dumped into the valley's main lake, and is the lake's most significant contributor to the kokanee population, a land-locked sockeye salmon.

Mission Creek is not only a vital link in the natural world, it has played a key role in the human history of this area as well. It provided a Native Indian fishery; supplied irrigation water for farming settlers; and even supported gold-mining operations as recently as the 1940s. Mission Creek still serves a large agricultural area of 4054 hectares (10,135 acres).

The Native name for Mission Creek was N'wha-kwi-sen, which means smoothing stones. The French settlers named Mission Creek Rivière de L'Anse au Sable, or Sandy Cove River. It was renamed Mission Creek in honor of the Oblate Mission established in 1859 by Father Charles Marie Pandosy.

Fig 22:
A runner on the Mission Creek Greenway. (Photo © Judie Steeves.)

Significant features include Layer Cake Mountain which rises 350 feet above the floor of the canyon near Gallagher's Canyon Golf Course, and a spectacular waterfall near the City of Kelowna boundary.

Gold was discovered in Mission Creek in 1861 by William Pion (Peon), and in 1898 Dan Gallagher (Gallagher's Canyon) preempted land on the creek. He passed away in 1950. As much as $80,000 worth of gold was mined, all downstream from Gallagher's Canyon.

Community pitched in.

From 1996 through 1997 a grassroots community fund-raising effort led to creation of a public stream-side corridor called the Mission Creek Greenway. It is a three-metre wide pathway along the north side of the creek, from its outflow at Okanagan Lake, seven kilometres to Mission Creek Regional Park. In future phases, the intent of the Friends of Mission Creek, who spearheaded the community effort, is to continue the pathway for a further 11 kilometres to the waterfall. This is a joint-use creekside trail through the City of Kelowna for walkers, joggers, cyclists, wheelchairs and equestrians. Consideration and cooperation is essential among the different users in order to prevent conflicts.

With its ancient cottonwoods often meeting overhead, and dense undergrowth, this is a cool, refreshing walk on a hot Okanagan summer day. Viewing platforms and interpretive signs point out such features as swampy areas where a dramatically different ecosystem supports birds, reptiles and plant growth quite different from that in the majority of this arid valley. Although it is a natural corridor, this pathway is city-style, not a wilderness hike. With large numbers of feet, wheels and hooves tramping the trail, no green growth has a chance to mar its surface, but the creek burbles and rushes alongside you all the way.

Start at either end.

To walk upstream, begin by driving south off Highway 97 (Harvey Avenue) in Kelowna at Pandosy Street. Continue past the Kelowna Regional Hospital, a total of 4.8 kilometres to Mission Creek. Don't be alarmed if you suddenly find you're on Lakeshore Road after crossing KLO Road. It's just a street name change. Rather than crossing over Mission Creek on Lakeshore Road, make a left turn across the road, and park at the entrance to the 48-acre Mission Creek Greenway. There's an interpretive kiosk at the entrance with information about the greenway, how it came to be, and what its features are. You can walk from here to Gordon Drive and back, or arrange to be picked up there. You can continue farther along to Benvoulin Road; or hike the whole seven kilometres to Mission Creek Regional Park. You could also begin your trip on the greenway from the park, by turning east off Highway 97 at Leckie Road, and following Leckie a couple of blocks directly into Mission Creek Regional Park.

Watch the kokanee spawning.

This is one of the largest parks in Kelowna, although it's a Central Okanagan Regional District-maintained facility. An autumn feature of this 92-hectare (230-acre) park is the interpretive tours of the kokanee spawning channel that's been built adjacent to Mission Creek. It is an attempt to provide ideal habitat for the little fish to lay their eggs for maximum survival of the fry. Expect the red-flushed kokanee to be fighting their way back upstream to spawn beginning around September 10 most years, and continuing for about a month. The freshwater salmon die after laying their eggs, usually in the fourth year of their life.

There's also an environment educational centre in a new log building in the park, with displays specific to the park and the valley, and there's a composting education garden adjacent. The park has a picnic area, playground, grassy areas and an informational kiosk, as well as a network of trails other than the Mission Creek Greenway.

In fact, there are seven hiking routes from less than one kilometre to more than four kilometres in length in the park other than the greenway, a total of more than 12 kilometres of easy hiking. Check the information available at the kiosks near the parking lot. All are on the south side of the creek, so you must cross the bridge spanning the creek to begin your hike. You may choose the perimeter loop trail of 3.5 kilometres, the lookout trail loop of 1.8 kilometres, the four-kilometre upstream loop, 1.3-kilometre downstream loop, the 2.3 kilometre pond loop or the spawning channel loops. During your walk, take the time to watch for some of the park's 130 bird species, and some of the complex aquatic ecosystems. Beware of poison ivy.

Cycling is permitted on the greenway, the main trail from Hall Road to the dike and along dike surfaces, but not on other trails. Dogs must be kept on a leash at all times while in the park, and their owners are expected to clean up after them.

•••

17

Trans Canada Trail

By Judie Steeves

Statistics: For maps, see pages 176, 69, 140, 110

Distance:	In all, 15,000 kilometres, across Canada.
Travel Time:	Your choice.
Condition:	Variable.
Season:	With appropriate transportation and clothing, all.
Topo Maps:	Kelowna 82 E/NW (1:100,000).
	Penticton 82 E/SW (1:100,000).
Forest Maps:	Penticton Forest District Recreation Map.
	Merritt Forest District Recreation Map.
Communities:	Midway, Rock Creek, Beaverdell, Carmi, Kelowna, Naramata, Penticton, Summerland, Faulder, Princeton, Coalmont, Tulameen and Brookmere.

The Trans Canada Trail is planned as a multi-use trail from the Atlantic Ocean, traversing every province, to Vancouver Island and the Pacific Ocean, including a spur trail from Calgary, Alberta, to the Arctic Ocean. That spur travels through BC for about 1300 km, routed through Fort McMurray.

When completed, it will be the longest trail in the world. Its visionaries picture it as a unifying force, binding the various parts of Canada together in celebration of the year 2000. It is a three-metre wide pathway for the use of walkers, cyclists, horse riders, skiers and snowmobilers. It will be built by volunteer groups throughout the country, on existing pathways and such corridors as abandoned railway lines.

The backbone of the Trans Canada Trail in BC is the Kettle Valley Railway corridor, which is basically the route it takes through the Okanagan. See the *West Kettle Route — Highway 33* section, on page 72. With a few deviations, the trail follows the provincial government-owned KVR corridor from Grand Forks through Midway (so-named because it's midway across the province) to Rock Creek, close to the international boundary. It parallels the winding Kettle River, crossing it at the Kettle River Provincial Park. It continues through the campground, where campsites hug the river on both sides of the trail, to

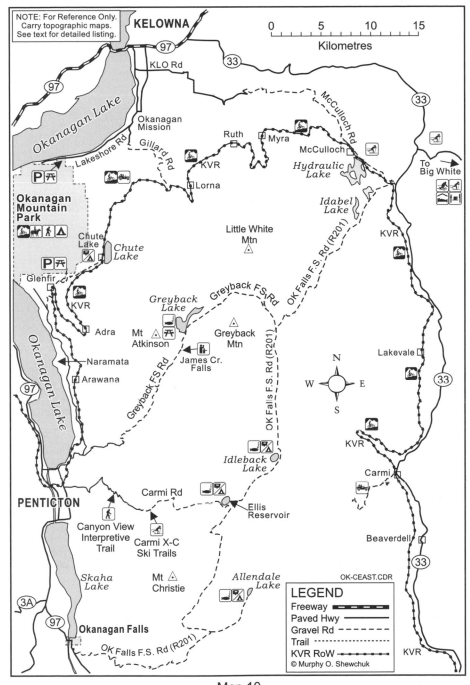

Map 10
Much of the Kettle Valley Railway (KVR) right-of-way is now part of the Trans Canada Trail across southern British Columbia.

Westbridge, at an altitude of 750 m (2,500 feet). It then branches off to follow the clear and cold West Kettle River north along the valley bottom, through historic mining settlements, intriguing with abandoned digs and the shells of old log structures.

Through some of these now-shrunken communities, the trail is used by local roadways. Some communities offer services such as cafes, hotels and other accommodation for the traveller, as well as historic points of interest.

The trail can be accessed from Highway 33 at dozens of points along the Kettle Valley. It is fairly smooth and level throughout, with a gradual incline to the 1300 m (4,300 feet) summit at McCulloch Station.

In places hikers, cyclists or skiers must deviate from the historic rail route around a farmer's field or rancher's pasture before re-joining the rail corridor on the other side. Agricultural taming of the landscape is part of the beauty of this valley that soaks in the sunshine between granite cliffs.

The KVR corridor and Trans Canada Trail leaves the Kettle Valley, but retains its name, near Cooksen Station. For a dozen kilometres or so there are a number of attractive wilderness campgrounds such as at Arlington Lakes, Idabel Lake and McCulloch Lake. There are also excellent resort accommodations, featuring both summer and winter recreation. See the *McCulloch Road* section on page 79 and *McCulloch Trails* section on page 82.

From Myra, the next historic station on the KVR, to Ruth, the trail clings to the mountainside through Myra Canyon. See the *Myra Canyon / KVR Corridor* section on page 84. This 12-kilometre section features some of the most spectacular scenery on the route. It winds high above the canyons and creeks as it passes over 18 wooden and steel trestles and through two tunnels on the eastern rim of the Okanagan Valley.

The awe-inspiring trestles and tunnels continue to be a feature of the trail's route from Ruth, where the Little White Forest Service Road connects the trail with Kelowna, to Arawana near Penticton.

Between Ruth and Lorna Stations the Crawford Trail from Kelowna meets the Trans Canada Trail and follows along it for a short distance, before turning off on its way up to Little White Mountain. See the *Crawford Hiking Trails* section on page 87.

The Gillard Creek Forest Service Road is another vehicular access route from Kelowna to the trail, or to Chute Lake Resort and campground. See the *Chute Lake Loop* section on page 91.

From Chute Lake to Penticton the Trans Canada Trail is downhill. It features some fabulous panoramic views of Okanagan Lake along the way. At Adra Station, between Chute Lake and Glenfir Stations, it also has the longest tunnel on the route. There are a number of access routes to the Trans Canada Trail from Naramata from just before Glenfir, to beyond Arawana Station.

Some will pass by some of the many small wineries and vineyards that have made the the the Okanagan Valley famous.

The Trans Canada Trail pavilion opened in Penticton in the fall of 1998, commemorating some of the many people whose donations made this trail a reality across the country. The route goes around orchards and follows city streets and paved pathways through Penticton. It then crosses the Okanagan River before beginning its climb up the sage-covered clay cliffs overlooking Okanagan Lake on the way to Summerland.

Just before it reaches Trout Creek you can take a diversion from it to tour the botanical gardens at the Pacific Agri-Food Research Centre (formerly the Federal Summerland Research Station), including the new xeriscape demonstration garden. Have your picnic on the lawns after you inspect the gardens. Here, the Trans Canada Trail crosses Trout Creek over the highest steel trestle bridge of its type in North America, before entering West Summerland Station. From the Trout Creek Trestle to Faulder Station is the only section with train tracks remaining. The Kettle Valley Steam Train carries visitors along the route from the Research Station through Summerland and then Prairie Valley.

The route then follows Trout Creek up a steady incline through the historic stations of Faulder, Crump, Kirton and Demuth to Thirsk. Here a chain of little lakes, Thirsk, Osprey, Link and Chain, feature BC Forest Service recreation sites and good fishing. From Osprey Station through Jellicoe, Erris, Jura and Belfort the route is downhill again into Princeton. See the *Princeton-Summerland Road* section, starting at page 141, for details.

From Princeton, it winds along the picturesque Tulameen River to the historic settlements of Coalmont and Tulameen. There's a slight incline as the trail gains altitude to Brookmere. On the way it passes Otter and Thynne Lakes and Otter Creek, and Manning, Thalia and Spearing Stations.

North of Brookmere, the Trans Canada Trail follows Brook Creek down to the Coldwater River and then parallels the Coldwater River southwest to the Brodie "Y". While the CPR line continued north through Kingsvale, Pine and Glenwalker Stations to Merritt, the trail takes parts of the old KVR route southward from Brodie. The exact route was uncertain at the time of writing, but it was expected to follow the Coldwater valley and Coquihalla canyon to Hope.

For more information on the Princeton to Hope section of the Trans Canada Trail, consult *Coquihalla Country, A Guide to BC's North Cascade Mountains & Nicola Valley*, by Murphy Shewchuk (ISBN 0-929069-10-2). See page 224 or check out the Sonotek Publishing Ltd. Web site at http://www.sonotek.com for details.

•••

18

West Kettle Route - Highway 33

By Murphy Shewchuk

Statistics:	For maps, see pages 69, 80 & 176.

Distance: 129 km, Hwy 33, Rutland to Rock Creek.
Travel Time: Approximately two hours.
Elevation Gain: Approximately 925 metres.
Condition: Paved throughout, some steep grades.
Season: Open year around.
Topo Maps: Kelowna 82 E/NW (1:100,000).
                 Penticton 82 E/SE (1:100,000).
                 Grand Forks 82 E/SE (1:100,000).
Forest Maps: Penticton Forest District Recreation Map.
                 Boundary Forest District Recreation Map.
Communities: Kelowna & Rock Creek.

Placer gold, fingers of silver, an abandoned railway and a ski resort that rivals Europe's best may appear to be an unusual combination, but Highway 33 provides access to all of them and much more.

This 129-kilometre-long highway links the central Okanagan with the Boundary Region. On the way, it passes through the West Kettle River valley — a dry, timbered region rich in both scenery and history. This is a quiet part of the province; still largely unspoiled by modern hustle and bustle.

The north end of Highway 33 begins at its junction with Highway 97 in Rutland, a Kelowna community. (Just a word of warning, the next gasoline service station is at Beaverdell, 79 kilometres down the road.) It ends at Rock Creek, at the junction with Crowsnest Highway 3 near the Canada-U.S.A. boundary, 52 kilometres east of Osoyoos.

Follows Mission Creek.

Highway 33 passes through the heart of Rutland before beginning a steady southeast climb out of the Okanagan Valley. Rangeland, scrub brush and pine forests gradually replace the orchards that have helped make the Okanagan Valley famous.

After allowing one last glimpse of the sprawling city below, the road opens to a view of the timber-lined canyon of Mission Creek. Originally named Riviere L'Anse du Sable by the fur traders, Mission Creek was a busy gold placer creek for a short time in the mid-1870s. According to historian N.L. "Bill" Barlee, Dan Gallagher, the last of the old prospectors, eked out a living on the creek until the 1940s.

Approximately 24 kilometres east of Kelowna, the highway crosses Mission Creek and enters the Joe Rich Valley. During the period between the two World Wars, the remarkably rich black soil of the valley supported a lettuce market gardening industry. E.O. MacGinnis started the lettuce farming and made a fortune before everybody got into it, says one old-timer. The Joe Rich Community Centre marks the heart of the former market gardening enclave.

Big White Ski Resort.

Less than 10 minutes beyond the Joe Rich Valley community center, a junction marks the paved road that leads 24 kilometres east and up to Big White Ski Resort. From a start in the early 1960s, Big White has become the closest a westerner can get to a European ski experience. It is a ski village in the mountains, equipped with private chalets, condominium style apartments, and a hotel complex with ski-to-your-door accommodations for over 6,000 guests. A choice of restaurants, discos, lounges and a grocery store help round out the facilities. Oh yes! Chair lifts and T-bar lifts, numerous downhill runs plus cross country ski trails on top of 12 metres of average snowfall help complete the requirements for a memorable ski holiday. See page 77 for more information.

West Kettle Valley.

Just beyond the Big White junction is the Rock Creek — Kelowna Summit. At an elevation of 1265 meters (4,159 feet) it marks the divide between the Okanagan and West Kettle drainage basins. The summit also marks a change in the scenery from the narrow valley of Mission and Joe Rich creeks to a broader, drier valley, lightly timbered with aspen and pine.

Five kilometers past the summit, there is another major junction, this time to the right. The well-maintained Okanagan Falls Forest Service Road continues south past Idabel Lake to Okanagan Falls (see page 167). A secondary road parallels the former Kettle Valley Railroad bed as far as McCulloch Station before the railbed strikes across the mountainside to Penticton and the road winds down the mountainside to Kelowna. (See *McCulloch Road*, page 79, for details.)

Kettle Valley Railway.

Under the direction of Chief Engineer Andrew McCulloch, construction of the Kettle Valley Railway (KVR), a Canadian Pacific Railway subsidiary, was begun in the summer of 1910. By the end of 1913, tracks had been laid from Midway in the Boundary region to Mile 83, a short distance west of McCulloch Station. This long-awaited Coast-to-Kootenay railway was finally completed through the Coquihalla Canyon (north of Hope) on July 31, 1916.

Steam buffs will undoubtedly remember the Kettle Valley Railway as one of the last bastions of "real" railroading. With speeds that varied from 25 kilometres per hour (15 mph) on the tortuous mountain grades to 90 kilometres per hour (55 mph) on the flat valley floors, steam led the way. The Mikados, the Consolidations and a few old Ten-Wheelers pulled passengers and freight over some of the most difficult terrain in North America. In its heyday, the steam-driven cylinders powered the eastbound Kettle Valley Express from Vancouver through Hope, Penticton, Rock Creek, Midway and on to Nelson in 23 hours. In another five hours, the "Express" had arrived at Medicine Hat, Alberta.

A large washout permanently closed the Coquihalla section of the KVR in 1959 and the last passenger run from Penticton to Midway took place in 1964. Since then, despite protests and suggestions that the route could be operated as a tourist attraction, the tracks have been removed on the Penticton-Midway section, as well as the Coquihalla and most of the route between Okanagan Falls and Spences Bridge.

Carmi.

Back on Highway 33, about 73 kilometres south of Kelowna, the paved road passes the remnants of the former community of Carmi. There is little left to indicate that, in 1914, Carmi had two hotels (one of which remains standing), two stores, a shoe shop, a resident policeman and jail, and a railroad hospital. The railway and a gold mine were the source of income in Carmi. When the mine closed in 1936, the town was dealt a severe blow. The closure of the railway finished it off.

Six kilometres south of Carmi, on the outskirts of Beaverdell, the East Beaver Creek Road begins a winding route eastward around Curry Mountain to Christian Valley. If you're interested in a little backcountry exploring, there is a network of logging roads and a dozen Forest Service recreation sites in the mountains between Beaverdell and Christian Valley. The Boundary Forest District Recreation Map, available from most Forest Service offices in the area, has the details.

There have been silver mines on Wallace Mountain, to the east of Beaverdell, since the 1890s. The first claim was staked on the mountain in 1889, but was apparently allowed to lapse. In 1896, a flurry of staking took

Fig 23:
The "Country Inn", one of Carmi's pioneer hotels. (Photo © Judie Steeves.)

place and the West Kettle River soon saw three new communities, including Carmi, Beaverton and Rendell. Later Beaverton and Rendell, only a short distance apart, were united under the name of Beaverdell.

Several mines operated profitably during the first half of the twentieth century. The Bell Mine, for instance, produced 350,000 ounces of silver between 1913 and 1936. The Highland Bell Mine, the site of more recent activities, was formed in 1936 through the amalgamation of the Bell and the Highland Lass claims. The silver was in veins "like the fingers on my hand," remembered miner Charlie Pasco of the day in 1945, when he first came to work for the old Highland Bell.

Beaverdell Hotel.

The Beaverdell Hotel, one of the oldest operating hotels in British Columbia, is itself a museum piece. It is certainly one of the more colorful places to visit in the community, particularly on a Friday or Saturday night.

Logging is the main industry of the West Kettle Valley today. The majority of timber harvested is pine and, according to one logger, most of it is hauled by truck to the mill at Midway.

Throughout the length of Highway 33 there are many spots where self-contained recreational vehicles can park for the night. However, the first privately-operated roadside campground on the southward journey is the West

Kettle Campground, 16 kilometres south of Beaverdell. It is an inviting location, laid out among the pines.

A kilometre or two farther south, a gravel road winds westward to Conkle Lake Provincial Park. See *Conkle Lake Loop*, page 175.

The West Kettle River and the Kettle River join at Westbridge. A secondary road follows the Kettle River northward, past the settlement of Christian Valley, eventually joining Highway 6 near Monashee Pass, east of Lumby.

Kettle River Park.

A short drive south of Westbridge lies the Kettle River Provincial Park campground. Set in the pines at a bend on the west bank of the river, this picturesque spot contains 49 campsites, picnic tables and an opportunity to swim, fish or cycle. The area is also ideal for the artist or photographer. In the summer months, the nearby irrigated hay fields are lush green, while outside the range of the sprinklers, the foliage is typical of the interior semi-desert plateau country.

Rock Creek.

Rock Creek is the southern terminus of Highway 33 and the end of the 129-kilometre drive from Kelowna — plus side trips, of course. Rock Creek was also the best-known placer gold creek in the Boundary region of British Columbia. Discovered in 1859 by Adam Beam, the creek was worked extensively from 1860 to 1864. At the peak of activity at least 500 miners scoured its gravels. Historians estimate that well over 250,000 ounces of gold — then worth $16 per ounce — was recovered from the creek before the paydirt played out and the miners moved north to the Cariboo. The creek saw limited action again during the recessions of the 1890s and 1930s. With the present price of gold, and the state of the BC economy, there may again be prospectors searching for the elusive Mother Lode.

Today, Rock Creek is the center of a busy agricultural community. Patient ewes and prancing lambs liven up the fields in the spring, while the yellow arrow-leaved balsamroot brighten the open slopes.

Midway, 19 kilometres east of Rock Creek on Crowsnest Highway 3, is well worth the visit regardless of your ultimate direction. The Kettle River Museum, officially opened in Midway in 1977, is an excellent source of information on the history of the Kettle Valley.

The West Kettle Route — Highway 33 — seems left out of the hustle and bustle of today. But, if you are interested in a skiing holiday, or a camping, fishing or back-country exploring vacation, this may be an advantage — not a disadvantage.

•••

19

Big White Ski Resort

By Judie Steeves

Statistics:	For maps, see pages 69 & 80.

Distance:	55 km from Kelowna.
Travel Time:	45 minutes to an hour from Kelowna.
Condition:	Paved road to resort.
Season:	All.
Communities:	Near Kelowna.

Big White Ski Resort is both big and white, with more than 2,075 acres of skiing, second in size only to Whistler-Blackcomb, and more than 6,000 beds on the hill. With the village at an elevation of 1768 metres (5,800 feet) and an annual snowfall of 750 centimetres (24.5 feet), it's white from October or November through April or May.

Boasting dry, light, champagne powder skiing, Big White offers world-class skiing and snowboarding, with a ratio of 18 per cent gentle slopes for beginners, 56 per cent long, cruising runs for intermediates and 26 per cent exhilarating steeps and deeps for the more advanced thrill-seekers.

There are more than 100 marked runs, accessed by 10 lifts, including four high speed quads like the new $4.5 million Gem Lake Express featuring 710 vertical metres of skiing. In addition to both day and night downhill skiing, there's 25 kilometres of alpine cross-country trails, access to more than 100 kilometres of snowmobiling tours, a snowboard park with both a 137-metre expert and beginner/intermediate half-pipes, and even an outdoor ice rink.

Modern mountain village.

Big White was established in 1963 and has been growing rapidly since 1985, with more than $110 million invested in the resort since then. The modern village is mid-mountain and features breath-taking scenery overlooking the Monashee Mountains.

Fig 24:
The daycare facilities at Big White are an important part of their service.
(Photo BWS-075 © Murphy Shewchuk.)

Accommodation at over 20 different sites varies from hostels to luxurious hotels or condominiums, and the numerous eateries range from pubs to family restaurants, to specialty offerings such as sushi, Italian food or fine dining. Clubs and bars are a part of the nightlife, and there are grocery stores and liquor outlets in the village as well.

Recent additions include the $10 million Kettle Valley Lodge operated by the Coast Resort, featuring 57 luxury rooms in the heart of the ski village, a 200-seat restaurant and other skiers' amenities. The $5 million Legend Condominium Hotel opened in late 1998 adjacent to the Plaza Quad Chair, with 30 suites and condominiums, and the luxurious Normerica Post and Beam Townhouses opened across the street about the same time. The resort is in the middle of a $65 million expansion, including a new kid's centre and daycare in the village centre and a teen centre.

Everything is ski-in and ski-out. Ski schools, a community school, a gift shop, ski shop with equipment rentals and sales, a hot tub, jacuzzi, sauna, racquetball, tennis, squash, indoor swimming pool and conference rooms are all available on the mountain.

•••

20

McCulloch Road

By Murphy Shewchuk

Statistics:	For map, see page 80.

Distance:	40 km, Highway 33 to downtown Kelowna.
Travel Time:	Up to one hour.
Elev. descent:	Approximately 925 metres.
Condition:	Gravel road with some steep sections.
Season:	May be closed in winter, slippery when wet.
Topo Maps:	Kelowna, BC 82 E/NW (1:100,000).
Forest Maps:	Penticton Forest District Recreation Map.
Communities:	Kelowna, Rutland and East Kelowna.

If you're looking for some fishing, backroad exploring and beautiful scenic views — with the option to explore a few Kettle Valley Railway trestles or strap on the cross-country skis, McCulloch Road is the answer. The upper or east end of McCulloch Road begins at Highway 33 in the West Kettle Valley, 40 kilometres southeast of the junction of Highway 97 and Highway 33 in Rutland, or six kilometres south of the junction to the Big White Ski Resort. (See *Big White Ski Resort* page 77, for details.)

With the junction of Highway 33 and McCulloch Road as kilometre 0.0, the first major side road is less than one kilometre to the northwest. The well-maintained Okanagan Falls Forest Service Road to the south will take you past Haynes Lake and Idabel Lake Resort. If you follow it far enough, you can descend to the Okanagan Valley at Penticton or Okanagan Falls with opportunities to fish, hike and explore along the way. However, as this is an active logging road it would be wise to restrict your exploring to weekends. (See *Okanagan Falls F.S. Road* on page 167 for details.)

Staying on McCulloch Road, a junction at km 4.5 marks a short side road leading south to the Hydraulic (McCulloch) Lake reservoir and several small Forest Service recreation sites. Fishing, cycling and cross-country skiing are the main pursuits of the area (see *McCulloch Trails*, page 82). The lakes serve as reservoirs for the residents and orchards of Kelowna.

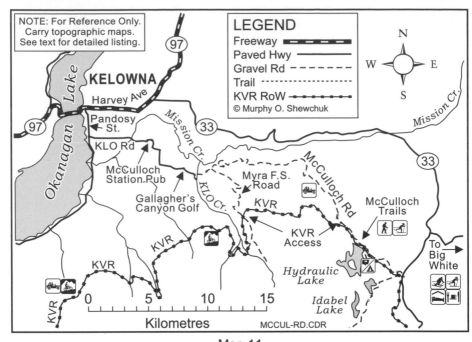

Map 11
McCulloch Road — Downtown Kelowna to Highway 33.

The trackless remains of the Kettle Valley Railway (KVR) parallel the road for a short distance before continuing their descent to Naramata and Penticton, via Chute Lake. McCulloch Station, near km 6.0, served as the KVR station for Kelowna. Stage coaches and freight wagons made the hair-raising trip to and from the orchard community on a regular basis. See the *West Kettle Route — Highway 33* section, starting on page 72, for more information on Andrew McCulloch and the Kettle Valley Railway.

A rough side road near km 8.5 leads south to Myra Canyon and the KVR right-of-way (see *Myra Canyon KVR Corridor*, page 84).

Remnants of wooden irrigation flumes can be seen as the road descends into the Okanagan Valley. A rough side road leads through the trees to an opening near km 21. Here you'll get an excellent view of East Kelowna with basalt columns in the foreground and Mount Boucherie in the distance.

Beyond the viewpoint, the road descends through a mix of grasslands and light timber. Switchback turns provide a bit of excitement for those unfamiliar with mountain roads, but good brakes and extra caution are all that is really needed to make the descent.

The basalt columns that were far below at the viewpoint a few minutes earlier are now just across a narrow valley near km 24. A short distance farther along, the road crosses Hydraulic Creek as it carries whatever water hasn't been used for domestic and irrigation purposes.

Viewpoint for valley.

In 1890, in what was probably the first move towards irrigating the dry benches above Kelowna, the Lequimes built an irrigation ditch from what was then called Canyon Creek, near km 28, to the upper bench that is now East Kelowna. The Kelowna Land and Orchard Company (KLO), formed in 1904, bought up the Lequime estate and the irrigation system. The water system is now part of the Southeast Kelowna Irrigation District.

The gravel of McCulloch Road gives way to pavement just before Gallagher's Canyon Golf Course (km 29). Farther down the road, vineyards soak up the sun on the slopes.

A viewpoint of the city of Kelowna (km 33) with its orchards and a back-drop of hills to the west presents still another reason why this is the largest community in the Okanagan Valley. McCulloch Road ends a short distance farther along, but if you wish to continue down toward Kelowna and Highway 97, follow KLO Road west after crossing Mission Creek.

First known as Riviere L'Anse du Sable, Mission Creek took its present name from the settlement first established in 1860 by Father Pandosy. The Priests' ranch at Okanagan Mission is believed to be one of the first in the area to use irrigation with water rights on Mission Creek issued in April, 1874.

Mission Creek Regional Park, in the centre of greater Kelowna, is well worth a side trip. The 92-hectare (230-acre) park contains more than 12 kilometres of hiking trails, a childrens' playground and a kokanee spawning channel — all in a mixed forest and river setting. To get there, turn north on Benvoulin Road and then east on Springfield Road (see *Mission Creek Greenway,* page 65).

Turn left (south) on Benvoulin Road, km 37, to explore the Pandosy Mission grounds near the corner of Benvoulin Road and Casorso Road. Casorso Road winds northwest to join KLO Road, which in turn runs into Pandosy. After exploring the Pandosy Mission, you can also turn north on Benvoulin Road to Highway 97, a distance of about four kilometres. If you continue on KLO Road at the Benvoulin Road junction, turn right on Pandosy and it will take you to Harvey Avenue (Highway 97). If you are now totally confused, before heading for the hills stop for a city map at the Kelowna Chamber of Commerce office on Harvey Avenue.

•••

21

McCulloch Trails

By Judie Steeves

Statistics:	For map, see page 80.

Travel Time:	You can decide.
Condition:	Well-maintained.
Season:	Ski here in winter; hike in summer.
Topo Maps:	Kelowna 82 E/NW (1:100,000).
Forest Maps:	Penticton Forest District Recreation Map.
Communities:	Kelowna.

More than 100 species of wildflowers have been documented on the McCulloch Trail system which winds through the forest near McCulloch Reservoir (Hydraulic Lake) east of Kelowna. The Nordic Cross Country Ski Club, Central Okanagan Naturalists' Club and Canada Trust's Friends of the Environment Foundation opened phase one of the Mildred Wardlaw Nature Trails in July, 1999. In all, 81 species of wildflowers and such wildlife as the Great Gray Owl are found in the area.

Mildred Wardlaw was the daughter of Emily and Dave Wardlaw, who was employed by the South East Kelowna Irrigation District in the 1930s. Mildred, who died in 1995, was steward of the Brown Lake Ecological Reserve.

The 52 kilometres of trails vary in length from half a kilometre to several kilometres. The trail system is at an altitude of 1280 metres (4,200 feet), so the biggest show of flowers is usually in early summer rather than spring.

All roads lead there.

The McCulloch Cross Country Ski Trails are located near the intersection of McCulloch Road (see page 79), Highway 33 and the Okanagan Falls Forest Service Road (see page 167). They can be reached from Kelowna via either Highway 33 off Highway 97, or along McCulloch Road via KLO Road and Gordon Drive off Highway 97 in Kelowna. (See the map on page 80.) Parking and the trailhead is off McCulloch Road across from the McCulloch Lake Resort. There are two fairly primitive Forest Service Recreation Sites for camping adjacent to Hydraulic Lake, and near Minnow Lake. There are more than eight lakes in the area, most stocked with rainbow trout. On the south side of McCulloch Road, trails loop from Idabel Lake Resort on Idabel Lake, to the Kettle Valley Railway line, and along Haynes, Minnow and Hydraulic Lakes. As well there is a canoe route from the McCulloch Forest Service Recreation Site around a couple of the islands on Hydraulic Lake to a portage between it and Pear Lake. From there you could cross Pear Lake to another short portage to Haynes Lake, then across a corner of that lake to Minnow Lake, and back to the recreation site.

Fig 25:
Canoeing is a popular past-time.
(Photo KAA-199 © Murphy Shewchuk.)

Diversity's the key here.

The Ministry of Forests calls this an integrated use area because it's managed for such diverse values: Hydraulic Lake is the McCulloch Reservoir providing water to residences and farms in the southeast area of Kelowna. Working with the ski club, a series of trails have been created and maintained in the area for public use all seasons of the year. The KVR corridor, now part of the Trans Canada Trail, provides world-class opportunities for cyclists, and there are other outdoor recreation uses as well. There is recreational fishing at several of the lakes in the area, and there's ample wildlife viewing opportunities, as well as good hunting. Rangeland permits are let by the ministry for local ranchers to allow their cattle to graze some of the Crown-owned land in this area. The ministry manages the harvest of timber on Crown-owned land in the area, as well as replanting, thinning and other silviculture practices. There's a strong link to BC's settlement and economic history in the section of Kettle Valley Railbed that cuts through this area, and in its name. Andrew McCulloch was the chief engineer during the construction of the KVR in the early part of the 1900s, and a nearby station on this rail line was named after him as well as the road and reservoir.

•••

22

Myra Canyon KVR Corridor

By Judie Steeves

Statistics: For maps, see pages 69 & 88.

Distance:	12 kilometres through the canyon.
Travel Time:	About four hours from Myra to Ruth station.
Condition:	Recently upgraded, level and well-maintained.
Season:	Spring, summer and fall.
Topo Maps:	Kelowna, BC 82 E/14 (1:50,000).
Forest Maps:	Penticton Forest District Recreation Map.
Communities:	Kelowna.

S pectacular views draw more than 30,000 people annually from all over the world to hike and cycle through Myra Canyon along the historic Kettle Valley Railway corridor, just 40 minutes from downtown Kelowna. Steel tracks were built through this steep-walled rocky canyon in the early 1900s, and the line was completed in 1914. They were removed in the 1980s because the railway was no longer used. However, the intricate steel and wooden trestles spanning creeks and cuts in the canyon remained behind, a legacy of the visionaries who created this transportation link. Those historic artifacts were considered an engineering marvel in their day, and are still awe-inspiring today, with the highest reaching 55 metres (180 feet) from its base to the wooden ties. In all, there are 18 trestles — 16 wooden and two steel — and two tunnels in this 12-kilometre stretch of the old railway bed.

In 1993, following both death and injury from falling from the trestles, the community formed the Myra Canyon Trestle Restoration Society. The members coordinated an upgrading of the trestle crossings and construction of 1.2 metre high handrails to prevent people from falling to the rocks far below. In two years there were donations of thousands of metres of lumber, an estimated 80,000 nails and more than 10,000 hours of volunteer labor. They constructed a one metre (three-foot) wide board walkway, complete with handrails, across each of the trestles. From corporations to kids, everyone got involved to create a safe walking and cycling corridor at the 1200-metre (4,000-foot) elevation around the city's southeast slopes.

Getting there.

The Myra Forest Service Road, which provides access from Kelowna to the KVR line at Myra Station, was upgraded by the provincial Ministry of Forests in the summer of 1998. That 8.5 kilometres is now a good gravel road suitable for a two wheel drive family vehicle. The parking lot at the intersection with the KVR has also been enlarged. To reach it from Highway 97 in Kelowna, turn south off that highway onto Gordon Drive at the Capri Hotel, continuing out to KLO Road. Turn east (left) and follow KLO, then McCulloch Road until you reach the turnoff to the Myra Forest Service Road, between crossings of KLO Creek and Hydraulic Creek. (See the *McCulloch Road* section on page 79 for more information.)

An alternative, but very rough-surfaced route is the Little White Forest Service Road, reached via June Springs Road, which accesses the KVR at the Ruth Station end of Myra Canyon instead of the Myra Station end. Take the same route from Highway 97, but turn off McCulloch Road just past Gulley Road, onto June Springs. It's 4.6 kilometres along the Little White Forest Service Road to the KVR.

Just a beginning.

Myra Canyon is actually just one part of a 600 kilometre long provincially-owned recreation corridor along the former KVR line from Grand Forks through Midway, Rock Creek, Beaverdell, Carmi, Myra Canyon near Kelowna, Penticton, Summerland, Princeton, Coalmont, Tulameen, Brookmere and Merritt to Spences Bridge. In various places, it's still used for transportation of logs, gravel, minerals and sightseers, by trucks, cars, motorbikes, bikes and boots. However, much of the public corridor has been designated as the route of the Trans Canada Trail. (See the *Trans Canada Trail* section starting on page 68 for an overview of the route.)

Created as a transportation link between the mineral-rich interior of the province and the trading port on the Pacific Coast, the KVR was intended to prevent BC resources and business from going south to the United States in the early years of this century. To carry minerals to the Pacific Coast, it traversed mountain ridges and forested slopes; rolling farmland and rangeland and crossed steep gorges and roaring rivers. In Myra Canyon, the route still clings to the rocky mountainside, as it spans bubbling brooks and rushing waterfalls, and takes you through mysterious tunnels and deep timber.

If you have more time, or feel adventuresome, you could follow the KVR route 140 kilometres southeast of Myra, through McCulloch to Midway. You could also carry on in the other direction, from Ruth to historic stations at

Fig 26:
Cycling the KVR in the Myra Canyon area. (Photo © Gordon Bazzana.)

Lorna, Chute Lake (it is 11 kilometres away and there's a full-service fishing resort there as well) Glenfir, Arawana and Penticton. The Gillard Creek Forest Service Road from Chute Lake Road in Kelowna crosses the KVR just west of Lorna. The Crawford Trail (see page 87) crosses the KVR between Ruth and Lorna.

In mid-summer, when it's hot in the valley bottom, it's cooler up on the KVR. In fact, be prepared at all times of the year for temperatures that are a few degrees cooler at this higher elevation. Although there are pit toilets now provided along the route, it's basically a well-maintained corridor through rugged wilderness, so be prepared with drinking water, something to snack on, if not a meal, and suitable clothing, including comfortable, stout walking boots or shoes. Expect to take out everything you take in, so you and your children can enjoy this piece of preserved wilderness another day.

•••

23

Crawford Hiking Trails

By Judie Steeves

Statistics:	For maps, see pages 69 & 88.

Distance:	6 km to KVR; 2.3 on KVR; 9.5 km to Little White.
Travel Time:	2-3 hours to KVR; 1 hour on KVR; 4-5 hours on way to Little White.
Condition:	Most trails are well-maintained.
Season:	Dependent on elevation.
Topo Maps:	Kelowna, BC 82 E/14 (1:50,000).
Forest Maps:	Penticton Forest District Recreation Map.
Communities:	Kelowna.

The main Crawford Trail is like a trunk from which you could quite literally get lost in a network of branching trails southeast of downtown Kelowna. It includes a portion of the historic Kettle Valley Railway (KVR) corridor and features panoramic views across steep canyons to Okanagan Lake far below. At the beginning of the trail, you'll hear Bellevue Creek as it falls 20 metres through a narrow, rocky gorge. In the middle, stately mariposa lilies dot the hillsides; chipmunks scour the pathway for tidbits, and grouse will startle you with their sudden awkward flight into the bushes. At the top of the last trail section, you will find a beautiful alpine meadow and tarn.

Built at the turn of the 20th century.

The trail to Crawford Lake near the top of Little White Mountain was constructed at the turn of the century. It provided access to an open flume system used to carry irrigation water to the Crawford fields. Sections of the old flume still lie rotting in the underbrush along the canyon rim. Growth of a different kind has now sprouted in the Crawford fields. The asphalt and concrete of Crawford Estates has replaced the flora of earlier decades.

Start anywhere.

You can embark on these trails at several points, depending on the season, your appetite for exercise, your fitness level, and whether you want to spend a

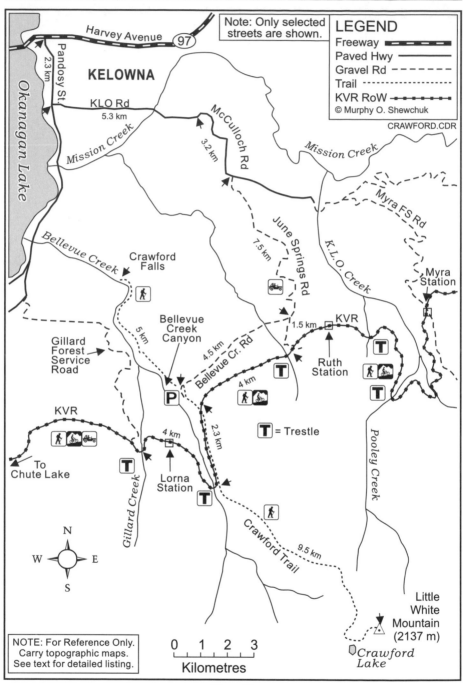

Map 12
Crawford Hiking Trails and the Myra - Ruth - Lorna section of the KVR.

Fig 27:
Cyclists on the KVR in the Myra Canyon area. (Photo © Gordon Bazzana.)

few hours, a whole day or a weekend hiking. You may wish to arrange for pickup at an alternate access point so you don't have to return on the same trail you set out on.

To reach the lowest access point to the trail, take Gordon Drive south off Highway 97, near the Capri Hotel in Kelowna. Drive 7.3 kilometres south on Gordon to DeHart Road and turn east onto DeHart, which makes a right turn uphill after several long blocks. Take Crawford Road to the right, then turn right onto Stewart Road West, at the end of Crawford Road. Turn right onto Westridge Drive, left onto Canyon Ridge Crescent, then right onto Canyon Falls Court, all within a few blocks. Park here in the cul-de-sac at Canyon Falls Court, and you'll see the pathway heading uphill from there along the rim of the canyon. It's a steady six-kilometre climb from the 510-metre elevation of the trailhead to 1050 metres, where the trail intersects with Bellevue Creek Forest Service Road. This is the second option for an access point to the trail, to either hike down to Crawford Estates, or up to the intersection with the Kettle Valley Railway corridor, another 2.3-kilometre hike.

At the Bellevue Canyon trestle on the KVR you leave the rail corridor to head uphill to Little White Mountain to continue along the Crawford Trail. It's 9.5 kilometres farther, at an elevation of 2137 metres, but there's a fabulous 360-degree viewpoint. There's a primitive campsite not far from the KVR along this last leg of the trail, complete with pit toilet, bear cache and picnic table. You should also be prepared for some rough spots along the trail as it is subject to damage from spring runoff. This section of the trail once served as a horse trail up to the fire lookout tower on Little White. It once carried the telegraph line to the tower, too, as the remnants can attest.

You could also access the Crawford Trail system from the Kettle Valley Railway route. The trail intersects the KVR between the Ruth and Lorna Stations, about four kilometres from the Little White Forest Service Road, more than six kilometres from the site of the former KVR Lorna station.

Trails get diverse use.

The Crawford Trail begins in the City of Kelowna and travels through a section of the Central Okanagan Regional District, but most of it is on land owned by the province of BC. The first part climbs along the rim of Bellevue canyon, 150 metres or so above Bellevue Creek. This lower portion of the Crawford Trail gets regular use from mountain bikers and backcountry horsemen, and both groups hold regular race events in this area. The races are usually posted, but be aware that these are multi-use trails and observe good trail etiquette.

The trail is well-marked, but generally keep to the right at trail intersections through the canyon, rather than taking trails to the left.

Fig 28:
On the Crawford Trail.
(Photo © Judie Steeves.)

Make sure you know where you're going if you leave the main trail, and use your compass and map. The main trail continues along the canyon rim past where Gillard Creek Canyon comes into Bellevue Creek Canyon, not far before the Bellevue Creek Forest Service Road meets the trail. Shortly after that, the trail enters the KVR corridor between the Ruth and Lorna Stations, and follows it for a couple of kilometres, until the Crawford Trail takes a turn to the east, and you head up to Little White Mountain. The grade isn't too steep except for the last bit up Little White Mountain itself.

It's breathtaking — in more ways than one.

•••

24

Chute Lake Loop

By Murphy Shewchuk

Statistics:	For maps, see pages 88 & 92.

Distance:	77 km, Hwy 97, Kelowna to Hwy 97, Penticton.
Travel Time:	Two to four hours.
Condition:	Some rough gravel, may be closed in winter.
Season:	July through October.
Topo Maps:	Kelowna, BC 82 E/NW (1:100,000).
	Kelowna, BC 82 E/14 (1:50,000).
	Summerland, BC 82 E/12 (1:50,000).
Forest Maps:	Penticton Forest District Recreation Map.
Communities:	Kelowna, Naramata and Penticton.

The Kettle Valley Railway right-of-way, between McCulloch Station and Naramata, has become a favorite travel route for motorcyclists, mountain bicyclists and backroad explorers. Because of the easy grades and spectacular scenery, efforts have been under way for more than a decade to have the route preserved and maintained as a linear park. Through the hard work of many and the impetus of a coast to coast to coast Trans Canada Trail, much of the former KVR right-of-way has been designated for use as part of the national trail.

It should be emphasized that this is a travel-at-your-own-risk route. At the time of writing, parts of the railway right-of-way were being used as an active logging road and still other sections, particularly the tunnels, require caution. Fortunately, considerable work has been expended on the trestles through the Myra Canyon, making them much safer, but also making them off limits to motor vehicles. Vehicle drivers can avoid the Myra Canyon section by gaining access to the KVR right-of-way via the Gillard Creek F.S. Road. Chute Lake Road bypasses the Adra Tunnel and the south end of the KVR right-of-way which has also been designated as part of the Trans Canada Trail. At the time of writing, there was no restriction against vehicles on the Gillard Creek to Chute

91

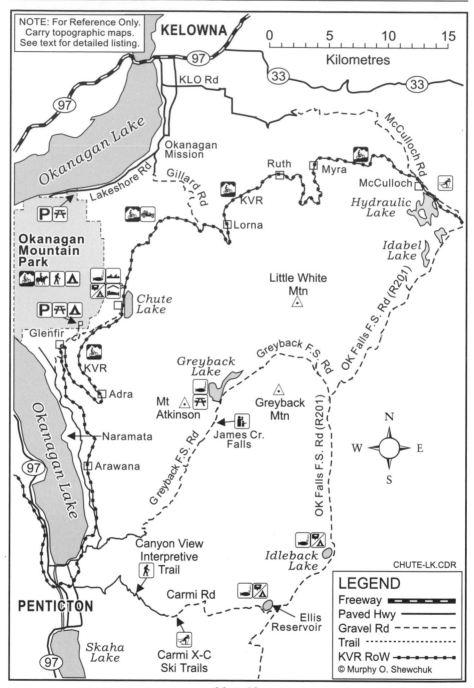

NOTE: For Reference Only. Carry topographic maps. See text for detailed listing.

KELOWNA

0   5   10   15
Kilometres

97
97
KLO Rd
33
33

Okanagan Lake
Lakeshore Rd
Okanagan Mission
Gillard Rd
Ruth
Myra
McCulloch Rd
McCulloch
Hydraulic Lake
KVR
Lorna
Idabel Lake

P
Okanagan Mountain Park
P
Glenfir
Chute Lake
Little White Mtn
OK Falls F.S. Rd (R201)

KVR
Adra
Greyback Lake
Mt Atkinson
James Cr. Falls
Greyback Mtn
Greyback F.S. Rd

Naramata
Okanagan Lake
97
Arawana
Greyback F.S. Rd
OK Falls F.S. Rd (R201)

N
W   E
S

Canyon View Interpretive Trail
Idleback Lake
CHUTE-LK.CDR

PENTICTON
Carmi Rd
Ellis Reservoir

LEGEND
Freeway
Paved Hwy
Gravel Rd
Trail
KVR RoW
© Murphy O. Shewchuk

Skaha Lake
97
Carmi X-C Ski Trails

Map 13
Various routes between Kelowna and Penticton, east of Okanagan Lake.

Lake section of the KVR. In fact, logging trucks and industrial equipment were using this route, posing a hazard for any unwary traveller. The hazards, however, have done little to discourage cyclists from making the long, scenic run from McCulloch Road or Gillard Creek Road to Naramata.

It's all downhill.

From a lazy man's perspective, the most enjoyable direction in which to follow the KVR route is from high above Kelowna, down to Naramata, particularly if you are on a bicycle. With the junction of Highway 97 (Harvey Avenue) and Pandosy Street as your kilometre 0.0 reference, follow Pandosy Street south, continuing on as it becomes Lakeshore Road. Leave Lakeshore Road where it makes a right turn at the flashing light at km 9. Follow Chute Lake Road up the hill, generally keeping to the left. Watch for the entrance to the Gillard Creek F.S. Road, before you reach the Cedar Creek #6 Firehall.

The Gillard Creek Road is a well-used forest access road. Although steep and dusty, with a few switchback turns and narrow sections thrown in for excitement, it should pose few difficulties in dry weather. As a safety precaution, it may be smart to leave the road to the logging trucks on weekdays.

At one time, the regular route from Kelowna to Chute Lake was via the Chute Lake Road, but by the summer of 1991, it was virtually blocked by a major washout 8.5 kilometres from the junction with Lakeshore Road. A bypass had been chewed around the washout, but it was too steep for two-wheel drive vehicles and many normal 4x4's.

North to Myra Canyon or south to Chute Lake?

After climbing approximately 700 metres (2,300 feet) in the 8.8 kilometres from Chute Lake Road to the KVR right-of-way, the time comes to make a decision. If you're planning a bicycle trip to Naramata, you can follow the right-of-way east (up the track) for a few hundred metres to a wide, safe parking area near the old Gillard Creek trestle, and begin your cycle touring. If you decide to continue left (east), the tall, curved steel Bellevue Creek trestle is about 4.5 kilometres east of the Gillard Creek Road/KVR junction and is well worth a visit. A network of logging roads and trails lead from the east side of the trestle southeast past Crawford Lake to the 2,137 metre (7,011 foot) summit of Little White Mountain. It's about 9.5 kilometres from the trestle to the summit. Information on this and other hiking trails in the area can be found in the *Crawford Hiking Trails* section on page 87.

If you choose to go right (west) at the Gillard Creek Road/KVR junction you'll begin the gradual descent to Chute Lake and Naramata. The right-of-way is fairly narrow with little room to pass a cyclist, let alone a logging truck or another vehicle. Fortunately, visibility is generally good and there are frequent wide sections to pull over.

Lebanon Lake, approximately 26 kilometres from downtown Kelowna (Hwy 97), is the first major landmark on the now-southward descent. The rough road to the west at the south end of the lake is the continuation of the old Chute Lake Road. If you are riding a mountain bicycle or a 4x4 with excellent clearance, you could consider returning to Kelowna via this route, but there are no guarantees the road will be easy, or even passable.

The KVR right-of-way continues south another 5.9 kilometres to the Chute Lake Resort at the former site of the Chute Lake station. At an elevation of 1,160 metres (3,950 feet) Chute Lake can be a cool oasis in a hot Okanagan summer or a snowmobiling haven in a dry Okanagan winter.

Chute Lake Resort.

Gary and Doreen Reed have operated the Chute Lake Resort since 1975, catering to fishermen, hunters, snowmobilers, cross-country skiers and just plain vacationers who want to get away from the city for a weekend. Chute Lake, says Gary Reed, is high enough and cool enough to keep the rainbow trout firm and tasty year around. To make it easier for the drop-in fisherman, the resort offers log cabins, lodge accommodation, campsites and a licensed dining room, if you aren't into cooking. Gasoline- and electric-powered motorboats, canoes and rowboats as well as fishing tackle are also available.

Bring up the subject of hunting, and Gary Reed will show you the snapshots of the #3 and #5 record Boone & Crockett whitetail bucks taken in the nearby mountains. According to Gary, George West of Victoria took the #3 buck (a B&C score of 173) in 1987. Fred Metter, also of Victoria, took the #5 buck that same year with a B&C score of 169 points. He will also tell you about the herd of elk that is attracting plenty of attention. Moose, once a scarcity this far south, are now thriving in the upland marshes.

The junction at the south end of Chute Lake is a place for decision making. If you are in a vehicle, you can follow the steep, winding gravel road for about 11 kilometres down to Naramata Road and a further 20 kilometres south to downtown Penticton. If you are a cyclist, you can follow the steady grade of the Kettle Valley Railway as it snakes down the mountain, passing two tunnels, rock ovens and spectacular viewpoints before reaching a man-made dead-end at Smethurst Road above Naramata.

KVR route.

With the junction at the gate of Chute Lake Resort as your kilometre 0.0 reference, follow the railway grade as it carves a gentle arc across the mountainside. You'll have the option of rejoining Chute Lake Road near km 2.5 and again via the Elinor Lake F.S. Road near km 9.3. Watch for the foundation of a railway water tank near km 10.5 and the extra wide right-of-way of the passing track of Adra before reaching the 489 metre (1,604 foot) long Adra Tunnel. The

Fig 29:
A rock oven near the Adra Tunnel. (Photo OKO-375 © Murphy Shewchuk.)

tunnel carves a curve within the mountain and a weak spot in the roof near the mid-point is slowly caving in. At last check, the tunnel had been barricaded and a hiking/biking trail bypasses it. The Elinor Lake Road, mentioned earlier, can also be used to get down to the next level of the right-of-way.

The right-of-way now traverses the mountainside in a northwesterly direction. Watch for a wide spot in the grade near km 14.8 just before it enters a rock cut. If you've found the right wide spot, you can follow a fairly well-used trail up the hillside to a fine specimen of the rock ovens that once served the railway construction crews. (If you bypassed the tunnel via Elinor Lake Road, back-track a few hundred metres up the railway grade.) According to several sources, including Bob Gibbard of nearby Glenfir, these ovens were used by the railway construction camp cooks during 1912 and 1913 when baking for the hungry, hardworking crews. A regional park has been established to protect these unique ovens as relics of an important part of our past. Although we only managed to find one complete oven on our trip down the KVR, Bob Gibbard suggests that there are half a dozen such locations between Chute Lake and Naramata.

Elinor Lake F.S. Road again crosses the right-of-way at km 15 and between that crossing and the hairpin turn at Glenfir (km 20.8) there are several opportunities to photograph Naramata and Okanagan Lake with the next traverse of the railway far below. A short, dusty side road at Glenfir also provides the opportunity to rejoin Chute Lake Road.

Little Tunnel.

There are several more excellent viewpoints near km 24, but one of the most spectacular is at the mouth of the Little Tunnel at km 25.5. Below you to the south, the scattered ponderosa pine and bunchgrass gives way to the neatly manicured orchards of Naramata and then the beaches and cityscape of Penticton. Skaha Lake disappears around the bend on the horizon. The winding descent on the KVR right-of-way ends at Smethurst Road at km 30 (Naramata Creek F.S. Road on the uphill side) and after leaving the KVR, it's little more than a kilometre down Smethurst Road to Naramata Road.

If you've made the trip on a hot, dusty day, it's less than a kilometre to Robinson Avenue and then two kilometres downhill to Naramata's fine beaches.

Highway 97 and the beaches at the foot of Okanagan Lake in Penticton are about 14 km south of the junction of Smethurst Road and Naramata Road.

Chute Lake Road.

Again, with the Chute Lake Lodge as your km 0 reference, Chute Lake Road offers an only slightly less spectacular descent to Okanagan Lake — with the opportunity to detour into Okanagan Mountain Provincial Park.

The generally winding downhill run picks up steam near km 4.2 with an excellent view of Okanagan Lake — and a series of tight switchback turns that will keep your foot on the brake. A junction at km 6.1 marks the start of Gemmill Lake Road, a rough gravel road into Okanagan Mountain Park. The parking lot and the Mountain Goat trailhead (to Divide Lake) are about 1.6 km up the road. There is also a picnic site, but no vehicle campground at the trailhead.

Back on Chute Lake Road, there is another access to the KVR right-of way at km 7.6. The steep descent continues until you reach another junction and pavement at km 10.7. Go left (south) to Naramata and Penticton. The road to the north ends at a ranch gate.

You'll pass several excellent viewpoints along the way as you continue south. Depending on the season, you may find the birdwatching or wildflower photography worthwhile. You should see the junction to Smethurst Road near km 17.2 and the route to downtown Naramata at 17.7. As you continue south, your route winds through orchards and vineyards. Watch for the side road to Munson Mountain Lookout near km 28.3 — this may also be a good spot to check out the birds and flowers.

The road changes names several times before it reaches downtown Penticton, approximately 31 kilometres from Chute Lake.

•••

25

Okanagan Mountain Park

By Murphy Shewchuk

Statistics: **For maps, see pages 92 & 98.**

Distance:	20 km, Hwy 97, Kelowna to north entrance.
	27 km, Hwy 97, Penticton to south parking lot.
Travel Time:	Approximately one half hour from highway.
Season:	South entrance may be closed in winter.
Topo Maps:	Peachland, BC 82 E/13 (1:50,000).
	Summerland, BC 82 E/12 (1:50,000).
Forest Maps:	Penticton and Area.
Communities:	Kelowna, Peachland and Penticton.

Okanagan Mountain Provincial Park offers you a truly diverse spectrum of outdoor pursuits. Because of its large land mass and wide elevation range — 1200 metres (3,900 feet) between lakeshore and mountain summit — the park contains a wide variety of ecosystems. A semi-desert wilderness on the lakeshore headlands blends into lush, green forest in the sub-alpine plateau.

Secluded coves and sandy beaches highlight the park's Okanagan Lake shoreline, with six marine camping areas for overnight boat camping. Inland are spectacular Wildhorse Canyon and Goode's Creek Canyon, cutting deeply north and south through the mass of Okanagan Mountain. More than 24 kilometres of connecting trails suitable for hiking, mountain biking and horseback riding lead through the canyons and into four spring-fed mountain lakes located along forested upper mountain ridges. You may see mule deer, elk and black bear and even an occasional mountain goat and cougar. Ospreys build their massive aeries in the tall trees near Norman, Baker and Divide lakes.

Established in 1973, after years of lobbying by the Okanagan Similkameen Parks Society, the park encompasses 10462 hectares (25,841 acres) of wilderness on Okanagan Mountain and spectacularly rugged Okanagan Lake foreshore.

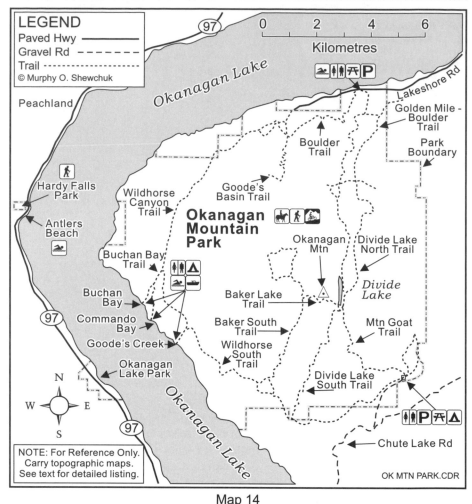

LEGEND
Paved Hwy ———————
Gravel Rd – – – – – –
Trail ·······················
© Murphy O. Shewchuk

Map 14
Okanagan Mountain Provincial Park and the Peachland - Summerland Area.

Fascinating cultural diversity.

Okanagan Mountain Provincial Park has a fascinating cultural history as well. Indian pictographs can be found on canyon walls and outcrops in several places. Early missionaries, fur traders, cattlemen and miners traveled a series of now overgrown Okanagan Mountain trails more than a century and half ago. Scattered old homesteads are evidence of attempts to settle this rugged landscape. Horse-logging was common up until the 1930's, and cattle are still grazing on the eastern boundary of the park. Despite all the human activity, the park remains a relatively undisturbed wilderness area.

Access from Kelowna and Penticton.

The northern boundary of Okanagan Mountain Park can be reached from Kelowna by turning south off Highway 97 (Harvey Avenue), a few blocks from the floating bridge, onto Pandosy Street, (kilometre 0.0). Pandosy Street soon becomes Lakeshore Road as you follow it through Okanagan Mission, keeping right at the light at the junction of Lakeshore and Chute Lake Road (km 9.0). If you are planning to spend a day or two in the hills, consider stopping for refreshments at the Cedar Creek, St. Hubertus or Summerhill Estate Wineries near km 13.

Bertram Creek Regional Park, near km 14, is another recreational option on the way to the mountain. After a day of horse riding, hiking or mountain biking, it may be a necessary stop for a swim before facing the city.

Divide Lake Trail.

Rimrock Road, near km 15, provides access to the start of the Divide Lake Trailhead. This 10 kilometre route follows an old microwave site access road to Divide Lake and the peak of Okanagan Mountain. A gate two kilometres up Rimrock Road bars vehicles from using the microwave site access road and parking is limited to only a few vehicles.

About two kilometres farther along Lakeshore Road is a parking lot and entrance sign to Okanagan Mountain Park. There are toilets, a horse loading ramp and a swimming beach nearby, but no overnight camping.

Wildhorse Canyon.

After passing through several small subdivisions, Lakeshore Road ends at km 20 in a wide cul-de-sac. Parking here is also limited, but a very rough, enticing trail angles down to the lake. A few hundred metres before the end of the road, a sign on the hillside marks the start of the ancient trail into the upper end of Wildhorse Canyon. The trail, though wide and easily navigated on foot or mountain bicycle, climbs steadily, gaining about 200 metres in two kilometres before leveling off. Near the crest it is joined by portions of the Boulder Trail and Goode's Basin Trail. An up-to-date map, available from BC Parks, and topographic maps (see the chapter header for details) are essential before heading too far into the north end of the park.

Okanagan Mountain Park has approximately 25 kilometres (15.5 miles) of unobstructed shoreline with ready access to the trail system at Buchan Bay, Commando Bay and Goode's Creek. The south-facing slopes surrounding these access points are classic examples of the dry environment that is said by some to be a northern extension of the Sonoran Desert of the southern U.S.A. Sagebrush, bunchgrass, prickly-pear cactus, ponderosa pine and poison ivy eke out an existence wherever moisture gathers. Pacific rattlesnakes are frequently sighted along the trail, but given a wide berth, they tend to be wary of humans.

Commando Bay.

The Commando Bay trail, across the slopes and into the foot of Wildhorse Canyon, is an easy, picturesque walk that is best tackled in early morning before the sun turns the sheltered draws into a bake-oven. The canyon trail is a pleasant walk along an old road that was once promoted as the ideal route for a highway from Kelowna to

Fig 30:
An early morning hike on the Commando Bay Trail.
(Photo OMP-027 © Murphy Shewchuk.)

Penticton. Wilderness lovers should be thankful that saner heads prevailed.

Several trails offer access to the southern part of the park from Penticton and Naramata via Naramata Road and Chute Lake Road. With the five-way junction of Main Street, Westminster Avenue and Front Street in downtown Penticton as km "0", follow Front Street northeast to Vancouver Avenue, then follow the signs to Naramata. Continue past Naramata to Chute Lake Road (km 20), then follow the steeply climbing Chute Lake Road for another five kilometres to the Gemmill Lake Road (marked with a sign to Okanagan Mountain Park). A narrow road winds through the evergreens for another 1.6 km to the South Parking Lot and a tenting campground near Chute Creek.

Mountain Goat Trail.

The Mountain Goat Trail, in the southeast sector of Okanagan Mountain Park, is aptly named. It starts off at the south parking lot, accessible from Chute Lake Road, and climbs steadily through semi-open timber to Divide Lake, just east of Okanagan Mountain summit. In keeping with the park's role to conserve the wilderness experience, the trail has no graveled pathways and no toilets along the way. It is unsuitable for mountain bicycles and a challenge to skilled horsemen on skilled horses. It is a steady climb up and around granite bluffs, over boulders and between trees.

The BC Parks map says the trail is 4.7 km long and a three hour hike one way. Add another half an hour if you're over 40. You can also count on one half to three quarters of that time for the return trip.

Carry plenty of drinking water.

Although Divide Lake is a cool, clear spring-fed lake at an elevation of 1500 metres (4,900 feet), carry plenty of water. For a mid-summer jaunt up the Mountain Goat Trail, plan on carrying at least one litre of water per hiker. There are no trustworthy creeks along the way. In fact, most of the creek beds are likely to be bone dry. Because of the wildlife in the park, the water is also likely to be unsafe even if it is flowing.

If you haven't been frightened off by this preamble, you'll probably enjoy this hike. Among the reasons to consider it is the relatively short distance from your vehicle to the heart of the park plus the opportunity for a cool, private swim in an upland tarn. An additional reason to make the climb is the relatively easy access to Baker and Norman lakes. Both lakes have excellent fishing for pan-sized trout and are downhill from Divide Lake.

Fig 31:
A wildlife tree near the Mountain Goat Trail.
(Photo OMP-008 © Murphy Shewchuk.)

From a naturalist's or photographer's perspective, getting there is half the fun. The trail starts off in a damp upland environment with evergreens, alder and vine maple shading queen's cup, thimbleberry and star-flowered Solomon's seal. Oregon grape grow profusely at all elevations along the trail. As you climb away from Chute Creek, the growth reflects the drier climate. White bunchberry blossoms, columbine and lupines add color to the slopes in early summer, later replaced by the red bunchberries and black huckleberries that could add a dainty touch to your bannock.

Not everyone thinks of food when they hike, poor souls. If scenic views turn you on, you'll be able to catch a few glimpses of Giants Head Mountain and the south end of Okanagan Lake. But Divide Lake is the real beauty up here. It is a steep-sided mountain crevice filled with cool, clear green water. It will take you about 15 minutes to walk the length of it, skirting the six-metre cliffs that make up the east shore. You may find a few ledges suitable for sunbathing or fishing, but you won't find a beach. You may, however, find a few picnic tables and a pit toilet nearby.

•••

26

Bear Road

By Murphy Shewchuk

Statistics:	For map, see page 103.

Distance:	66 km, Okanagan Connector to Westside Road.
Travel Time:	Two to three hours.
Elevation Diff.	1300 metres, Pennask Lake to Okanagan Lake.
Condition:	Rough gravel, may be closed in winter.
Season:	July through October.
Topo Maps:	Tulameen, BC 92 H/NE (1:100,000).
	Kelowna, BC 82 E/NW (1:100,000).
	Vernon, BC 82 L/SW (1:100,000).
Forest Maps:	Penticton Forest District Recreation Map.
Communities:	Peachland, Westbank and Kelowna.

Bear Road begins (or ends, depending on your direction of travel) at its junction with Westside Road approximately 8.5 kilometres north of Highway 97 and 1.7 kilometres north of the Bear Creek Provincial Park main gate. It climbs steadily as it cuts a wide arc northwest and then southwest up to the Pennask Plateau. The upper terminus is at its junction with Sunset Main Road near the Pennask Creek overpass on the Okanagan Connector of the Coquihalla Highway. Although the junction is within sight of the freeway, the nearest access to the Connector (Highway 97C) is at the Sunset Main Road interchange approximately 6.5 kilometres to the west. (See *Sunset Main to Summerland*, starting on page 109, for details.)

The elevation where it passes under the Connector (Highway 97C) is 1600 metres (5,250 feet) so Bear Road may not be passable until mid or late June. But when it is open, it is a pleasant, though sometimes bumpy, alternative to the freeway — an alternative that allows access to several Forest Service recreation sites and some of the finest trout lakes in the BC interior.

Bear Road is an industrial forest road and should be approached with caution, particularly on weekdays between 6:00 a.m. and 6:00 p.m. Although it is

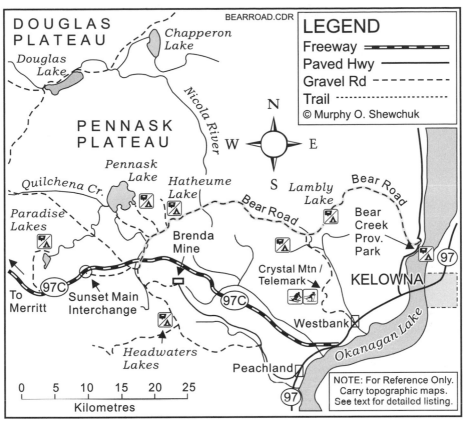

Map 15
Bear Road and the Pennask Lake area.

generally wide enough to pass an oncoming vehicle, the sharp turns and dust can make visibility difficult.

Roadside kilometre markers, used by the radio-equipped logging trucks, can also serve as a reference to you when exploring the region. One important point to consider, should you stray off the main roads, is that the markers usually count down to the nearest highway or mill yard. In this case "0K" appears to be the log dump at the shores of Okanagan Lake, a short distance north of Bear Creek Provincial Park. If you are unsure of which way to find civilization, following the decreasing numbers is a safe bet.

Dirt Bike Heaven.

Bear Road initially climbs northwest as it clings to the benches along Lambly (Bear) Creek Canyon. There are a few wide areas where it is safe to pull off the road and enjoy the view down the canyon to Okanagan Lake. De-

103

BEAR CREEK MOTORCYCLE TRAILS

THE TRAILS IN THIS AREA ARE MAINTAINED BY THE KELOWNA DIRT BIKE CLUB, IN COOPERATION WITH THE B.C. FOREST SERVICE.

• Yield to logging traffic and watch for Forest Workers
• Avoid wetland and marshy areas
• Avoid hill climbs next to and above creeks and roadways
• Report illegal dumping
• Pack out what you pack in
• Respect the right of others to enjoy this area
• Keep to the right when meeting other trail users
• Yield to other riders moving uphill
• Do not disturb wildlife or livestock
• Respect public & private property
• Slow down and use caution when approaching others

To contact us or obtain more information on KDBC trail networks or to join our club please fax (250) 765-3436

Support Project Stealth: excessive noise is detrimental to our sport!

Fig 32:
Bear Creek Motorcycle Trails sign.
(Photo OKO-500 © Murphy Shewchuk.)

pending on where you choose to stop, you may notice a network of dirt bike trails through the pines on the benches below.

According to Ron Irnie, president of the 350 member Kelowna Dirt Bike Club (KDC), the club is the steward of the "Bear Creek Riding Area". The KDC encourages safe riding and environmental protection, including not allowing poorly muffled bikes. It holds many events each year for the beginner to the expert rider. The club welcomes visitors to their Wednesday night rides which start at the cattle guard approximately 1.5 km up Bear Road. Ron Irnie suggests that the Bear Creek Area offers the best riding in North American. For additional information, contact the KDC at (250)785-3436.

Terrace Road (8K), Bald Range Road and Esperon Road present opportunities for diversions into the plateau to the north and west. Keep left at all three junctions, following the "Bear Road" signs as your direction gradually changes to southwest.

Bear Lake.

The first major fishing opportunity is at Lambly (Bear) Lake, near the 23K marker. There is a private resort and a Forest Service recreation site on this lake, which also serves as a water reservoir for the Westbank Irrigation District. At an elevation of 1158 metres (3,798 ft), the 74-hectare (182.8-acre) lake should be high enough to sustain rainbow trout fishing well into the summer.

Lambly Lake takes its name from the Lambly brothers, a trio of pioneer settlers who came to the Okanagan Valley in the 1870s. According to an article in *Peachland Memories, Volume Two*, (pp. 426-430) the Lamblys were natives of Megantic County, Quebec, an area settled by United Empire Loyalists.

Robert Lambly, the first to arrive in the Okanagan, tramped in from the coast over the Hope Trail and initially settled in what is now the Enderby district. A year later he was joined by his brother Thomas who took up land nearby. Charles Lambly followed his brothers westward in 1878 and obtained work as a civil engineer in northern British Columbia. A decade later, Charles moved into the Enderby area to work on the construction of the Shuswap and Okanagan Railway. Charles soon entered the service of the Provincial Government, first as Assessor, and later as Mining Recorder, Gold Commissioner, Stipendiary Magistrate and still later, Government Agent. His first post was Enderby, as the young town at "Lambly's Landing" was later christened, but soon he was off to Rock Creek, where he spent the rest of his life.

The other Lambly brothers, Thomas and Robert, continued to live in the Enderby area until 1894. Some years earlier they had acquired land on the west side of Okanagan Lake at Trepanier Creek, with extensive range north and west of present-day Peachland.

The brothers had bought out William Jenkins who had located at Trepanier Creek in 1886, and on March 1, 1887 a pre-emption for D.L. 220 was registered to Charles A.R. Lambly, the first pre-emption in the district. Charles also purchased D.L. 490 in 1893, and his brother, Tom, bought D.L. 449 the same year. These properties all fronted on Okanagan Lake, and gave the brothers five kilometres of lakeshore. On the lakeside property at Trepanier they experimented with fruit growing, and pioneered the growing of soft fruits in that area.

"This was not the brothers' only activity in the area," states the article in Peachland Memories. "While ranging the horses and cattle on the hills they had done some prospecting, and had become the possessors of a number of likely-looking mining claims.

"This unfortunately led to a tragedy.

"Tom Lambly contracted a severe cold while doing some development work on claims west of Trepanier. This turned into pneumonia and he was taken across the lake to Kelowna for treatment, but to no avail, and he died there on Nov. 24, 1897."

Following the death of his brother, Robert Lambly moved back to Enderby to reside, after disposing of part of the Trepanier holdings. A short time later he moved with his wife and family to Alberta, where he operated a stock ranch in the foothills of the Rockies.

Jackpine Lake.

Jackpine Forest Service Road, between 26K and 27K, winds down through the Powers Creek Canyon to Westbank, passing side roads into Jackpine Lake and the Crystal Mountain ski area. See the *Crystal Mountain/Telemark* section on page 129.

Cameo Lake.

Bear Road continues to climb — now westward — reaching Cameo Lake near the 38K marker. There is a small Forest Service recreation site on the rock outcropping at the west end of the lake. Beyond Cameo Lake, forest roads lead into the headwaters of the Nicola River and several small lakes, including Windy Lake, near the 44K marker. Windy Lake also has a Forest Service recreation site.

Bicycle Trails.

The Mellin Lake Forest Service Road, just past the 48K marker, leads north into the Pennask Plateau. There are short hiking or cycling trails into Ellen Lake, Mellin Lake and Tim's Pond.

Beyond the 49K marker, the road markers begin a countdown to the junction with the Trout Main Forest Service Road near the Headwaters Lakes. The 20K marker is about 52.3 kilometres from Westside Road.

Hatheume Lake.

Hatheume Lake Road, near the 18K marker, presents another opportunity to explore the back-country and enjoy camping, fishing or a wilderness resort experience. Although, at 134 hectares (331 acres), Hatheume Lake is considerably smaller than nearby Pennask Lake, it too has a widespread reputation as a source of fighting rainbow trout. At the time of writing, Hatheume was a catch-and-release fly-only fishery with a further restriction of barbless hooks. There are medium-sized Forest Service recreation sites on Pinnacle Lake, the south side of Hatheume Lake and a resort on the northeast shore.

If you reset your odometer, and take the road north, you will pass Pinnacle Lake Forest Service recreation site near km 2.5 and reach a junction near km 3.4. The road to the right leads less than a kilometre to the Hatheume Lake Forest Service recreation site while the road to the left partly circles the lake, reaching Hatheume Lake Resort in another 4.6 kilometres.

Both recreation sites and the resort have been upgraded considerably in recent years.

Pennask Lake Provincial Park.

Your next possible detour is north to Pennask Lake. At 1041.29 hectares (2,572 acres) it is one of the larger lakes in the upland region. At an elevation of 1402 metres (4,599 ft.), it is also one of the highest. Check the latest fishing regulations, but at the time of writing, Pennask was a fly-only lake yielding prize rainbow trout up to three quarters of a kilogram (1.5 pounds).

The very rough six-kilometre long public road into Pennask Lake leaves Bear Road about 4.4 kilometres southwest of the access to Hatheume Lake. There is a 28-vehicle/tent campground on the southeast corner of the lake. Facilities also include a day-use/picnicking area, boat launch and pit toilets. No fee is charged and reservations are not available.

Fig 33:
The main lodge at Hatheume Lake Resort. (Photo NVG-1351 © Murphy Shewchuk.)

The public area was first established as a Class A Park on May 2, 1974, but was downgraded to a Recreational Area early in 1975. There were several reasons for the change: the new status would allow ranching interests to keep their cattle in the area; limited resource development would be allowed if it would not damage recreational values; but probably most important of all, it would limit park development and consequent pressures on Pennask Lake as the province's most important source of rainbow trout eggs. While facilities are still limited, the recreation area was recently upgraded to a park.

The construction of Coquihalla Highway Phase III — now known as the Okanagan Connector — prompted some major soul-searching on the part of BC Parks. The present rough access road limits the number of visitors to the recreation site, but with a major highway only a short distance away, pressure will certainly be felt to improve access and facilities at the lake.

Pennask Lake Lodge.

Pennask Forest Road, near the 13K marker, leads north into the plateau with a side road into a private lodge on the west shore of Pennask Lake.

James D. Dole, whose name is synonymous with Hawaiian pineapple, first visited Pennask Lake in September, 1927. Accompanied by his wife, Belle, two employees, and three friends who then managed the lodge at Fish Lake (Lac Le Jeune) near Kamloops, Dole camped for a week at the head of Pennask Lake.

In the book, *A Place Called Pennask*, Stanley E. Read writes that James Dole was in search of a dream — to be part of a fishing club that could control its surroundings. He wanted a lake of perfect fishing in a region teeming with attractions which he and his friends could call their own. He found it in Pennask Lake and moved quickly to gain control.

In a memorandum dated October 26, 1928, Dole wrote, "We believe that by controlling the land at shore-front we can maintain good fishing in this lake for a long time to come, and it is hoped that it will be kept as a fly-fishing lake solely and not be dredged... with tin shops and worms."

The Pennask Lake Club was established in 1929, and officially incorporated in June, 1930, as the Pennask Lake Company, Ltd. Membership was to be limited to 50 at a fee of $1,000 per member. Several prominent U.S. citizens joined the club, but the Great Depression dealt a series of setbacks before Dole's plans could materialize. The new lodge was under-utilized, resulting in deficits that Dole made up from his personal finances. It was not until the late 1940s, when the Pennask Lake Fishing and Game Club was formed, that new financial life was breathed into the operation — under Canadian control.

Three-way junction.

After passing under Highway 97C, Bear Road ends at a junction with Sunset Lake and Sunset Main roads. If you continue straight ahead (south), you can visit Brenda or McDonald lakes, and descend to Peachland or Summerland or go there via the Headwaters Lakes area. See the *Sunset Main to Summerland* section on page 109 for details.

The road to the right (west) offers a couple of options. The first junction to the right, after crossing Pennask Creek, will take you down the rough BC Hydro right-of-way to Douglas Lake or Quilchena. The main road west allows access to Highway 97C at the Sunset Main interchange, about 6.5 kilometres from the three-way junction.

If you find it too tough to make a decision, you can always go back the way you came — looking downhill all the way you'll find the scenery a little different.

•••

27

Sunset Main to Summerland

By Murphy Shewchuk

Statistics: **For map, see page 110.**

Distance: 90 km, Sunset Main Interchange to Summerland.
Travel Time: Approximately three hours.
Condition: Mostly gravel, some paved sections.
Topo Maps: Penticton 82 E (1:250,000).
Forest Maps: Merritt Forest District Recreation Map.
Penticton Forest District Recreation Map.
Communities: Merritt, Aspen Grove, Summerland.

There are as many reasons for backroad exploring as there are backroad explorers. The seasons often influence what you'll discover or what will interest you. However, if you're like me, as the snow retreats from the high country, you're off looking for whatever may be around the next corner. Sometimes what is around the next corner is an impassable washout or a snowdrift that still hasn't been melted by the sun.

We've all spent time proving that mudholes or snowdrifts really are deeper than we expected. However, when we discover a brightly lit field of wild-flowers or a grazing deer and fawn, we understand why we risk life, limb and the family sedan for a spring drive in the country.

The high country that surrounds the Okanagan Valley is a backroad explorer and wildflower lover's delight. Getting away from the city scene can be as simple as taking a walk in a park, but to get away from civilization and people involves a wee bit more effort.

If your base is in the central Okanagan, here is one way to enjoy a scenic tour and photograph the wildflowers. It involves half an hour's drive on the Okanagan Connector of the Coquihalla Highway and half a day or more of back country exploring. Although this trip includes active logging roads, some steep grades and loose gravel sections, it is often quite passable by ordinary car by late May or early June. It is probably safest to travel it on weekends and from a west to east (downhill) direction.

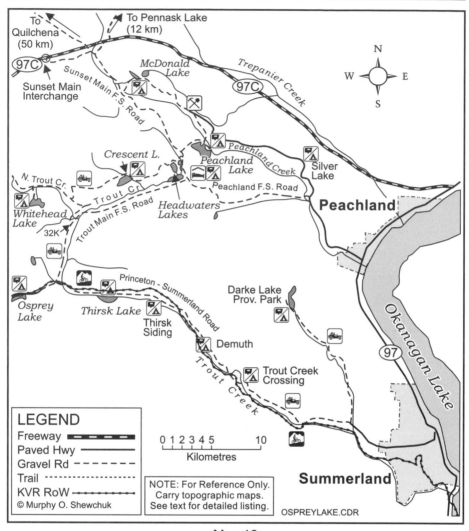

Map 16
Headwaters Lakes area and Princeton-Summerland Road.

Sunset Main Road.

For this Okanagan adventure, head 45 kilometres west of Peachland on the Connector (Hwy 97C) and take the Sunset Main Road exit about 10 km west of the summit. Reset your odometer at the cattleguard on the south side of the underpass and then head east along a gravel road that parallels the freeway.

Your first opportunity for diversion is near the 1K marker on the Sunset Main Forest Service Road. Look closely for an unmarked trailhead and an undeveloped parking area on the south (right) side of the road.

Although unmarked, the trail into Sunset Lake is well-used and easily wide enough to portage a canoe or drag a car-top boat. And it's only a few minutes walk. Game trails circle the lake, but you'll need a good set of gumboots and a sturdy walking stick to probe the mud holes. In addition to the lupines that do remarkably well here, you're likely to find ground dogwood and a host of other shade loving plants that have adapted to the short season at this elevation (1600 metres or 5,250 feet). Wildlife is also plentiful in the area. If you are early and quiet, you may see a mule deer browsing along the lake shore.

As you continue following the gravel logging road eastward, it swings away from the freeway through a clear-cut that is quickly regenerating. Depending on when you get around to making the tour, you may find the lupine still in blossom or fields of fireweed swaying in the wind. In late summer, the flowers may be a secondary attraction to rich, black huckleberries. The lush foliage also attracts the natural residents. Don't be too surprised to see white crowned sparrows, yellow bellied marmots and black bears foraging near the road.

Pennask Creek.

Several side roads lead off to new logging cuts and the high voltage power line, but the first major diversion is just before the Pennask Creek crossing near the 6K marker. A little-used road to the left crosses under the freeway near the creek and swings northwest along the north side of the freeway. This was once the main road across the plateau. Although rough, you could follow it westward to Quilchena or Douglas Lake, but now a questionable bridge across Quilchena Creek could make it impassable.

Back on Sunset Road, a short climb past the creek crossing will bring you to another junction. Bear Road, to the left (north), could take you past Pennask and Hatheume lakes and down to Okanagan Lake near Bear Creek Provincial Park. For now, swing right and continue southeast on Sunset Lake Road.

The timber in this area is older and the undergrowth a little different. Lupine, arnica, wild strawberries and columbine grace the roadside slopes. Watch for the potholes, washouts and washboard gravel surface as too little caution and too much speed could be disastrous.

Brenda and MacDonald Lakes.

A junction near the 11K marker offers a chance to do a little fishing and get a different view of the Okanagan Valley. To the left lies Brenda and MacDonald lakes, and a few side roads above the now-closed Brenda open pit mine.

To the right, Sunset Lake Road climbs over a saddle and skirts a box canyon that is the head of Peachland Creek. You may catch glimpses of the craggy cliffs of the canyon before you start the winding descent to the Headwaters Lakes area. There are signs of recent logging in this area and also signs that mark still more diversions.

Fig 34:
Loons frequent the upland lakes. (Photo BLO-038 © Murphy Shewchuk.)

A signpost near the 23K marker indicates a short detour into Peachland Lake (at last check, there was a bridge out on this route). About half a kilometre farther along, another post marks the route to Whitehead Lake via Peachland Forest Service Road. There are small Forest Service recreation sites at Peachland, Crescent and Whitehead lakes. Many of the lakes in the area have been developed or enhanced to hold irrigation water for the orchards and communities of the Okanagan Valley. These are no exception, but Whitehead Lake shows the least sign of water control work.

If you're not an altogether altruistic wildflower watcher, you may want to detour into one of these lakes to wet a few flies. If the roads are dry, the first two should be easily accessible, but unless there has been some maintenance done recently, the last two or three kilometres into Whitehead Lake could be a bit rough on the old family sedan. Here, a 4x4 pickup might be a better choice.

Regardless of your choice, if your timing is right, you could discover that the lodgepole pine stands near the Peachland Forest Service Road junction are carpeted in a solid mass of blue lupine.

Headwaters Fishing Camp.

If you've found the dusty road a little hard on your throat, you could detour into Headwaters Fishing Camp for a cold pop. Owners Roy and Verena

Bockstatt offer a tiny store and big-hearted hospitality. The Bockstatts left jobs in Switzerland in 1994 to move to British Columbia where, as Verena put it, "There is more elbow room!" They have since made renovations to many of the cabins in an effort to add to the year-around comfort of the fishing camp.

If you're interested in continuing your wildflower jaunt in the morning, you can rent a camping spot, a cabin, a boat or a mountain bike and take a break until the light is a little better for photography.

Meanwhile, back on the road, the next major junction is about 1.2 km past the entrance to Headwaters Fishing Camp. Peachland Road continues down to Peachland (no surprise here), while Trout Creek Road follows Trout Creek south for about 20 km to the Princeton-Summerland Road. If you are looking for wildflower diversity, follow the Trout Creek route to Summerland (See *Princeton-Summerland Road* on page 141.)

The gravel road passes alternately through several clear-cuts and old growth stands, with a corresponding variety of wildflowers. In addition to the plants I've already mentioned, look for fields of wild roses and Indian paintbrush, particularly near the 34K marker.

If you are heading to the southern Okanagan Valley, turn left at the Princeton-Summerland Road junction. As you continue past Thirsk Lake, you'll see a gradual change in undergrowth. The lower elevation and drier climate support semi-desert plants such as sedum and scarlet gilia. Lodgepole pine forests give way to scattered stands of ponderosa and huckleberries are replaced by saskatoons.

When you break free of the confines of the valley and the upper reaches of Trout Creek, you'll discover that the road is narrow and dusty, with few places to enjoy the spectacular view of the Trout Creek canyon. If you can find a safe spot to pull over, you may be surprised at the variety of wildflowers that survive the dry climate. The drying leaves of arrow-leaved balsamroot cover the slopes. Their yellow sunflower-like blossoms do their thing in April or early May. Closer to the ground lay the prickly pear cactus. You should consider yourself lucky to find one in blossom. You won't soon forget the delicate yellow-green-orange blossoms — or the sharp spines, should you sit down indiscriminately.

Your final journey to Highway 97 will be through the orchards of Summerland via Prairie Valley Road.

The total distance from the Connector to Summerland is about 90 km, hardly more than a jaunt for today's Sunday traveller. However, if you are as easily side-tracked as I am, you should bring your lunch, drinking water, a full tank of gas and plenty of film, and allow a full day.

Make it a lodgepole and lupine holiday.

•••

28

McDougall Rim Trail

By Judie Steeves

Statistics: **For map, see page 115.**

Distance:	12-15 km of trail.
Travel Time:	Four or five hours.
Elevation Gain:	800 metres.
Condition:	Varies seasonally.
Season:	Spring, summer and fall.
Topo Maps:	Peachland, BC 82 E/13 (1:50,000)
Forest Maps:	Penticton Forest District Recreation Map.
Communities:	Kelowna, Westbank

Sweeping views of the Okanagan Valley and of Rose Valley Reservoir, tucked in a fold in the hills far below, are the reward for a steep initial climb on the McDougall Rim Trail. It's more than a 600-metre (2,000-foot) climb in altitude from the trailhead parking area on Bartley Road to where this trail finally levels out and you can catch your breath, but the view really is spectacular. That first hour (longer if you have to stop to breathe), offers an excellent example of the open dry hillsides typical of the Okanagan Valley.

During this part of the hike you are vulnerable to quick changes in weather. One spring when we hiked the trail, we experienced hot sunshine, a quick shower, a hailstorm, wind and cooler temperatures as we moved higher, until we hit muddy patches of snow. Although this is the most popular section of the trail, it does continue along the canyon rim above Rose Valley Reservoir and Lambly and McDougall Creeks. On the way, you pass through marshy areas, grassy meadows, heavy timber and around small ponds and lakes.

Getting there.

To reach the trailhead, leave Highway 97 at Bartley Road, about halfway between the communities of Kelowna and Westbank. Drive west past Byland's Nurseries through a gravel mining operation to where you'll see private property signs nailed to trees. Drive slowly and respect the fact that this narrow road winds through a small farming community. The road becomes gravel 1.5 kilo-

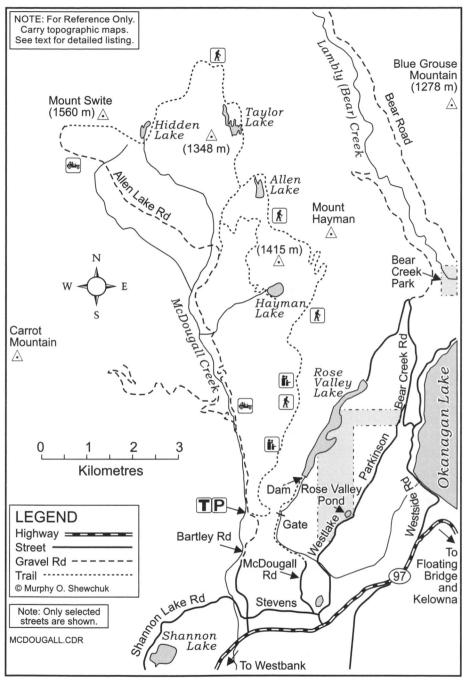

NOTE: For Reference Only.
Carry topographic maps.
See text for detailed listing.

Lambly (Bear) Creek

Bear Road

Blue Grouse
Mountain
(1278 m)

Mount Swite
(1560 m)

*Hidden
Lake*

*Taylor
Lake*

(1348 m)

*Allen
Lake*

Mount
Hayman

(1415 m)

Bear
Creek
Park

Allen Lake Rd

N
W   E
S

*Hayman
Lake*

Carrot
Mountain

Bear Creek Rd

McDougall Creek

*Rose
Valley
Lake*

Okanagan Lake

0   1   2   3
Kilometres

Parkinson

Dam   Rose Valley
Pond

Rose Valley
Pond

Westside Rd

To
Floating
Bridge
and
Kelowna

LEGEND
Highway
Street
Gravel Rd
Trail
© Murphy O. Shewchuk

Bartley Rd

Gate

Westlake

McDougall
Rd

97

Note: Only selected
streets are shown.

Shannon Lake Rd

Stevens

MCDOUGALL.CDR

*Shannon
Lake*

To Westbank

Map 17
McDougall Rim Trail and Rose Valley Lake area.

115

metres from the highway. You should reach the trailhead at three kilometres, just past a cattle guard. Park off the road in the small cleared area amongst the trees and head uphill along the trail.

Breathtaking views.

In spring these hillsides are marked by patches of brassy yellow spring sun-flowers, or arrow-leaved balsamroot (*Balsamorhiza sagittata*). In summer you'll likely find clumps of the shy pink bitterroot (*Lewisia rediviva*), with their delicate tissue-like flowers, clinging to the slopes. When the shimmering summer sun beats down on this southeast-facing hillside, the pines give off a distinctive, pungent odor. As the trail winds around the hill, views of the McDougall Creek canyon far below open up. There's sometimes a whiff of cool dampness from that quite-different environment.

The creek was named after Westside pioneer John McDougall, who once traveled with the Hudson's Bay Company horse brigades. In Dorothy Hewlett Gellatly's book, *A Bit of Okanagan History*, she says his sons had reputations as excellent and dependable guides and hunters.

Higher up this trail both the terrain and the scenery changes as you hike along the rocky Westside cliffs. Not far after that the trail levels off and a short diversion to the east leads to a spectacular, panoramic viewpoint. Don't get too close to the edge. In places it's straight down. Below is Rose Valley Lake, Lakeview Irrigation District's water reservoir, trapped in a fold in the hills. Farther off, Okanagan Lake spreads out between higher hills. The floating bridge and City of Kelowna are front and centre. Shift your eyes to the north and Vernon is almost visible, and to the south Rattlesnake Island, across Okanagan Lake, juts out from Okanagan Mountain Park.

A ferry captain.

The trail continues along the ridge line past a marshy area to an old road which will take you to Hayman Lake. It was named after a pioneer family whose patriarch, Captain Len Hayman, was skipper of the ferry on Okanagan Lake before the floating bridge was built between Westside and Kelowna.

The trail crests at an elevation of 1415 metres (4,640 feet), topped in the area only by Mount Swite to the northwest, and Carrot Mountain to the west.

The road back.

From here you can hike back to your car down either of a couple of old roads (washed out in spots) from Hayman Lake to the McDougall Creek logging road. You can also continue along the rim, but this part of the trail's not always well marked, so make sure you take a compass and map.

•••

116

29

Rose Valley Trails

By Judie Steeves

Statistics: **For map, see page 115.**

Distance:	Varies.
Travel Time:	Varies.
Condition:	Varies.
Season:	Year-round.
Topo Maps:	Peachland, BC E/13 (1:50,000).
Forest Maps:	Penticton Forest District Recreation Map.
Communities:	Westbank, Kelowna.

A spring-fed pond alive with the call of birds, and a larger water reservoir tucked into the valley in a fold between two hills are the two main features of a fairly new park between Kelowna and Westbank. There are two types of trails in Rose Valley Pond Regional Park. A short, easy walk takes you around the pond which is home to the dramatically-colored yellow-headed blackbirds, red-winged blackbirds, and a great variety of other birds and waterfowl. Take your binoculars, bird book and bug repellant. From there, the more ambitious hiker can strike off uphill on a trail through the forest toward the ridge which separates the residential area from its water supply. Be prepared: this is an undeveloped wilderness park with trails marked by usage rather than by signs.

Canoe, fish, hike or birdwatch.

To reach the pond, take Westlake Road off Highway 97, west at the traffic lights. Travel 2.9 km up Westlake Road and park in a small cleared area to the left off the road. The trail that takes you around the pond begins here, and the longer hike up to the ridge turns off the path around the pond near its south end. Another of the trails into Rose Valley Reservoir's watershed begins at the end of West Kelowna Road, west off Westlake Road immediately past Rose Valley Elementary School, which is adjacent to the pond. Another is at the end of Bear Creek Road, reached by a left turn off Parkinson Road, which is a continuation north of Westlake Road. This path takes you to the north end of Rose Valley Reservoir. To reach the dam at the south end of the lake, take Westlake Road west off Highway 97, then almost immediately turn left at Stevens Road, and right on McDougall Road. A sign informs you this is not a through road, since it ends at the dam. Drive through a gravel mining operation, up the hill to a fork in the road at 1.9 km. Take the left and either park and walk from here, or drive along a rough dirt road to a red gate, 2.8 km in total from the highway.

Be wary, I found a healthy patch of poison ivy not far along the road from this gate. "Leaflets three, let it be," is the old saying to remind hikers how to identify and avoid the irritation of this plant, with its shiny leaves in clusters of three. Park before reaching the gate so you don't block the road, which is access for irrigation district staff to maintain the water storage facility. It is an easy 1.5 to 2-kilometre walk in to the lake along a dirt road from here. Remember that this is the source of water for thousands of homes below, so enjoy the area with respect for those users. There's fishing on the lake, but only electric motors are permitted.

Lots of history.

Rose Valley Reservoir was created by an earth-filled dam which was built in 1949 and completed in 1951, when the Lakeview Irrigation District was incorporated. It holds water diverted from Lambly (Bear) Creek in what was once just a spring-fed marshy area between the hills. The project was part of efforts to re-settle the veterans of World War II. It involved subdividing and clearing the forest over what is now Lakeview Heights into parcels for farming, then providing water to them under the Veterans' Land Act. It was named after a Kelowna-area pioneer family named Rose. Oral history relates a story about one of the brothers who built a cabin on property in what is now the park, with the intent of settling there with his young bride. However, when she realized how isolated it was she refused to move there, and she never did.

More recent area residents marshalled their forces in the early 1990s when the small pond was about to be filled in and developed as housing for people instead of birds. They lobbied and raised funds and finally purchased the property containing the little wetland as a seed of public land from which a larger wilderness park could grow. The Central Okanagan Regional District now has a 10-year Crown lease on the land uphill from the pond, over the ridge that separates it from Rose Valley Reservoir, and intends to apply for a Crown grant for parkland when that expires. There is also a move to extend that parkland to include more of the watershed around Rose Valley Reservoir.

•••

30

Kalamoir Regional Park Trails

By Judie Steeves

Statistics: **For map, see page 120.**

Distance: More than 5 km of trails along Okanagan Lake.
Time: Depends where you enter and exit the trails.
Condition: Good.
Season: Year-round
Topo Maps: Kelowna 82 E/NW (1:100,000)
Forest Maps: Penticton Forest District Recreation Map.
Communities: Westbank, Kelowna

This long, narrow lakefront park features a typical sagebrush-dotted Okanagan hillside which has been left in its natural state, except for a network of trails. They will take you from near the Okanagan Lake Floating Bridge to Sunnyside, a Westside residential neighborhood. Kalamoir is a Central Okanagan Regional District Park that offers spectacular views of Okanagan Lake throughout its entire length.

The park drops about 200 metres in elevation from the top of the rocky hillside to the lake, so the trails are steep in places. However, it's neither a long nor a difficult hike. You should be able to circle the park in less than two hours.

Through Lakeview Heights.

From Highway 97, turn east at the Boucherie Road intersection, travelling up the hill 1.9 kilometres to Anders Road where you turn left, then right on Thacker Drive, just over a half-kilometre along. The first road to the left is Collens Hill Road which will take you down into the park, 3.9 kilometres in all from the highway. It's about another half kilometre down to the lake. Parking is available off Collens Hill Road at either the upper or lower parking areas, with lake views from each. Trails begin at each of the parking areas, heading both north and south along the length of the park, ending either at Sunnyside Drive in the south, or Casa Loma in the north. However, instead of leaving the park, you can loop back, taking the upper or lower series of trails instead of the same

119

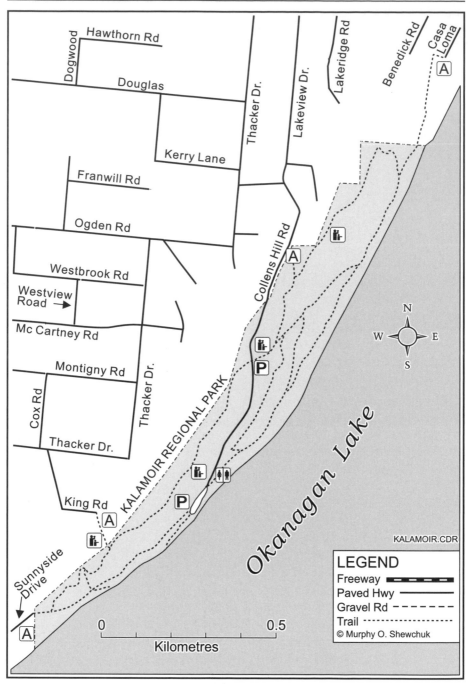

Map 18
Kalamoir Regional Park and east Lakeview Heights area.

Fig 35:
Yellow Bell (*Fritillaria pudica*).
(Photo WYB-020 © Murphy Shewchuk.)

one you first took, so you don't have to re-trace your steps. There are also access points, without much parking, at the end of Sunnyside Drive and also at the end of King Road off Thacker Drive, where there's also a viewpoint (see map on page 120).

Typical Okanagan habitat.

Early in spring these hillsides are cheery with bright yellow patches of arrow-leaved balsamroot or spring sunflowers that herald the arrival of spring in the Okanagan. Hidden among them, the careful observer will find single stems of graceful yellowbells, a fritillaria-family native plant. In summer, the delicate mariposa lilies dot these hillsides, often protected among patches of spiny prickly-pear cactus, which literally seem to jump from the ground to plant themselves in your bare calf. In June or July, they sport delicate, tissue-like yellow flowers that belie the spines underneath. Red patches of sumac leaves brighten the hillsides of brown grasses in fall as their leaves change color with cold nights.

Much of the network of trails is exposed, so it's a relief during summer days that they occasionally branch off down to a rocky beach where you can cool off in the lake. A bit of local history sits at the corner of Boucherie Road and Sunnyside. Here Quail's Gate Estate Winery's boutique is housed in the historic log Allison family homestead, which they called Sunnyside. It dates from 1873 when John and Susan Allison became the first European settlers on the west side of Okanagan Lake. Just up the road is the Mission Hill Winery, famous for its award-winning Chardonnay.

•••

Fig 36:
Prickly-pear Cactus (*Opuntia fragilis*).
(Photo WCA-081 © Murphy Shewchuk.)

31

Upper Glen Canyon Trails

By Judie Steeves

Statistics:	For map, see page 123.

Distance:	More than 4 km of trails in Glen Canyon Regional Park.
Travel Time:	It's up to you.
Condition:	Well-maintained.
Season:	Year around.
Topo Maps:	Peachland, BC 82 E/13 (1:50,000).
Forest Maps:	Penticton Forest District Recreation Map.
Communities:	Westbank.

On a hot summer day it's delightfully cool on the hiking trails along Powers Creek in Glen Canyon Regional Park. In all, this 65-hectare park features more than four kilometres of trails over a great variety of terrain and through changing wildlife habitat on both sides of Highway 97. You can take a short after-dinner constitutional or a day-long hike on the Glen Canyon network. The creek flows through a deep canyon separating the downtown community of Westbank from the newer residential area of Glenrosa, perched on the hillside to the southwest.

Powers Creek's canyon is not only an oasis of cool air on a hot summer day, it is also the route used by this rapidly-growing community's life-giving water supply. Originally that water was brought down from such high-elevation storage reservoirs as Jackpine Lake and Lambly (Bear) Lake, dammed in the 1920s by the Westbank Irrigation District. Using a system of laboriously-built wooden flumes, the water was carried to the first orchards and farms. Today it makes its way into the thousands of homes now growing on the fertile benchlands above Okanagan Lake. Portions of those old flumes still cling to the cliffsides along creeks throughout the Okanagan. They are a reminder of simpler times when the valley was sparsely populated, and a less sophisticated, above ground water supply was adequate.

The Central Okanagan Regional District maintains a still-growing network of trails along Powers Creek.

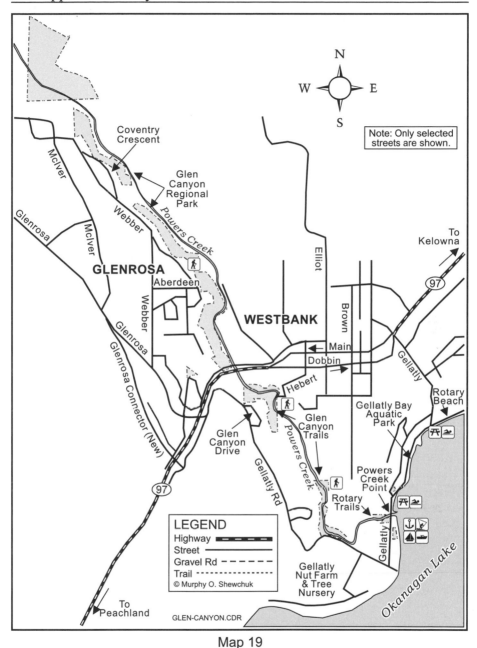

Map 19

Powers Creek, Glen Canyon Regional Park, Gellatly Bay Aquatic Park and surrounding area.

Access from Glenrosa Road.

The upper canyon trails can be reached from a number of access points in Glenrosa. To reach them, turn west off Highway 97 onto Glenrosa Road, then head up the hill until the road veers left. Instead, take Webber Road to the right, and drive along it to Aberdeen Road, which comes into Webber on the right. Turn right and follow Aberdeen Road the few blocks to its end where you can park. Another trail into the canyon can be reached from the cul-de-sac between Aberdeen and Dunbarton Road. You could also continue farther up Webber Road and turn onto Coventry Crescent to take either one of two trails down to the main

Fig 37:
A "hoodoo" rock formation in Upper Glen Canyon. (Photo © Judie Steeves.)

creek trail. Another option is to go farther up Glenrosa Road then turn right onto Gates Road at the Westside Firehall. Follow Gates Road to Salmon Road and turn left. At Canary, turn right until Bluejay. Turn left and park to enter the canyon, or right to McLeod Road, then left and park, for another entrance to the trails.

Most of the main trail leads you right along the winding creek, which gives off cool whiffs of misty dampness as it burbles along over the rocks. Powers Creek is critical to survival of the dense canopy of old cottonwoods, aspens, birch and maple trees that grow along the floor of the canyon. Higher up the canyon walls, ponderosa pine and Douglas fir are more common, along with such dryland vegetation as the bright brown-eyed Susans, saskatoon bushes and spiny Oregon grape.

Cliffs and hoodoos.

You can see weather-worn 100-metre-high cliffs and hoodoos across the canyon as you make your way out of the canyon or down to the creek. Rustic log benches allow you to sit and contemplate the forces that created these fascinating sandstone and conglomerate rock formations.

The most direct route to view them is by entering the canyon from Aberdeen Road, beginning at the Bruce Memorial. This stone memorial was established to honor Cst. Neil Bruce, an RCMP officer who was fatally wounded in April 1965 while attempting to arrest a suspect holed up in a nearby cabin.

Fig 38:
Bruce Memorial, near Aberdeen Road. (Photo © Judie Steeves.)

You may hike downstream to Highway 97 near Westbank's town centre, or upstream for a more ambitious workout and some spectacular views. In fact, you may continue on Crown-owned land upstream from Glen Canyon Regional Park to Black Canyon and beyond, but only the park trails are well-marked. Eventually, there may be a looping trail up the creek to a wilderness campsite, then across the creek and back down on the rim of the canyon along the historic Westbank irrigation pack trail. This trail leads up to the Lambly Lake reservoir. Also known as Bear Lake, it can be reached by Bear Road from Bear Creek Park or Highway 97C. See page 102 for details.

Downstream, kokanee spawning beds have been constructed by the Peachland Sportsman's Association. The canyon is home to more than 100 species of birds ranging from colorful woodpeckers and western tanagers to sparrows, crows and chickadees. You may also see a variety of mammals and reptiles, including the Pacific tree frog, garter, gopher and rattlesnakes, squirrels, skunks, mice, chipmunks, bear, deer, cougar, coyotes and porcupines.

Respect the park.

Follow regional district park regulations by keeping your dog on a leash and cleaning up after it. Use only designated trails and do not pick flowers. Using motorized vehicles on the trails, lighting fires or camping are not permitted.

•••

32

Lower Glen Canyon / Gellatly Aquatic Park

By Judie Steeves

Statistics:	For map, see page 123.

Distance:	More than 4 km of trails in Glen Canyon Regional Park, and downstream trails and parks.
Travel Time:	Fragmented trail sections so far.
Condition:	Well-maintained.
Season:	Year around.
Topo Maps:	Peachland, BC 82 E/13 (1:50,000).
Forest Maps:	Penticton Forest District Recreation Map.
Communities:	Westbank

Raised, rustic wooden walkways protect not only walkers' feet, but also the rare Okanagan ecosystem deep in the glen along Powers Creek in Glen Canyon Regional Park. Because of the shade in this deep canyon, and the extra moisture provided by a year-round stream, the plants that grow here are quite different from those that frequent the arid hillsides.

If you can climb stairs, these shady trails, with and without the wooden walkways, won't be too much of a challenge for you. The prize is a fabulous view, from Powers Creek Falls Bridge, of the rushing creek 24 metres below. Here the little creek has exerted its power over the years, wearing through the rock and creating deep undercuts in the canyon walls as it sped its way to the big lake.

To the Glen Canyon trails.

Access this trail network by turning east off Highway 97 at the Glenrosa/Gellatly junction. Head downhill for a half-kilometre on Gellatly Road. Park off Gellatly Road at a cluster of mail boxes, near the signed entrance to Glen Canyon subdivision. Look for stairs leading down into the canyon.

This walk probably won't take you more than an hour even if you smell the flowers along the way. In late summer, you can snack on a few wild blackberries, a rare opportunity in this valley's dry climate. The historic Hudson's Bay Company Brigade Trail which carried trappers and traders through the Okanagan in the early 1800's, followed part of this route. You tread in the footsteps of pioneers in this shady glen. On foot, you can exit at downtown Westbank on Hebert Road if you follow the pathway up toward the highway from this park.

To More Trails.

For a pleasant and easy lakefront walk, then a bit of birding, begin by turning southeast from downtown Westbank at the major intersection of Highway 97 and Gellatly Road. This is the intersection where you're bombarded by

Fig 39:
Gellatly Bay lakeside trail area.
(Photo © Judie Steeves.)

signs catering to those fast food urges. Drive down Gellatly Road toward the lake, and to dine outdoors, turn left at the bottom to Rotary Beach. Here picnic tables on a grassy stretch between the paved parking lot and the beach provide a pleasant setting for your meal. Sun yourselves on the adjacent beach, or have a swim before embarking on a 1.2-kilometre walk along the lakeside paths to the Rotary Trails. On the way, you'll pass under ancient willows and cross Smith Creek. When you reach the Gellatly Aquatic Park docks, you may see youngsters dive into the lake from the pilings. Your stroll will take you to a sandy beach at Powers Creek Point where the creek empties into the lake.

Rotary Trails.

Here the local Rotary club has created a kilometre long network of trails and bridges around a calm, heavily-treed portion of the creek, where birding is a treat. The Westbank Yacht Club and a public boat launch are across the road.

The clubhouse is in the historic *Pendozi*. According to Bill Chubb, a member of the Westbank Yacht Club, "It was originally built as a ferry for crossing from Kelowna to the Westside. It was built in Victoria, taken apart and rebuilt in Kelowna. The *Pendozi* was diesel-powered and had four propellors, two on each end."

Horses and history.
From your walk around Rotary Trails, you can either walk back for the car, or carry on in the opposite direction, past the Flying Horse Farm, where R.J. Bennett raises thoroughbred horses. The Bennett family is inextricably linked to the political history of this province. Russell (R.J.) Bennett is the son of one and brother of another former British Columbia Premier. Russell's father, senior statesman W.A.C. Bennett, served in the top position from 1952 to 1972, and his son Bill Bennett was first elected as Premier in late 1975.

Nearby is the historic Gellatly Nut Farm. It is known internationally for its unique nut breeding program begun in 1900 by the Westbank pioneer Gellatly brothers. Walnut, buartnut, chestnut and filbert trees up to 100 years old still grow at the lakefront orchard.

Stroll up the creek.
Pass by both history and horses to the next section of the lower Glen Canyon Trail. Walk (or drive) past the Flying Horse Farm, around the corner it's on, until you reach the next corner in Gellatly Road, where it turns north again and heads up the hill, a total of 2.4 kilometres from Rotary Beach. A new 1.4-kilometre section of the trail begins here and winds through the trees along the creek. Kokanee spawning platforms have been built in this section of the creek and are maintained by the Peachland Sportsman's Association. It's hoped in this way man can help compensate for some of the habitat damage he's caused to this struggling native land-locked salmon.

Local residents are spearheading efforts to complete the trail through private land along Lower Powers Creek to link this section with the glen trails at the Powers Creek Falls Bridge.

•••

128

33

Crystal Mountain / Telemark

By Murphy Shewchuk

Statistics:	For map, see page 103.

Distance:	11.5 km, from Hwy 97 in Westbank.
Travel Time:	One half hour.
Condition:	Paved, with gravel sections.
Season:	Year around. May need chains in winter.
Topo Maps:	Kelowna, BC 82 E/14 (1:50,000).
Forest Maps:	Penticton Forest District Recreation Map.
Communities:	Kelowna, Westbank and Peachland.

Crystal Mountain ski area (formerly Last Mountain), located 11.5 kilometres (seven miles) north west of Westbank, is geared to serve the family-oriented market. With only 10 per cent of the ski mountain rated as expert and the remainder evenly divided between beginner and intermediate, it's a good place to learn, practice technique or get back in shape to tackle the more demanding Okanagan ski mountains.

With a normal mid-December to late March season, Crystal Mountain also offers night skiing. Spring skiing starts early at Crystal Mountain — why not give it a try this February?

Telemark X-C Ski Trails are also located near Crystal Mountain. Access from Highway 97 is via Glenrosa Road on the south west outskirts of Westbank, with the large parking area nine kilometres from the highway. Telemark has over 32 kilometres of marked trails, groomed for classic and freestyle skiing. The area also has 2.5 kilometres of lit track for night skiing.

Summer can also be an interesting time in the area. You can continue northwest up Powers Creek for another 10 kilometres and then west for five kilometres into Jackpine Lake. Here a Forest Service recreation site can be your base for a little fishing, boating or camping. You can also continue farther north to Bear Road for further back-country exploring. (See the *Bear Road* section on page 102 for details.)

•••

34

Lacoma Lake Trail

By Judie Steeves

Statistics: **For map, see page 131.**

Travel Time: Allow at least 2 hours to hike each way,
                    plus time at the lake.
Condition: Trail is well-marked, easy to follow and maintained regularly.
Season: Spring (but it can be very wet), summer and fall.
Topo Maps: Peachland 82 E/13 (1: 50,000).
Forest Maps: Penticton Forest District Recreation Map.
Communities: Peachland.

Caught in the cup formed by steep surrounding hillsides, Lacoma Lake is an oasis of pristine wilderness. It can be reached by an 11-kilometre hike along a sun-dappled trail through the forest adjacent to Trepanier and Lacoma Creeks. Vibrant with wildlife, this serene little spot is a long but not difficult hike from Peachland, on a trail that was upgraded by the Canadian EarthCare Foundation in 1997 with a grant from Forest Renewal BC. They installed pit toilets at the trailhead, half-way along, and at the lake, and created primitive level campsites at all those spots as well.

Getting there.

The trailhead can be reached by turning east off Highway 97 onto Trepanier Bench Road, past Hainle Vineyards and First Estate Wineries, then along Cousins Road to Trepanier Road. Follow Trepanier Road as it twists and turns through rural acreage, finally changing from pavement to a rough gravel road about seven kilometres from Highway 97.

Continue to follow the main road to a cul-de-sac at its end, about 18 kilometres from Highway 97. Here a bridge used to cross Trepanier Creek until it was removed. This is the trailhead for the hike into Lacoma Lake. You'll find a pit toilet about 100 metres back from the end of the road toward Peachland. The first trail markers are high on the trees on the boulder-strewn road that parallels the last bit of the road to the cul-de-sac.

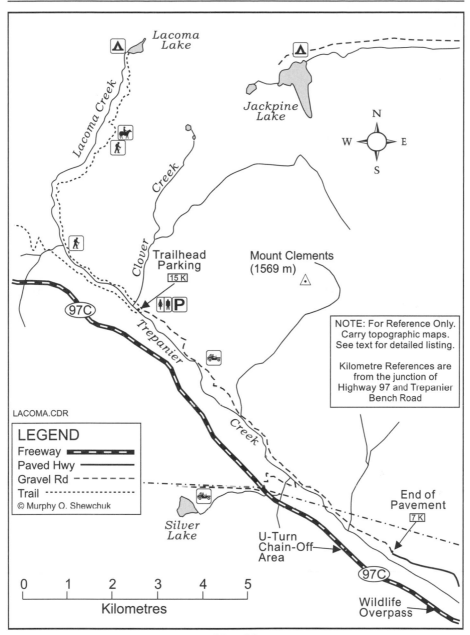

Map 20
Trepanier Creek Road and Lacoma Lake Trail.

Bird Haven.

A Great Blue Heron spread its enormous wings and soared over the little lake as we reached it. The call of the loon told us there were fish in this water as we parted the undergrowth and first set eyes on our goal. While we watched the wild scene before us, a belted kingfisher hovered over the water, plunged, then flew to the nearest branch with its breakfast. The loon danced atop the water, then dove, with a tremendous splash, and disappeared from the still surface.

Fig 40:
Black-capped Chickadee.
(Photo BCD-011 © Murphy Shewchuk.)

Waxwings, warblers, flickers, sparrows, chickadees, a sparrow hawk, a flock of swallows, some ducks, and several chipmunks all appeared in just the first few minutes.

Lacoma Lake is at an altitude of 945 metres (3,100 feet). On the dam built by Peachland pioneer families in the 1920s there are now three campsites and a firepit for the use of hikers.

It's the combination of Law, Coldham and Morshe family names that form the name of this little lake and creek. They built a crude log and rock dam with which to store water in the early years of the 20th Century. Those pioneer families needed to harness the potential of this bowl to hold water during spring runoff for use during the later dry summer months. That allowed them to irrigate their holdings far down-stream on the dry bench above Okanagan Lake.

It is said the first feet on this trail were those of the Okanagan First Nations people heading for powwows with the Nicola bands on the North Douglas Plateau. An aboriginal trail here is marked on the Archibald McDonald map of 1827 as Indian Road, reaching Okanagan Lake at "squ-ha" which meant "the bend."

Native people were followed in later years by European Peachland pioneers searching for a source of water they could control to keep their farms producing through the dry Okanagan summer. The first stretch of trail into the lake is the remnants of a road which provided access for the horses and vehicles used to maintain the dam. The road narrows after a time and clings to the edges of hillsides in places. Other sections are boggy from spring-fed tributaries to Trepanier Creek. There's a great viewpoint at the confluence of the valley that

Fig 41:
Lacoma Lake Trail. (Photo © Judie Steeves.)

holds Lacoma Creek, and that which opens up and bears Trepanier Creek. From there you can look far down the valley and across the creek and the Okanagan Connector Highway to the flat face of the tailings dam at Brenda Mine.

As you come closer to Lacoma Lake, you hike through huge patches of devil's club and false Solomon's seal. In late summer, you can spot the distinctive deep blue berry of the queen's cup or alpine beauty, which blooms here in early summer.

Prepare properly.

Before embarking on this hike, make sure you have adequate drinking water, comfortable hiking boots and something to snack on. At this altitude the weather can change suddenly, so be prepared. Don't travel alone and allow at least five hours for the return trip.

In addition, you should allow an opportunity to take the goat trail around the east side of the lake. Try to spend some time enjoying the peace, tranquility and wildlife there as well. Remember, too, that this is a source of drinking water for Peachland residents, and a pristine wilderness area, so pack out every single scrap you pack in.

•••

35

Hardy Falls Park

By Murphy Shewchuk

Statistics:	For map, see page 98.

Distance:	29 km, Kelowna to Hardy Falls Park.
	4 km, Peachland (Princeton Ave.) to the park.
Travel Time:	Approximately one-half hour from Kelowna.
Condition:	Paved highway (Highway 97).
Season:	Year around.
Topo Maps:	Summerland, BC 82 E/12 (1:50,000).
Forest Maps:	Penticton Forest District Recreation Map.
Communities:	Peachland.

Hardy Falls Park, on Peachland (Deep) Creek in south Peachland, is a cool oasis in what can sometimes be a hot landscape. A pleasant walking trail begins at a parking lot and picnic site on Hardy Street, just off Highway 97 on the southern outskirts of Peachland. The kilometre-long trail, complete with seven footbridges, leads to a splendid little falls hidden away at the head of a narrow canyon. Allow one-half to one hour to make the trip to the falls.

In April, the sunflower-like blossoms of the arrow-leaved balsamroot brighten the slopes and the yellow flowers of the Oregon grape add splotches of color to the underbrush. Kokanee, rainbow trout and carp spawn in the creek in season, while in spring a dipper nests in a crevice part way up the waterfall. In October, the Oregon grape fruit turns a dusty blue and crimson spawning kokanee dart about in the spawning beds in the creek.

Although the Hardy Falls Park sign was once marked with a "1972" date, the park had already gone through several incarnations by that year. It started off as an Order-in-Council setting aside 15.4 hectares (38 acres) in October, 1949. The BC Parks Branch established Antlers Beach Park in 1955, taking in Okanagan Lake waterfront and the creek-side property. At the time of writing, the park had been transferred to the Regional District of Central Okanagan.

Harry Hardy arrived in 1884.

According to Stella (Gummow) Welch in *Peachland Memories, Volume Two* (pp 379-384), "It was the fall of 1884 that Harry Hardy came down through the Okanagan Valley for the first time, and on New Year's Day, 1885, he got his first glimpse of what was later Peachland."

Harry Hardy soon "got a job with Bob Lambly. The Lambly Brothers had bought out the squatter, Bill Jenkins, at Trepanier and pre-empted District Lot 220, and Harry Hardy was sent down to look after the stock. Peachland became his home from that time on and he thus became the first permanent settler."

Irrigating with water from Trepanier Creek, Harry Hardy planted the first peach orchard in the Okanagan Valley in 1885. "In 1891 Hardy pre-empted land where the Gorman Brother's Mill now stands, its southern boundary being Hardy's Lake, known to old timers as the Turtle Ponds. At this property he planted about 200 fruit trees, one of the first orchards in the Westbank area." According to Stella Welch, "it would seem he cared for the two properties at the same time.

The first peaches at "Peachland".

"The first peaches ripened on the young orchard at Trepanier Creek gave the idea of a new venture to J.M. Robinson, energetic mine promoter. He had earlier induced a number of prairie farmers to invest in mining claims, and a little cluster of homes housed these venturing pioneers. But no ore was ever taken out, and Mr. Robinson's first taste of a delicious peach, which Mr. Hardy declared was nine inches around, opened up a whole new prospect. J.M. Robinson bought up pre-emptions in and around Peachland, paying Harry $600.00 for a pre-emption he had which extended from the lakeshore to the top bench, D.L. 1184. He sub-divided these into ten-acre plots, and went down to Winnipeg to sell them. John Gummow with his young family arrived from Winnipeg in December 1899, and the first orchard planted on the south side of the village came into being. His first crop of huge potatoes grown on this new and fertile land, with the aid of a plowed furrow as an irrigation ditch, inspired the disgruntled miners to buy up land for orchards, and the new settlement took form as a fruit-growing community.

"But," continues Welch, "Harry Hardy, in the meantime, left the Lambly Ranch to do a little prospecting on his own. After several disappointing years spent prospecting, Harry Hardy bought 10 acres of his own pre-emption back from J.M. Robinson, and started an orchard of his own. This was later sold and Harry spent the last years of his life in his little home in town. He passed on quietly March 21, 1947 at the age of 89 years."

•••

36

South Okanagan, Similkameen & Boundary

The South Okanagan, Similkameen and Boundary districts of BC have many similarities and many differences. At the lower elevations, the climate of all three is generally hot and dry in summer and moderate and dry in winter. Without the irrigation water pumped from rivers or captured in the hills, the bottomland would be as dry and barren as the nearby sage-covered hillsides.

But it isn't dry and barren — and that is one of the important attractions of the region. Where sprinklers cast their man-made rainbows, a virtual Garden of Eden flourishes. Cherries, apricots, peaches and plums are harvested as the summer progresses. Apples and pears are cultivated in many varieties and follow the soft fruit harvest. Grapes — raw material for the wine-making industry — grow on the slopes, row upon row.

What healthier form of recreation is there than fruit stand shopping?

Once you've filled your basket, you can head for the beaches of Okanagan, Skaha or Osoyoos lakes — or one of the dozen other lakes on the valley floor or in the nearby hills. You can practice your swing at one of many golf courses, ride an inner tube down the Okanagan or Similkameen rivers, or bird watch in the riverside oxbows or sagebrush-covered hills. If you are really serious about hills, you can explore Apex Provincial Park, Nickel Plate Provincial Park, Cathedral Provincial Park or the south slopes of Okanagan Mountain Provincial Park and bring back fine memories of the mountains.

If you choose not to hibernate in winter, the alpine region beckons. Strap on the slats and try skiing at the many ski resorts or cross country trails. Penticton has many fine restaurants and an excellent Library/Museum centre, while Osoyoos features a Spanish theme to go with the nearby pocket desert and Oliver is set halfway between Vaseux Lake and Osoyoos Lake.

Over Richter Pass, west of the Okanagan, lies the Similkameen, with more fruit stands per kilometre in Keremeos than probably any other place in Canada. Over Anarchist Mountain, to the east of the Okanagan, lies the Boundary District — and Doukhobor country. This narrow stretch of land has a heritage as rich as any in Canada.

The choices are many — and they're all yours.

•••

37

Okanagan Lake Park

By Murphy Shewchuk

Statistics:	For map, see page 98.

Distance:	25 km, Penticton to Okanagan Lake Park.
	35 km, Kelowna to Okanagan Lake Park.
Condition:	Paved highway, some four-lane sections.
Season:	Year around, north park closed in winter.
Topo Maps:	Summerland, BC 82 E/12 (1:50,000).
	Kelowna, BC 82 E/NW (1:100,000).
Forest Maps:	Penticton Forest District Recreation Map.
Communities:	Summerland, Peachland & Westbank.

O kanagan Lake Provincial Park is situated along the western shores of Okanagan Lake, a short drive north of Summerland and approximately 25 kilometres north of Penticton. Highway 97, continuing north to Peachland and Kelowna, passes directly through the park, dividing the terraced, developed campground sections below from the rocky hills above. The upper sections of the park typify the dry, semi-desert landscape for which the Okanagan Valley is famous.

Founded in 1955, Okanagan Lake Park is an example of park planning with the intent to create an area with a striking contrast to the native vegetation. In the latter part of the same decade, the first of more than 10,000 trees were planted in the foreshore area of the park. Today you can set up your camp in the shade of any one of a dozen exotic trees, including Manitoba, silver and Norway maples, Russian olive, Chinese elm, Lombardy poplar, and red, blue and mountain ashes. In the hills above, natural stands of ponderosa pine and Douglas fir continue to share the rocky landscape with sagebrush, bunchgrass, and cacti, as they have for centuries.

The extensive tree cover provides a haven for a tremendous variety of bird life. Many species, including cedar waxwing, quail, red-shafted flicker, western meadow lark, Lewis woodpecker, and several varieties of hummingbirds

can be spotted here with little difficulty. Along the many hiking trails
in the dry upland areas of the park,
you might well come across a
harmless gopher snake sunning itself quietly on a rocky outcrop, or a
colony of Columbian ground squirrels eyeing you suspiciously from
the safety of their burrows.

Lakeshore destination.

The park's recreational activities focus on the warm, clear waters
of Okanagan Lake. There is more
than a kilometre of sandy beaches,
and the opportunities for wind-
surfers, swimmers, sailors, fishermen, water-skiers, picnickers, and
sun worshipers are virtually limit-
less. Okanagan Lake Park is unusual in that it consists of two
campgrounds instead of one. The
park has a total of 160 vehicle/tent
campsites, 84 in the north campground, and another 76 in the south

Fig 42:
Early morning at Okanagan Lake Park.
(Photo OLP-029 © Murphy Shewchuk.)

campground. There are day use/picnic areas in both campgrounds, as well as
changehouses, showers, pit and flush toilets and boat ramps. Interpretive programs are usually provided from the end of June until the Labor Day weekend.

Because of the park's tremendous popularity, Okanagan Lake Park is on the
reservation system during the busy summer months. As is the case in many BC
provincial parks, Okanagan Lake has a resident campground host/hostess to
answer your questions and make your stay a pleasant and memorable one.

The boat ramp at Okanagan Lake Provincial Park is also a departure point
for the marine campgrounds and trails on the west slopes of 10000 hectare
(25,000 acre) Okanagan Mountain Provincial Park. It is also accessible by road
from either Kelowna or Penticton. (See the *Okanagan Mountain Park* section,
page 97, for details.)

•••

38

Giant's Head Mountain

By Murphy Shewchuk

Statistics:	For map, see page 140.

Distance: Approximately 5 km, Hwy 97 to summit.
Travel Time: Allow 1 to 2 hours, including hike to top.
Elevation Gain: 500 metres.
Condition: Mostly paved, very narrow and steep.
Season: Best in dry weather.
Topo Maps: Summerland, BC 82 E/12 (1:50,000).
Forest Maps: Penticton Forest District Recreation Map.
Communities: Summerland.

One of the finest viewpoints in the south Okanagan is in the heart of Summerland. Giant's Head Mountain, with a 360-degree perspective from 500 metres (1,640 feet) above Okanagan Lake, is the ideal point to get a true appreciation of the lay of the land.

Getting to the peak is relatively simple. If you are travelling along Highway 97 in upper Summerland, turn west on Prairie Valley Road, then south on Atkinson Road to Giant's Head Road. After a very short jaunt on Giant's Head Road, make a sharp turn to the right and head west on Milne Road. Watch for the signs and the stone gateway marking the start of the narrow switchback road to the picnic site near the top. Cars and smaller trucks should have little difficulty in dry weather, but leave your motorhomes, campers and holiday trailers at the parking area near the gate. From the parking area and picnic site near the top, several trails crisscross the ridge. The main route goes south and up with a switchback walking trail and a straighter route that has been gouged out of the mountain by errant 4x4s or ATVs.

Excellent view of the south Okanagan.

Markers clearly point out many of the local landmarks. Across the lake to the northeast is Okanagan Mountain and Okanagan Mountain Provincial Park. Across the lake to the east is Naramata, with several fine beaches. If you look carefully to the northeast, you may be able to pick out the twisting path of the

Kettle Valley Railway as it descends from Chute Lake on its way to Penticton. Just below you to the south is the community of Trout Creek and the Pacific Agri-Food Research Centre (formerly the Summerland Agricultural Research Station). Okanagan Lake, Skaha Lake and Vaseux Lake lie progressively farther south. Nearer to the south and southwest, you should be able to pick out the meandering path of the Kettle Valley Railway as it begins its steady climb out of the Okanagan Valley on its way to Princeton. With the Summerland, BC (82 E/12) topographic map as a reference, you may be able to visually follow Prairie Valley Road as it heads up Trout Creek and then cross-country to Princeton.

If map reading doesn't enthral you, you may be interested in the excellent variety of dry-country wildflowers and shrubs that cling to the mountain slopes. Yellow avalanche lilies and arrow-leaved balsamroot dominate the scene in April and May, but a closer look will reveal shooting stars, scarlet gilia and a host of other plant species. Saskatoon bushes thrust forth their white blossoms before most other plants bear any leaves, showing clumps of white on a drab brown slope. By early summer, the purple fruit attracts birds, chipmunks and anyone interested in a little variety in their berry pies.

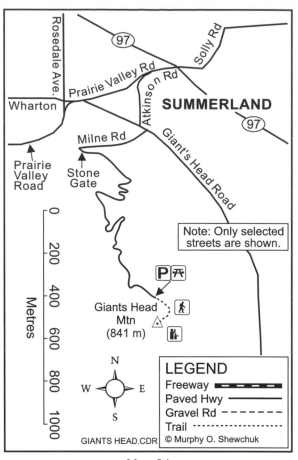

Map 21
Giants Head Mountain — Summerland.

•••

39

Princeton - Summerland Road

By Murphy Shewchuk

Statistics:	For maps, see pages 110 and 140.

Distance:	95 km, Summerland to Princeton.
Travel Time:	Two to three hours.
Elev. Gain:	860 metres.
Condition:	Mixed paved and gravel sections.
Season:	Best in the dry months.
Topo Maps:	Kelowna, BC 82 E/NW (1:100,000).
	Tulameen, BC 92 H/NE (1:100,000).
	Princeton, BC 92 H/SE (1:100,000).
Forest Maps:	Penticton Forest District Recreation Map.
	Merritt Forest District Recreation Map.
Communities:	Summerland and Princeton.

Visit the Sumac Ridge winery, stock up at the local fruit stands, fill up with gasoline and groceries and prepare to head for the hills in search of some fine trout lakes, hidden Forest Service recreation sites and the last remnants of the famous Kettle Valley Railway.

The Princeton-Summerland Road follows much the same route across this section of the Interior Plateau as the former Kettle Valley Railway. Called Prairie Valley Road in Summerland, the eastern end of this upland backroad begins at a set of traffic lights on Highway 97 in upper Summerland. This backroad is paved for the first 13 kilometres and the last 45 kilometres, with some rough gravel sections in the Trout Creek canyon area.

With the junction of Prairie Valley Road and Highway 97 as your kilometre 0.0 reference, follow the road as it winds through the village and out into an orchard-covered prairie that certainly isn't obvious from the main highway. Watch for the signs marked Osprey Lakes as you climb into the dry hills above Summerland.

141

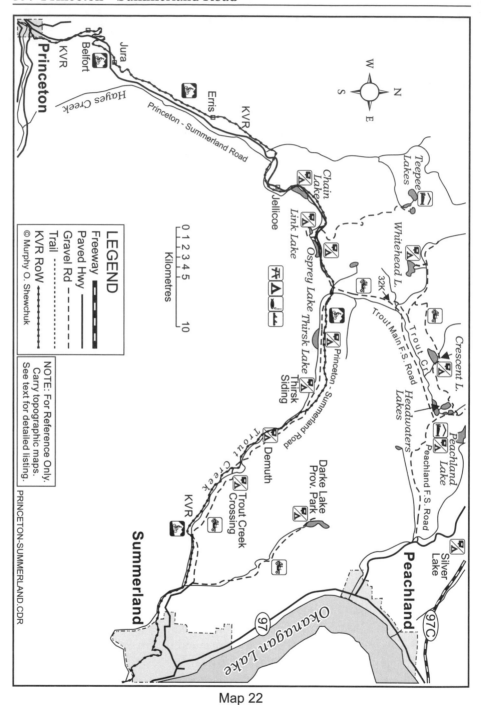

Map 22

Princeton-Summerland Road.

Fig 43:
Arrow-leaved balsamroot (*Balsamorhiza sagittata*) brighten the slopes in spring.
(Photo WAB-101 © Murphy Shewchuk.)

Darke Lake Park.

Bald Range Road, at km 11.0, is your first major junction. The road to the left continues up into the highlands, gradually getting narrower and rougher as it passes Darke Lake (Fish Lake). Bald Range Road, to the right, climbs away from the valley and up to a narrow bench high above Trout Creek. This is the truly scenic route to the Osprey Lakes and Princeton, and for the next 10 kilometres it offers several spectacular views of the Trout Creek Canyon and its arid rangeland. Wildflowers dominate the slopes in late April and May, but by July everything has a distinct brown look about it.

Brown gives way to green as the road crosses Trout Creek, near km 25.0, at the bottom of the Trout Creek valley. Forest Service campgrounds (basically a table or two and a pit toilet) have been established at several places along the creek for the cyclist, fisherman, hunter and itinerant tourist. The only service provided is the flat space among the trees. Carry in drinking water, fuel and supplies and carry out any garbage. These campsites do have their advantages, for even in mid-summer quiet solitude can be had with the only sounds being the yodel of a not-too-distant coyote and the gurgle of the stream.

Trans Canada Trail.

A minute's drive beyond the Trout Creek bridge, the road crosses the railbed of the former Kettle Valley Railway. The last train ran over the section from Spences Bridge to Okanagan Falls in May, 1989, and the twin steel rails have been removed. The province has since purchased the railway right-of-way. At the time of writing, much of the route from Brookmere to Midway had been designated as part of the Trans Canada Trail.

Thirsk Lake, at km 42, is a reservoir for the orchards and residents of the Summerland area, storing precious water for the hot summer months. Lake levels fluctuate significantly during the irrigation season as the water that begins in the Headwaters Lakes area is released via Trout Creek.

Trout Main F.S. Road, to the right at km 48.5, leads north to the Headwaters Lakes area with options to detour east to Peachland or northwest to Highway 97C and the Pennask Lake area. See the *Sunset Main to Summerland* section on page 109 for more information.

Popular fishing lakes.

Osprey Lake, (at km 51) Link Lake and Chain Lake form the popular Osprey Lakes chain near the summit of this backroad. Fishing is fine throughout most of the summer because of the altitude. Driving conditions also improve considerably as the rest of the road to Princeton is now paved.

Fig 44:
Princeton Castle, a 1910 cement plant.
(Photo PRN-442 © Murphy Shewchuk.)

Switchback or hairpin turns are common on mountain roads, but not nearly so common on railways. After seriously considering a number of alternative routes to Princeton, Kettle Valley Railway (KVR) Chief Engineer Andrew McCulloch used the undulating grasslands to his advantage when he designed the line's descent into the Allison Creek Valley north of Princeton. From the Separation Lakes area, near km 87, the railway line makes four wide loops down the hillside as it follows Belfort Creek to the valley floor. The road crosses the railway right-of-way several times, offering glimpses of the switchback loops between the low rolling hills.

Princeton-Summerland Road joins the Old Hedley Road and Highway 5A on the northern outskirts of Princeton, near km 94. Directly across the highway, another side road leads to the old mining towns of Coalmont and Tulameen and Otter Lake Provincial Park, but that's another trip.

Princeton, a community of 4,000 at the junction of Highway 5A and 3, at km 95, is the gateway to the dry interior for those travelling east on the Crowsnest Route. It was once known as Vermilion Forks because of the red ochre deposits nearby. More on the history of the region can be obtained from the museum and archives on Vermilion Avenue, near the Princeton city centre.

•••

40

Green Mountain Road / Nickel Plate Road

By Murphy Shewchuk

Statistics:	For map, see page 146.

Distance: 60 km, Penticton to Highway 3 near Hedley.
Travel Time: One to two hours.
Elevation Gain: 1,640 metres.
Condition: Partly paved; some rough gravel sections.
Season: Nickel Plate to Hedley may be closed in winter.
Topo Maps: Penticton, BC 82E/SW (1:100,000).
                 Kelowna, BC 82E/NW (1:100,000).
                 Princeton, BC 92H/SE (1:100,000).
Forest Maps: Penticton Forest District Recreation Map.
Communities: Penticton, Keremeos and Hedley.

The backroad from Penticton to Hedley via Nickel Plate Mountain has a historical significance that dates back to the late 1800s. In more recent years, the Penticton end has been the subject of Aboriginal land claims. Check the current status at the Penticton Indian Reserve administration office. If the road is signed or blocked, you may wish to use the route from Highway 3A near Yellow Lake.

In order to take advantage of Forest Service kilometre markers and still provide a guide for the complete trip from Penticton to Hedley via Apex and Nickel Plate, this description is broken into three parts. The first takes in part of the Green Mountain Road from Penticton to the junction to Apex Mountain Resort. The second part covers the route to the ski resort, and the remainder describes the route from Apex past the Nickel Plate Mine to Hedley.

Green Mountain Road suffers from an identity problem, for it is called Fairview Road when it heads east off Channel Parkway (the Highway 97 bypass) in the heart of Penticton's riverside industrial area. For the sake of this

145

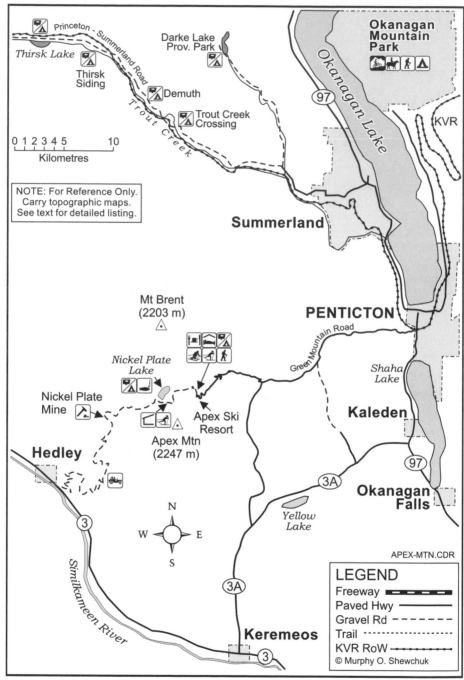

Map 23
Penticton - Apex Ski Resort - Hedley area.

book, the junction with Channel Parkway is considered to be kilometre 0.0. The first dozen kilometres of this paved road pass through Penticton Indian Reserve with the opportunity for backroads exploring to Farleigh Lake.

Marron Valley Road, at km 12.6, provides an alternate route to Highway 3A north of the Twin Lakes golf course, but at the time of writing, it was posted with "No Trespassing" signs. The term "marron" has French connections dating back to the fur brigade days. One of its meanings refers to "fugitive" or "wild" and could be related to the wild horses that once roamed the valley. But another meaning is related to chestnut which could also refer to a horse or the reddish-brown fall colors of the surrounding semi-desert hills. Word relationships such as this make the study of place names an interesting, but inexact science.

Marron Valley Road passes the T6 Ranch, then follows a switchback route up the hillside until it overlooks Aeneas Lake near km 5.0. From this midpoint, it follows a route apparently surveyed by the ubiquitous sidehill gouger until it joins Highway 3A approximately 11 kilometres southeast of Green Mountain Road.

Green Mountain House.

It was near the junction of Green Mountain Road and the road to Apex Ski Resort that the first Green Mountain House (km 19.8) was built. Ezra Mills, the master carpenter of Keremeos, built this roadside stopping-house for Leonard Albert Clark. L.A. Clark was born in Vermont in 1840, and after a stint in the American Civil War on the side of the north, he began a westward trek. He married in Iowa, learned irrigation lay-out in Colorado, railroad grading in Washington state and had a livery stable in Northport, Washington. By 1893, Clark and family were living in Calgary, Alberta, where he installed an irrigation system. He later continued in the same line of work for the Coldstream Orchards at Vernon, BC

After trying his luck in the Klondike in 1898, he returned to the Okanagan where he was contracted by M.K. Rodgers of the Nickel Plate Mine to build a road from Penticton to the mine. Clark and his crew began work August 10, 1900. Leonard Clark faced one of the toughest challenges of his varied career as he surveyed feverishly to keep ahead of the construction equipment, but he completed the rough wagon road by that Christmas.

His route left Penticton and wound up the sand hills on the south side of Shingle Creek, joining the present route of Green Mountain Road about eight kilometres from the Catholic Church on the Indian Reserve. From that point to the mine, nearly 50 kilometres, the route has changed little — a credit to Clark and his crew with their horse-drawn slip scrapers, hand tools, drill steel and blasting powder.

Clark recognized the potential of the area, and with his son Garry, pre-empted about 400 hectares (1,000 acres) of land in the Green Mountain District, named by him after his boyhood Green Mountains of Vermont. Green Mountain House thrived with the steady traffic of freight wagons to and from the mine and the thrice-weekly stage run over the soon-opened road to Olalla and points west in the Similkameen Valley.

Apex Ski Resort.

When efforts began to develop the Apex Mountain Resort in 1960, the original road to Beaconsfield Mountain (near Apex Mountain) proved woefully inadequate and a new road was started. Mostly single-lane at first, the road has been steadily improved by the Ministry of Highways until today the road to the ski resort is two-lane and paved.

The junction of the Green Mountain Road and the road to Apex, 21 kilometres southwest of Penticton, serves as the km 0.0 reference for the mid-section of this route. From the junction, the road climbs steadily toward the Apex ski area, passing Shatford Road near km 4.0. (Shatford Road winds north then northwest, providing access to the Sheep Rock trailhead near km 6.3 and the Mt. Brent trailhead near km 9.0.) At first the timber is scattered, but fir and lodgepole pine soon dominate the view.

Hedley-Nickel Plate F.S. Road.

Apex Village is reached at km 11.5 and the junction to the Hedley-Nickel Plate F.S. Road is well marked at km 13.0. Apex Mountain Ski Resort initially developed the reputation of being on a challenging, technical mountain. The first view of the ski runs from the day lodge still does little to allay the beginner's fears, but today the hill appeals to the recreational skier without taking away the challenge that the serious racer enjoyed. For the cross-country skier, ski clubs and the Forest Service maintain an extensive network of trails in the surrounding area. For additional information, see page 151.

Hedley-Nickel Plate F.S. Road begins in the upper levels of the Apex village (reset your reference to kilometre 0.0) and passes through an area marked for X-C skiers and snowmobiles at km 2.0. The Hedley Creek-Nickel Plate F.S. Road detours to the right, near the height-of-land and although it is very rough and boulder-strewn, it can be followed west to Nickel Plate Provincial Park on the north shore of Nickel Plate Lake. To get to the park beach, drive or walk west for about 2.6 kilometres and then turn south at a huge boulder. It's less than a kilometre from the boulder to the lake, but unless you are driving an ATV or a 4x4 with exceptional clearance, it is probably safest to park near the boulder and walk the rest of the way. The lake is at an altitude of 1900 metres (6,230 feet) so the fishing should stay good even during the summer while the swimming is likely to be a bit on the chilly side.

A junction at km 5.0 offers a few options for hiking or backroads exploring. Although there have been recent changes, roads and trails led south to Apex Mountain. Depending on the current state of the road and your vehicle, you can drive part of the way and walk the remaining distance to the peak of 2247 metre (7,372 foot) Apex Mountain. The total distance is about four to five kilometres, so take drinking water, a lunch and plenty of time. Other forest roads may end in log cuts or mudholes, so use caution.

The Nickel Plate Mine Road to the right has been variously marked by a "Mascot Gold" or "Corona Corporation" sign, but the best reference is the electric power line that leads to the open-pit mine site.

Nickel Plate Nordic Centre.

Nickel Plate Nordic Centre, less than a kilometre down the gradual descent, is the focal point of a 25-kilometre network of groomed and track-set cross-country ski trails — with more on the way. An additional 20 kilometres of back country ski trails are accessible from the Nordic Centre. A fine log building serves as a rendezvous and a warming hut for this relatively new operation. Work first started here in May, 1989, and by fall, the trail clearing was well underway. Sale of the logs removed from the trail system helped finance the grooming and the cabin. The system opened in February, 1990, in time for the Penticton Winter Games.

Nickel Plate Lake F.S. Recreation Site is less than two kilometres north of the junction near a creek crossing at km 7.0. Although not as attractive as the park at the north end of the lake, access is much easier for some excellent fly-fishing. The Nickel Plate Road, keeping left, follows Cahill Creek southwest, descending across a lightly-timbered mountain before reaching the open-pit Nickel Plate gold mine at km 12.5.

The operation here is not a new discovery. In fact, the Nickel Plate Mine, 1200 metres (4,000 feet) above Hedley, was one of BC's first successful hardrock mining operations. Except for a few short breaks, it operated steadily from 1904 to 1956.

From 1900 to late 1909, when the Great Northern Railway reached Hedley, four-horse teams plied the Nickel Plate Road in regular procession, hauling heavy mining and milling equipment from Penticton to Nickel Plate. Once the mine began producing, the teams did not return to Penticton empty.

According to Geoffrey Taylor in *Mining* (Hancock House 1978): "Every month two gold bricks came down to Penticton under special guard and were sent by Dominion Express to Seattle. Concentrates were sacked and hauled by horse-drawn wagon at $9 per ton to Penticton and from there by rail to the smelter in Tacoma. On the return journey the wagons would bring back supplies to Hedley at a contract rate of $20 per ton. The round trip usually took about a week."

The history of the Hedley Mascot operation also goes back to the turn of the century when the Mascot fraction, a triangular claim in the heart of the Nickel Plate orebody, was staked. The owners of the Nickel Plate mine were never able to come to suitable terms with Duncan Wood, owner of the Mascot fraction. In 1934, Hedley Mascot Gold Mines was formed to exploit the Mascot claim and neighboring claims. The ore contained a variety of minerals. For instance, in 1941, 22,477 ounces of gold, 2,755 ounces of silver, 1,300,000 pounds of copper and 2,250,000 pounds of arsenic were produced. In the half century of their first life, the mines on Nickel Plate Mountain produced one and one-half million ounces of gold and four million pounds of copper, worth a total of almost $50 million at the time of production.

Switchback descent.

To this point, the backroad has been descending steadily from near the Apex Ski Resort, but after passing the mining operation, it begins to take the process seriously. At first, the timber hides the steepness of the slope, but then the open hillside, dotted with aspen groves, makes the narrow, sometimes muddy switchback descent much more obvious.

A cattleguard and fence at km 21.0 marks a good spot to pull off the road, park and hike to the lip of a nearby rock bluff for an excellent view of the Similkameen Valley, both to the east and west. Caution is advised as there are no guard rails and a fall from the bluff means certain death.

Just beyond the viewpoint area, the road passes through a narrow rock cut and across a section of cliff face that is likely to convince even the bravest backroader to slow down. Once past the cliff, the road continues a steady switchback descent across a slope covered with sagebrush and bunchgrass. Visibility is good — and needed because the narrow road offers few places to safely pass oncoming vehicles. The Nickel Plate Road ends at Highway 3, 26 kilometres from the Apex Ski Resort and 60 kilometres from Penticton. If you're approaching it from the southwest, look for the road opposite St. Ann's Catholic Church, a few minutes drive east of Hedley.

•••

41

Apex Mountain Resort

By Judie Steeves

Statistics:	For map, see page 146

Distance:	32 kilometres from Penticton.
Travel Time:	Less than an hour from Penticton.
Condition:	Well-maintained.
Season:	All.
Topo Map:	Penticton, BC 82 E/5 (1:50,000).
Communities:	Penticton.

Apex was initially developed in 1969, and is now the largest ski resort in the south Okanagan with 56 marked runs served by one high speed detachable quad, a triple chair, t-bar and a platter.

The resort features 16 per cent novice, 48 per cent intermediate, 18 per cent advanced, and 18 per cent expert skiing. In all, there are 222 hectares to ski, including 25 hectares of machine made snow. The average snowfall is 548 centimetres. The mountain has a vertical rise of 605 metres with skiing from mid-November to mid-April. Snow boarders will enjoy the snowboard park on Claimjumper or the half-pipe on the Okanagan Run.

Apex Village features a range of accommodations, from The Inn, with 90 rooms, hot tubs and a fitness room, to condominiums or the RV park. You can grab a quick bite to eat at the Longshot Cafeteria, or relax at the bar and grill; the Gunbarrel bar or restaurant, or at the Rusty Spur. There's also a teen centre, outdoor hot tubs, jacuzzi and sauna, child care, ski schools, a skating rink, grocery store, liquor outlet, snowboarding, ski shop and rentals, snowmobile rentals and tours and sleigh rides.

The village is at an elevation of 1629 metres, while the peak is at 2247 metres. There is an extensive network of trails for the Nordic skier with 12 kilometres of trails at Apex Village, including a one-kilometre loop that's lit for night skiing. Just six kilometres away is the Nickel Plate Nordic Centre with 30 kilometres of groomed trails and 20 kilometres of back country trails.

•••

151

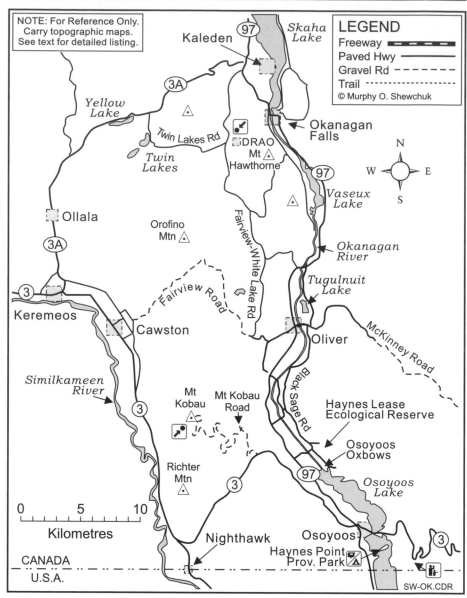

Map 24

Southwest Okanagan area.

42

White Lake Road

By Murphy Shewchuk

Statistics: **For maps, see pages 152 & 154.**

Distance:	32 km, Oliver to Hwy 97 near Kaleden.
Travel Time:	Up to one hour.
Elevation gain:	Minimal.
Condition:	Paved, with some gravel sections.
Season:	Maintained year around.
Topo Map:	Penticton, BC 82 E/SW (1:100,000).
Forest Map:	Penticton Forest District Recreation Map.
Communities:	Oliver, Okanagan Falls and Penticton.

Clothed in the history of the Okanagan, and of British Columbia, White Lake Road began as an Indian trail. It became the path that David Stuart, of John Jacob Astor's Pacific Fur Company, followed in 1811 for the first European incursion into the valley. In 1821, it became part of the Hudson's Bay Company fur brigade trail between Fort Okanogan on the Columbia River and Fort St. James in northern British Columbia. The last fur brigade, with perhaps 200 loaded horses, their packers, families and dogs, the beaver-hatted factor and his piper in the lead, camped in the roadside meadows where Hereford cattle graze today.

The establishment of the Canada-U.S.A. boundary in 1846 led to the abandonment of the route as a brigade trail, but as the nineteenth century wore on, it became the route of gold-seekers and cattle drivers heading for the Cariboo. Along it Father Pandosy traveled on his way to establish the church's presence at Okanagan Mission near Kelowna in the late 1850s. As the century closed, this Okanagan backroad echoed to the sounds of creaking wheels and snorting horses as the freight wagons loaded with supplies headed for the gold camps of Camp McKinney and Fairview.

With the main traffic light on Highway 97 in downtown Oliver as kilometre 0.0, follow 350th Avenue as it climbs westward. Soon becoming Fairview Road, it leaves the village and orchards to continue up through the sagebrush

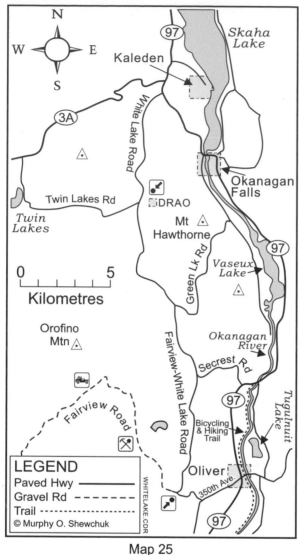

Map 25
White Lake Road and Oliver - Kaleden Area.

and greasewood-dotted slopes. Irrigated vineyards cut into the domain of the greasewood, producing one of the Okanagan Valley's finest cash crops.

A stop-of-interest sign near the junction of Fairview Road and White Lake Road, km 4.5, gives a brief glimpse of the long-gone community of Fairview, spawned by the discovery of gold, the Okanagan's oldest cash crop, in a nearby valley. See the *Fairview Road* section (page 156) for more information.

White Lake Road follows a dry bench northward, skirting stands of ponderosa pine, sumac bushes which turn flame red in autumn, and small ranches complete with children on horses. Although paved, this backroad deserves caution to avoid domestic animals and other sight-seeing drivers. The side valley begins to broaden, with homes nestled at the base of the cliffs. Another backroad, Secrest Road near km 12, winds down Park Rill to join Highway 97, north of Oliver.

Green Lake Road, km 16.0, marks the junction to yet another road down to the Okanagan Valley. After passing through the community of Willowbrook, it winds northeast around Mount Hawthorne, past Mahoney and Green Lakes as it descends to the Okanagan River near Okanagan Falls. Before joining Highway 97 at the bridge, it offers several excellent views of the valley and the highlands to the east.

Fig 45:
One of several star-scanning antennae.
(Photo DRA-008 © Murphy Shewchuk.)

Beyond the junction, the White Lake Road starts climbing gently at first, then more steeply as the road curves upward between the grassy hills and rock bluffs. Near km 22 the valley opens to a sometimes dry pond (White Lake) and the antenna farm of the Dominion Radio Astrophysical Observatory (D.R.A.O.). The junction with Twin Lakes Road, km 24, presents the option of heading west to Olalla and Keremeos or continuing north to Kaleden. The road to the west (left) passes the Twin Lakes junction (eight kilometres) and joins Highway 3A near Yellow Lake, while the White Lake Road continues north, past the observatory.

The Dominion Radio Astrophysical Observatory can be an extraordinary sight when you first catch a glimpse of the group of giant parabolic antennae pointing skyward. Your questions can be answered at the visitor centre which is open daily.

Visitors are asked to park in the lot next to the White Lake Road, at km 25.0, and walk into the site so that vehicle ignition noise does not interfere with the sensitive radio receivers that are part of the operation. These receivers, coupled to the huge parabolic antenna and the pole-top antenna array, are used to study radio emissions from our own sun, moon and planets as well as distant nebulae, supernovae (exploding stars), dark gas clouds and the Milky Way.

In addition to the computer-controlled receivers located at White Lake, computers link the receivers here with those at the Algonquin Radio Observatory near Ottawa, Ontario. This simulates an antenna with a 3074-km baseline for studies of remote galaxies.

From the radio observatory to Highway 97, the road winds generally downhill with a few steep narrow sections to add to the excitement, particularly after a snowfall or a heavy rain.

White Lake Road emerges from this side valley, at km 32, to join Highway 97 approximately one kilometre south of the junction of Highway 97 and Highway 3A near Kaleden.

•••

43

Fairview Road

By Murphy Shewchuk

Statistics:	For maps, see pages 152 & 158.

Distance:	8 km, Keremeos to Cawston.
	24 km, Cawston to Oliver.
Travel Time:	Approximately 1 hour.
Elevation Gain:	700 metres (2,300 feet).
Condition:	Narrow, some rough gravel.
Season:	May be closed in winter.
Topo Maps:	Penticton, BC 82 E/SW (1:100,000).
Forest Map:	Penticton Forest District Recreation Map.
Communities:	Keremeos, Cawston and Oliver.

airview Road, linking Cawston in the Similkameen Valley and Oliver in the Okanagan Valley, provides a glimpse of the colorful mining history of the region. The western end of the road can be approached from several points between Keremeos and Cawston. In the following description, I have followed Upper Bench Road from Highway 3A because of the special attraction of the historic Keremeos Grist Mill. This route also usually has light traffic, and the scenic contrast of the orchards below the stark mountainside presents some interesting photographic opportunities.

The junction of Highway 3A and Upper Bench Road, one kilometre north of the junction of Highways 3 and 3A makes a good starting point (kilometre 0.0) for a leisurely trip over Orofino Mountain. Upper Bench Road parallels the valley eastward, cutting a path through the orchards and along the barren cliffs.

Keremeos Grist Mill.

The Keremeos Grist Mill, less than a kilometre from Highway 3A, is the first stop along the way. Keremeos Creek gurgles through the sheltered vale, providing motive power for the giant wheel and a welcome reason to meander around the site. This grist mill is the only nineteenth-century mill in British Columbia that still has most of its machinery intact. This includes the original flour mill, a Eureka buckwheat screen, grain chute and a corn grinding machine.

The original mill was built in 1877 by Barrington Price, who had pre-empted land near Keremeos in 1873. The water-powered mill was operated by John Coulthard after 1885, and served the needs of the Similkameen Valley for almost 20 years before stiff competition from larger mills forced it to close.

In 1974, the mill and adjacent log building were designated an historic site and restoration was begun. The Keremeos Grist Mill was officially reopened in 1985, and has since been steadily improved.

Fig 46:
Keremeos Grist Mill, Upper Bench Rd.
(Photo KER-315 © Murphy Shewchuk.)

Beyond the grist mill, the road passes through the orchards and then along the base of the barren mountain. This country is too dry for timber at the lower elevations, and all that thrives are the desert plants more common to the Cascade Mountain rain-shadow much farther south in Washington and Oregon.

Orchardists advertise fresh fruit and vegetables in season, and some of the best spring asparagus comes from Keremeos. Local bee keepers also sell orchard blossom honey and beeswax candles. Upper Bench Road continues east until it merges with Highway 3, east of Cawston. However, Lowe Drive, at km 7.7 marks the start of the mountain road to Oliver.

Closed in winter.

Because of the option to leave Highway 3 at Cawston, the junction of Lowe Drive and Upper Bench Road has been chosen as kilometre 0.0 of the backroad over Orofino Mountain. It is worth noting that the road may be closed in winter. It is not recommended for vehicles other than cars and pickups.

The pavement ends at km 1.2, and as though not to waste any time getting away from the Similkameen Valley, the road quickly begins a northeast climb up Blind Creek. The desert environment, complete with ponderosa pine, sagebrush, prickly-pear cactus and the sunflower blossoms of arrow-leaved balsamroot in spring, gives way to gullies lined with cottonwood and aspen.

About the same time as the surroundings get a little damper, the steep grade and tight corners give way to a wider road with an easier grade at km 3.7. The

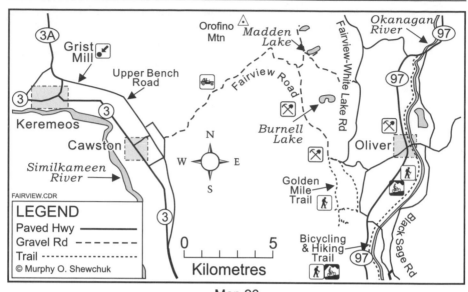

Map 26
Fairview Road: Keremeos — Cawston — Oliver.

climate continues to change as the road reaches the height-of-land at km 10.0. Now the timber is Interior fir and vine maple bushes hang over the narrow road where it swings near the creek. Watch for cattle — they seem to believe that they have the right-of-way by virtue of being there first.

The road now swings south as it descends into the Okanagan Valley. A side road north to Ripley Lake at km 12.2 and another at km 14.1 offer diversions for the backroad explorer. Ripley, Madden and Burnell (Sawmill) lakes are regularly stocked with rainbow trout. All three lakes have small Forest Service recreation sites complete with car-top boat access.

Fairview Camp.

Mill foundations, waste dumps and open shafts at km 16.9 mark the location of the Fairview gold and silver mines. Gold was first discovered in the area in 1887, writes Karen Witte in a brief Historical Sketch of Fairview. Fred Gwatkins and George Sheenan staked what was later to become the discovery claim of the Stemwinder Mine, the primary instigator of the Fairview Camp. The Stemwinder interests were soon sold to an American and British syndicate and the two-decade first life of the mining camp began when the original Fairview Camp was established near the mine site in 1890.

On August 12, 1892, the first newspaper in Oro, Washington, (now Oroville) published the following account about Fairview: "This camp is in the same gold belt we are, and proves beyond a shadow of a doubt that this is the most extensive mineral belt in the known world."

In 1893, the Golden Gate Hotel (later nicknamed the "Bucket of Blood") opened for business. Within a short time, residential buildings and other commercial developments, including the Miner's Rest, the Fairview, and Moffatt's Saloon, were built on the precarious slopes of the gulch.

But Fairview didn't become a thriving community until the settlement moved down to the mouth of the gulch in 1897, at km 19.3 overlooking present-day Oliver. On July 1, 1899, celebrations marked the opening of the Fairview Hotel (the Big Teepee), the most elegant hostel in the Interior.

The fire that destroyed the Big Teepee in 1902 signaled the end of Camp Fairview. The gold quartz veins became harder to mine as the miners worked deeper. By World War I, the only real activity was the wrecking bar as salvagers recovered the lumber and machinery from the townsite and mills.

The Fairview mines gained a new lease on life on January 31, 1934, when U.S. President Roosevelt raised the price of gold from $20.67 to $35.00 per ounce. Gold properties all over the continent saw renewed interest.

Robert Iverson worked at the Fairview Amalgamated Mines in 1938. "They had two horses in use pulling a train of five one-ton cars." writes Iverson in the Okanagan Historical Society 48th Report. "My job was helping load and unload the train. Between 100 and 150 tons over two shifts were normal. Between 40 and 50 men were employed, including those employed at the mill."

The start of World War II forced the closure of the Fairview and Morning Star properties, but in the half dozen years of renewed operation, they produced 14,000 ounces of gold and 152,000 ounces of silver.

A junction at km 18.2 marks a side road down to south Oliver while the main road keeps left to the junction of Fairview Road and White Lake Road at km 19.3. The gravel road gives way to pavement near the junction and the green orchards of the Okanagan Valley present a contrast to the stark grassland slopes dotted with sagebrush and greasewood in what some claim to be the driest part of Canada.

A nearby stop-of-interest sign offers a glimpse of Fairview's past:

FAIRVIEW GOLD
The 1890s held high hopes for the lode gold mines
such as Stemwinder, Morning Star and Rattler. By 1902,
when the Fairview Hotel or "Big Teepee" burned, the
golden years were over. Fairview's population dwindled
as miners left for more promising prospects. But some
settlers, lured by the natural attractions of the
Okanagan Valley, remained to profit from the lasting
wealth of its abundant resources.

The "Big Teepee" was the centre of a community that included livery stables, offices, several stores and houses, a school and a government building. Today all that remains of the original buildings is the jail which was moved and reassembled adjacent to the museum in downtown Oliver.

A concrete irrigation flume that passes under the street at km 23 deserves more than a passing glance, for in it is the real gold of the Okanagan Valley. Irrigation in the Okanagan grew out of necessity with techniques that were a carry-over from the water diversion practiced by placer miners. Some of the first water licenses in the Okanagan were recorded in the early 1870s, but serious irrigation didn't begin in the Oliver area until after World War I.

The South Okanagan Lands Project began in 1919, when the BC government bought out private holdings amounting to about 9,300 hectares (23,000 acres). A gravity system was constructed to take water from Vaseux Lake. Water was carried across the valley through a siphon that had pipes large enough for men to work inside. The dam and siphon were officially opened by BC Premier John Oliver in 1921, but it was not until 1927 that the project, with 100 km of flumes and laterals, was completed and the first irrigation water served the whole area.

Without the foresight and determination of pioneer politicians such as "Honest John" Oliver, the beautiful green orchards and vineyards would still be "just the haunt of jack rabbits and rattlesnakes."

Golden Mile Trail.

If you are interested in a closer look at both the man-made and the natural ecosystems, consider a hike on the 10-kilometre-long Golden Mile Trail.

No! This isn't a case of faulty metric conversion. The name refers to a narrowing of the Okanagan Valley at Oliver that has contributed to the desert microclimate. The three-to-four hour circle route extends from the Fairview townsite south to Road 7 (328 Avenue) and includes the desert hillside as well as orchards, vineyards and three wineries. Extensions added in 1998 further the value of the interpretive trail network.

Downtown Oliver.

Fairview Road joins Highway 97 at km 23.6 in the heart of Oliver. If you are looking for more exercise, you could consider the 18.4-kilometre-long bicycling and hiking trail that extends south to Osoyoos Lake from the McAlpine Bridge on Highway 97, just north of Oliver. Across Highway 97 and the Okanagan River, you can continue an eastward trek to Mount Baldy and old Camp McKinney. North of the junction, Highway 97 continues on to Penticton while to the south lies Osoyoos and the U.S. border.

•••

44

Mount Kobau Road

By Murphy Shewchuk

Statistics:	For maps, see pages 152 & 162.

Distance:	20 km, Highway 3 to Mount Kobau F.S. Rec. Site at summit.
Travel Time:	Approximately 1 hour.
Elevation Gain:	1190 metres (3,900 feet).
Condition:	Good gravel road, some rough sections.
Season:	Closed in winter.
Topo Maps:	Keremeos, BC 82 E/4 (1:50,000).
Forest Map:	Penticton Forest District Recreation Map.
Communities:	Keremeos, Cawston and Osoyoos.

Mount Kobau, roughly half way between Keremeos and Osoyoos, has what could be described as one of the finest "backroads" in the province. The one million dollar gravel road to the summit was originally built to service a $22 million observatory project that was never completed.

German origin.

The name, according to *An Historical Gazetteer of Okanagan-Similkameen*, is believed to be of German origin. It appears on George Dawson's map of 1877, but the reason for it has not been determined. To the early settlers, the south slope was known as Richter Mountain, the north end as Old Timers' Mountain and the high central cone as The Big Knoll. The local Natives called the cone, Nice Top.

Mount Kobau road leaves Highway 3 at the summit of 682 metre (2,237 foot) Richter Pass. The pass takes its name from Francis Xavier Richter, a pioneer cattleman who drove 42 head of cattle through it in 1864. Richter later settled in the area and built a comfortable home near the pass in 1887.

The first "road" had been cut through the pass in 1865 as part of the Dewdney Trail. It was later improved to wagon road status, but stagnated for a century until the southern route of Highway 3 was opened between Keremeos and Osoyoos in July, 1965. The Hon. Frank Richter, son of the original pioneer, in his ribbon-cutting speech, recalled the great changes of the past century and the "fantastic" future that beheld the Richter Pass Highway and Mount Kobau.

He spoke glowingly of the multi-million dollar Queen Elizabeth II Observatory planned for Mount Kobau. "In time, the observatory will become world famous for people from all over the world will flock to this installation..." wrote Kathleen S. Dewdney in a description of the opening.

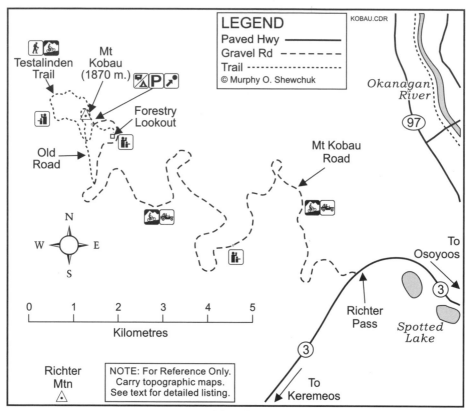

Map 27
Mount Kobau Road and Testalinden Trail.

Queen Elizabeth II Observatory Project.

The Observatory project was originally announced on October 28, 1964. But despite the Queen's name and glowing support from local politicians, it was never completed. Less than four years later, on August 29th, 1968, the government announced it would scrap the $22,000,000 observatory.

According to a report in The Osoyoos Times of September 5, 1968 "Close to $4 ½ million has now been spent on the project. One and a half million dollars was spent on the 150-inch blank that was cast in Corning, New Jersey. Over one million dollars was spent on the 11 miles of road built to the top of the 6200 foot mountain. The balance was on studies and engineering."

Mount Kobau Star Party.

The Mount Kobau Star Party, held every August near the dark-of-the-moon, has been attracting astronomers – amateur and professional – since 1984. Each year, over 150 dedicated deep-sky enthusiasts trek to the Forest Service recreation site atop Mount Kobau, dotting it with tents, trucks and telescopes.

As it is with most Forest Service rec sites, this one has a "pack it in, pack it out" camping policy. Sky watchers have discovered the reward for such simplicity is access to the clearest, steadiest of skies.

The Mount Kobau Star Party is geared to those who are prepared to "rough it" in pursuit of smog-free star watching. On Mount Kobau, city conveniences are exchanged for the necessary Spartan rigors familiar to serious observers: dim red lights at night, restricted noise during the morning sleep, limited amenities, and mountain- top isolation.

However, it isn't only a night-shift eye-to-the-telescope experience. In the past, guest specialists have brought along displays of meteorites and presented various other programs during the daylight and early evening hours. The nearby Dominion Radio Astrophysical Observatory is also a must see. (See the *White Lake Road* section on page 153.)

For more information, contact the: Mount Kobau Astronomical Society, P.O. Box 20119 TCM, Kelowna, BC, V1Y 9H2.

Getting to the top.

The Kobau Lookout Forest Service Road leaves Highway 3 about 10.5 km east of the Nighthawk junction. It is a wide gravel road with a few washboard sections and a few switchbacks. There are a number of excellent spots to enjoy the view of Osoyoos Lake and the south end of the Okanagan Valley.

For most travellers, the Mt. Kobau Forest Service rec site is the end of the road. However, it needn't be the end of the exploring. There is a one kilometre walking trail to the Forest Fire Lookout. If you are fortunate, you may find Ken Bushey there, as he has been spending his summers on Mount Kobau since the early 1990s.

Testalinden Trail.

The four to five kilometre long Testalinden Trail winds south and then west as it circles the summit of Mount Kobau. It offers some fine views of the Similkameen Valley before returning via the original road along the mountain top.

•••

163

45

Ellis Ridge / Carmi Trails

By Judie Steeves

Statistics:	For maps, see pages 69 & 165.

Travel Time: Less than an hour to several hours.
Condition: Well-marked, well-maintained trails.
Season: All.
Topo Maps: Penticton 82 E/SW (1:100,000).
Forest Maps: Penticton Forest District Recreation Map.
Communities: Penticton.

The dark spires of burned tree trunks rise out of clouds of newly-green bushes and undergrowth in the Ellis Ridge area east of Penticton — a stark reminder that a devastating forest fire here in 1994 claimed 5500 hectares of forest land and 18 homes. The foam of bright green undergrowth is also a reminder that new life springs from the ashes of a forest fire, and in fact is sometimes dependent on fire. That's a hint that parts of this valley are virtually a desert in terms of annual rainfall. In the hot summer months a spark can set off tinder-dry grasses, quickly blackening a lush green mountainside.

Garnet Fire Interpretive Site.

The force of fire and the wonder of water's effects in this ecosystem are the focus of two short trail systems created at the informative Garnet Fire Interpretive Site on the Ellis Ridge above Penticton. It's just a few kilometres from the Carmi Cross Country Ski Trails, 17 kilometres of well-marked trails used in winter for cross-country skiing, and in summer for hiking .

To get there.

From Main Street in Penticton, take Carmi Avenue east past Penticton Regional Hospital, winding through subdivisions, then uphill into acreage with an obvious recent history of fire. It's nine kilometres from Penticton to the Garnet Fire Interpretive Site and 13 kilometres to the Carmi Cross Country Ski Trails and toboggan hill. This back road continues on through to the Okanagan Falls

Forest Service Road (see page 167), and as the Carmi Creek Forest Service Road, ultimately to Beaverdell.

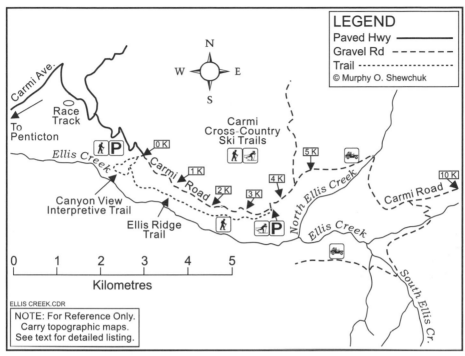

Map 28
Ellis Creek — Carmi Cross Country Ski Trails area.

Canyon View Trail.

The Canyon View Trail shows hikers a forest recovering from a major wildfire, with spectacular views of the Ellis Creek Canyon (where the fire began), Penticton, and surrounding forest.

The Okanagan is called a fire-dependent ecosystem, where fire is a natural event that changes and rejuvenates — part of maintaining a healthy, sustainable forest. Historically this ponderosa pine and bunchgrass ecosystem burned every five to 10 years. These frequent natural wildfires quickly burned fuels on the forest floor, cleaning up dead and diseased plant debris, and leaving behind the ashes that provide mineral nutrients to nourish the soil. Every 100-150 years more devastating fires occurred. The thick, layered bark of ponderosa pine and Douglas fir trees protects the living tissues. Bunchgrass thrive on the mineral-rich, ash soil left behind by fire, while their deep root balls survive surface fires which actually enhance the seed development of other plants.

In recent years, man has intervened in the natural process, preventing fire to protect both the timber resource and human communities. Ironically, that allows the build-up of fuels on the forest floor and ultimately endangers the human communities and timber man intended to protect. Wildland-urban interface areas, where human homes butt up against wild ones, are now recognized as particularly threatening situations because of the danger of fire moving from one type of home to the other with catastrophic consequences.

The good news is that on the wildland side, the dead and dying trees now provide food sources, storage, shelter, nesting holes, hunting and resting perches for wildlife. The fallen trees and branches make nesting areas for mice, voles and ground birds, while frogs, toads and salamanders and skinks stay moist and cool in their shade. Insects are attracted to the weakened trees and woodpeckers, sapsuckers and songbirds peck and drill into the wood for insects, ultimately excavating nesting cavities for themselves, as well as for bats and owls. Martens, squirrels and chipmunks use the cavities for nesting and for storing food.

Ellis Ridge Trail.

Water is a scarce and valuable resource in this ecosystem. Just how valuable is the focus on the Ellis Ridge Trail, where hikers are shown how important it is to care for water resources to sustain communities and maintain healthy forests. Both water and the watersheds from where it flows are essential to all life. In the Okanagan, snowfall is the dominant form of all the water used both for irrigation and domestic purposes, with 90 per cent coming from the season's snowpack. Every 25 centimetres of snow equals 2.5 centimetres of water. In some parts of the Okanagan, the annual average precipitation is only 20 centimetres, while the provincial average is 150 centimetres, and on the west coast of BC, the average is from 500 to 750 centimetres.

The trail takes walkers on a short trip with three scenic viewpoints, to look at the community watersheds, lakeshore zones, and streamside and riparian areas. In contrast to the dry forest high on the ridge, in such gullies as Ellis Canyon the riparian zones are green ribbons of life, with aquatic plants, shrubs, and trees filtering surface water before it reaches the creek. Stream corridors support a wider variety of plants and animals than any other habitat, and act as transportation corridors for some animals.

Returning to the main road, a further 3.5 kilometres will take you to the Carmi Cross Country Ski Trails, which include several viewpoints over their length.

•••

46

Okanagan Falls FS Road (R201)

By Murphy Shewchuk

Statistics:	For map, see page 69.

Distance:	80 km, Okanagan Falls to McCulloch Road.
Travel Time:	Two to three hours.
Elevation gain:	860 metres (2,820 feet).
Condition:	Gravel industrial road, rough in spots.
Season:	May be closed in winter.
Topo Maps:	Beaverdell, BC 82 E/6 (1:50,000).
	Wilkinson Creek, BC 82 E/11 (1:50,000).
	Penticton, BC 82 E/SW (1:100,000).
	Kelowna, BC 82 E/NW (1:100,000).
Forest Maps:	Penticton Forest District Recreation Map.
Communities:	Okanagan Falls and Kelowna.

The weekend wanderer may find the Okanagan Falls Forest Service Road (R201) to be a welcome break from the paved highways through the bottom of the Okanagan Valley. Coupled with the backroad through the *Grizzly Hill / Dee Lakes* area (see page 34) it can be part of route from Okanagan Falls to Lavington with only a short stretch of black-top on Highway 33, near Joe Rich Valley.

Weekends are safest.

Weekend is the key word here. This is an industrial road and the logging trucks are wider and longer than normal. Expect tree-length loads between 4:00 AM and 4:00 PM weekdays with the usual lighter traffic during the off-hours and on weekends and holidays. A Weyerhaeuser person I spoke to suggests that you avoid using the road during the hauling times, but if you can't, be sure to follow a radio-equipped vehicle. Wherever you travel in the back country, it is wise to use extra caution on weekdays because of the logging truck traffic.

Shuttleworth Creek.

In an attempt to keep things as simple as possible and to allow you to join the route at one of several locations, I will use the Forest Service kilometre markers as a general reference with the Weyerhaeuser mill scales as the 0K base. The simplest way to find the Okanagan Falls Weyerhaeuser mill is to start from the corner of Main Street

Fig 47:
Porcupine — handle with care.
(Photo PRC-017 © Murphy Shewchuk.)

(Highway 97) and 9th Avenue in downtown Okanagan Falls. Drive east to the end of 9th Avenue and turn right (south) and follow Maple Street south, watching for the mill on your left (east). Look for signs marked R201 on the road that skirts the main mill yard.

The first three kilometres of Okanagan Falls F.S. Road (R201) is an un-gated route through private land. Again, use caution and watch for industrial equipment. Beyond the mill, this route climbs steeply up the south side of Shuttleworth Creek. There are several opportunities to get a good view of the canyon and the Okanagan Falls area between 5K and 10K. A road to the right (south) near 12K can take you east to Solco Lake and, if you are really persistent, to Conkle Lake and the West Kettle Valley. The latter destination could require dry weather and a 4x4 vehicle.

Allendale Lake.

Another junction to the right (this time to the east) near 18K and a bridge marks the start of the road to Allendale Lake. It is about six kilometres in, but the Forest Service recreation site there may be a good base for some upland fishing. Beyond the Shuttleworth Creek bridge, the road swings northwest, climbing less steeply for about four kilometres before leveling off at an elevation of about 1525 metres (5,000 ft). While there are a few side roads along the way, the next major diversion is near 37K where you have the opportunity to follow Carmi Road down Ellis Creek to Penticton. (See the *Ellis Ridge / Carmi Trails* section on page 166 for more information.)

Idleback Lake.

The next major diversion is at Idleback Lake, near 43K. The large Forest Service recreation site here is an excellent base for fishing and canoeing. However, my wife, the swimmer, was not impressed with the cold water and muddy bottom.

Greyback Road.

If you are interested in a fine lake with a better bottom for swimming, consider detouring west to Greyback Lake. Greyback F.S. Road joins Okanagan Falls F.S. Road (R201) near the 57K marker. If you take this option, keep left at the Canyon Lakes F.S. Road junction and continue climbing west and then southwest to the height of land (1675 metres or 5,500 feet) near 63K. Keep left at a gated junction near 65K and you should reach a narrow side road down to Greyback Lake near 69K. This is a Penticton water reservoir, so be extremely careful with any pollutants.

Greyback F.S. Road continues southwest for about 17 kilometres to the suburbs of Penticton, but I would not recommend the last 15 kilometres for anything but a tough 4x4 pickup or dirt bike. However, if you are interested in a bit more exploring, you might follow the road for about two kilometres to the James Creek Falls Trailhead. Here a wide trail winds through the trees for about 100 metres to a viewpoint. If you want a closer, intimate look at the falls, you can climb down a rough trail through a natural rock cut to the valley floor. Mid to late afternoon will be the best time to see the falls lit by the sun.

Back on Okanagan Falls F.S. Road (R201).

North of the junction at 57K, Okanagan Falls F.S. Road (R201) crosses Wilkinson Creek and continues northeast across the uplands. You may want to stop to check out the granite quarry near 68K or Myra F.S. Road at 70K. Although we didn't explore it all the way, Myra F.S. Road could lead you across the ridge and down to the Kettle Valley Railway right-of-way (now part of the Trans Canada Trail). See the *Myra Canyon KVR Corridor* section, starting on page 84, for details.

If you are looking for a better class of accommodation than a Forest Service recreation site, you could consider Idabel Lake Resort at 75K. You could also continue north to the junction with McCulloch Road at 78K and go west to McCulloch Lake Resort. And if a fishing resort isn't your style, you can take a short jaunt east to Highway 33 and continue on to Big White Ski Resort or down the hill to Rutland and Kelowna.

•••

47

Mount Baldy Loop

By Murphy Shewchuk

Statistics:	For map, see page 171.

Distance:	53 km, Oliver to Highway 3 near Bridesville.
Travel Time:	Two to three hours.
Elevation gain:	1450 metres (4,750 feet).
Condition:	Gravel, rough in spots.
Season:	Maintained all year around, muddy in spring.
Topo Maps:	Penticton, BC 82E/SW (1:100,000).
Forest Maps:	Boundary Forest District Recreation Map.
	Penticton Forest District Recreation Map.
Communities:	Oliver, Bridesville and Osoyoos.

Backroads explorers are often forced to resort to armchair travelling when the snow closes in on the mountains of British Columbia. This is usually the time to repair fishing equipment, overhaul the vehicle and sort the photographs taken on previous trips into BC's heartland.

There are exceptions, of course, and one is the McKinney Road — Mount Baldy Road loop through the Okanagan Highlands from Oliver to Bridesville. The attractions include BC's Okanagan desert, mountain climbing, rockhounding in old gold diggings and — the reason for year round access — cross-country skiing at the Mt. McKinney Nordic Ski Trails and alpine skiing at the Mount Baldy Ski Area.

Starts in the heart of Oliver.

The traffic light at 350th Avenue and Highway 97 in the heart of Oliver serves as kilometre 0.0 and a suitable landmark for the start of this backroad trip into the highlands. Formerly Park Drive, 350th Avenue crosses the Okanagan River near the light. McKinney Road (362nd Avenue) swings right off 350th Avenue less than half a kilometre from the traffic light on Highway 97.

If you're hell-bent on heading for the hills, take McKinney Road. However, if it's hotter than Hades — as it can be in Oliver — continue straight ahead on 350th Avenue and 79th Street to 370th Avenue (formerly Harrison Way) and then take 370th Avenue and 81st Street to the public beach on Tuc-Ul-Nuit Lake. Also known as Tugulnuit Lake, this spring-fed swimming hole is a welcome break before tackling gravel and dust.

McKinney Road suffers from a minor identity problem with a sign at km 1.1 identifying it as Camp McKinney Road just before it crosses a concrete irrigation flume. At the junction with Sand Point Drive at km 1.9, the "Camp" is dropped.

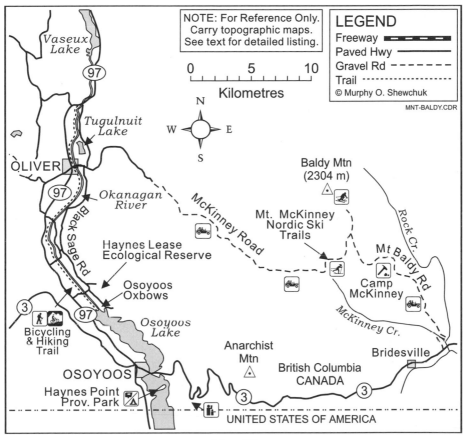

Map 29

Oliver - Mnt Baldy - Bridesville area.

Okanagan desert.

McKinney Road enters the Inkaneep Indian Reserve and as the paved road swings around a sandy knoll, sagebrush and ponderosa pine begin, leaving the fruit orchards behind. This land is typical of the desert that existed before irrigation turned the bottomland into orchards. It is barren, desolate and HOT.

171

Greasewood, sumac and the occasional clump of bunchgrass cling desperately to the sand dunes that were once under an ancient glacial lake.

Farther up the road, the effects of water are again visible with the desert on one side of the road and on the other side, near Wolfcub Creek, lush green hay fields. Water makes a major difference in this region which is considered to be an extension of the Sonoran Desert of New Mexico.

The road continues to climb southeast into the highlands. Near km 8.0 the desert gives way to another symbol of the dry country — ponderosa pine trees. They are scattered over the hillside, providing resting cattle with pockets of green shade among the clumps of bunchgrass.

A small lake near km 16 (14K on the roadside markers) marks the end of the pavement. A close look at a detailed topographic map, or the view from a low-flying aircraft, will reveal countless small man-made lakes and ponds in southern British Columbia's high country. Some of these were originally developed to store water for gold mining operations. But most were built to collect the water from winter snows and June rains. Water needed for grazing cattle and hay fields when the hot, rainless summer winds sweep up from the American southwest.

Colorful larch trees.

The stands of ponderosa pine gradually mix with interior Douglas fir and then needle-shedding larch as the road climbs eastward up the slopes of the Okanagan Highland. In September and October, the larch changes color, adding splashes of yellow to the background of evergreen forest.

A sharp corner near km 22.0 should be treated with respect — the loose gravel and occasional sand trap leave little room for mistakes. Although more than a bit dusty (depending on the season), McKinney Road is wide and well-built.

Mt. McKinney Nordic Ski Trails.

A sign on the south side of the road near km 27 marks the trailhead for the Mt. McKinney Nordic Ski Trail network. The 15-kilometre-long trail system, built on a network of old logging roads, is composed of a pair of stacked loops, each approximately seven kilometres in length. In addition to cross-country skiing, the trails are suitable for nature walks and equestrian use in the summer.

Mount Baldy Ski Hill.

A junction near km 36 marks the last short leg of the trip to Mount Baldy. A short 2.6 kilometre drive up the mountain to the left (north) lies the headquarters of the Mount Baldy alpine ski operation. According to Bill Hatton, a pioneer of the region since 1920, Mount Baldy ski resort had its beginnings in the mid-1960s with the Borderline Ski Club. The Club was formed in 1939 and operated on nearby Anarchist Mountain before moving to the privately-operated Mount Baldy in 1968. In his book, *Bridesville Country*, Hatton writes that a ski tow was set up on the Hedlund ranch on the east side of Anarchist Summit and served local skiers for several years before they embarked on the ambitious project of developing Mount Baldy. It took hard work, but the sight of happy skiers on the sunny slopes using the T-Bar tow and a dozen runs is an appropriate monument to their efforts.

In 1985, the club managed the ski races associated with the BC Winter Games held at Mount Baldy. This was the peak of the resort's activity, and it then slid downhill when the operators ran into one of the low-snow years that plague all ski resorts. After closing for the 1986-87 season, Mount Baldy has re-opened with a flourish under the careful management of the Borderline Ski Club. The mountain serves skiers from the South Okanagan, Similkameen and West Kettle districts with regular skiers arriving from south of the border in Washington State. The main attractions are its friendly, family-oriented atmosphere and every type of run from beginner to advanced.

Halloween trees.

The "Halloween Trees," left over from a forest fire that gave the mountain its bald appearance, provide Mount Baldy's trademark as well as a challenging and interesting backdrop to glade skiing at the higher elevations of the mountain. And when the mist rolls in, the "Halloween Trees" stretch out their gray arms in a way that triggers the imagination and justifies the name.

Mt. Baldy Road, to the right of the junction at km 36, was once the only access to the ski resort. It follows McKinney and Rice creeks down to join Highway 3 at the Rock Creek Bridge, a few kilometres east of Bridesville. The descent toward Highway 3 offers a number of excellent views of the grasslands of Anarchist Mountain and the desert country far to the southwest.

Camp McKinney.

Today, the Camp McKinney workings, five kilometres from the Mount Baldy junction, are a jumble of abandoned mine shafts, deep crevices, waste heaps, rusting mining equipment and barbed wire fences. It's a dangerous place for stray man or beast, but it wasn't always so.

According to N.L. Bill Barlee in *Gold Creeks and Ghost Towns*, Camp McKinney was born in 1887 as one of the earliest lode gold camps in British Columbia. "By 1893," writes Barlee, "the camp was roaring on the strength of excellent assays from claims like the Cariboo, Amelia, Alice, Emma and Okanagan."

The Cariboo-Amelia claim later developed into the premier mine of the camp, even paying dividends to shareholders. By 1901, the population of the camp stood at 250, with hotels, stores, a school and a church among the ameni-

ties of the community. Three years
later the Cariboo Mine closed and
within months Camp McKinney
became a ghost town.

Forest fires in 1919 and 1931
destroyed most of the original town
and all that remains is a small, decaying log cabin of indeterminate
age.

Gold, silver, lead and zinc.

A short note in the BC Minister
of Mines Report for 1943 states that
two groups operating in the old
Cariboo-Amelia claim mined 736
tons of ore, yielding 388 ounces of
gold, 628 ounces of silver, 7,219
pounds of lead and 5,381 pounds of
zinc. A much newer head frame,
shaft and service buildings, a short
distance east of the decaying cabin,
mark more recent efforts to rekin-
dle interest in Camp McKinney.

Beyond the mining camp, the
gravel road continues its descent
through stands of larch (tamarack)

Fig 48:
Mining structure at Camp McKinney,
September, 1985.
(Photo OKO-196 © Murphy Shewchuk.)

and lodgepole pine before emerging into the grasslands near the McKinney
Creek crossing, approximately 51 kilometres from Oliver. A short drive farther
and the road climbs up through a sand cut to the benchland high above the junction of McKinney Creek and Rock Creek.

The Oliver — Mount Baldy — Bridesville loop joins Highway 3 at the
western approach to the Rock Creek Bridge, one of the tallest bridges on Highway 3. From this point, pavement leads west to Osoyoos via Anarchist Summit
or east to the community of Rock Creek in the Kettle Valley.

A provincial park at Johnstone Creek, a short drive to the east, is an excellent campsite before continuing backroads exploring. If you are interested in
camping a little farther off the highway, a gravel road near Johnstone Creek
winds northward to Conkle Lake Provincial Park. See the *Conkle Lake Loop*
section, page 175, for details.

•••

48

Conkle Lake Loop

By Murphy Shewchuk

Statistics: **For map, see page 176.**

Distance:	21 km, Highway 33 to Conkle Lake.
	25 km, Conkle Lake to Highway 3.
Travel Time:	Up to one hour on each leg.
Elevation gain:	450 metres.
Condition:	Rough gravel road.
Season:	Best in dry summer weather.
Topo Maps:	Penticton, BC 82E/SW (1:100,000).
Forest Maps:	Boundary Forest District Recreation Map.
Communities:	Rock Creek, Beaverdell and Osoyoos.

If you're looking for someplace to get away, Conkle Lake Provincial Park, northwest of Rock Creek, is well worth exploring. Three-kilometre-long Conkle Lake, the dominant feature of the park, lies in a generally north-south direction, with an inviting, sandy beach at the north end. While the beach doesn't offer serious competition to the beaches at Skaha Lake or Okanagan Lake, it is for this very reason that Conkle Lake attracts repeat visitors. At an elevation of 1067 metres (3,500 feet), Conkle Lake is slow to warm in the early summer, but when the beaches on the valley floor are sweltering hot, this upland lake can still be very pleasant.

Three ways in — all rough.

There are three public routes to 124-hectare (306-acre) Conkle Lake — and all of them are best described as rough and not recommended for motor homes or vehicles pulling trailers. Judging by the number of motor homes and trailers at the park when we last camped there, the recommendations mean little to those determined to "get away from it all."

What is probably the most used and least difficult route winds north from Crowsnest Highway 3, 44 kilometres east of Osoyoos and approximately half

way between Brides-
ville and Rock Creek.
The signs on John-
stone Creek West
Road warn of the diffi-
culties, but the first
few kilometres are
merely steep, twisting
and dusty. The transi-
tion from open grass-
lands to lodgepole pine
and then to marshland
and cedar-lined creek
beds is fairly quick.
Signs mark the route to
Conkle Lake at most of
the junctions, particu-
larly where much
newer logging roads
can create confusion.
Much of the road is
single lane with inter-
mittent opportunities
to pass oncoming traf-
fic and virtually no op-
portunity to pass any
slowpoke in front of
you. Caution is essen-
tial and a good four-
wheel-drive vehicle is
a definite asset. A
junction approxi-
mately 24 kilometres
from Highway 3 marks
the start of the last
short, steep run up to

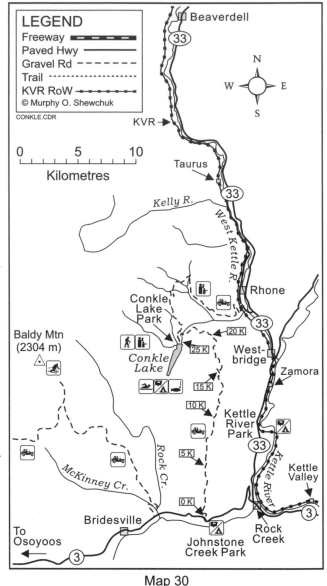

Map 30
Conkle Lake Provincial Park access and KVR RoW.

the lake and provincial park. To the left is the park, while straight ahead is the
backroad to Highway 33 near Rhone.

Tom Evans of Oliver has been fishing Conkle Lake almost every year since
1934. With his help and additional information from Jack Coates, another Oliver resident, I was able to piece together a bit of the puzzle that is the history of
Conkle Lake.

Gold nearby.

According to these gentlemen, two trappers had cabins near the lake well before the 1931 Camp McKinney forest fire destroyed a vast tract of timber north of the Rock Creek bridge. Sullivan and Ripperto were their names, it seems, and they were noted for the private telephone line that they had strung between their cabins. Tom Evans also remembers that Ripperto rawhided high grade gold ore out of a mine he had on one of the nearby mountainsides.

The original road into the lake was a corduroy road, made by laying poles crosswise on a route cut through the upland marshes, put in from the south via Little Fish Lake.

"I've driven it, but it was a real tough drive." says Jack Coates, of Oliver. "It must have been put in way back in the teens or early 20s."

By 1945, that road had disappeared, flooded by beaver dams and overgrown with timber and windfalls. In 1955, Frank Martin bought the land on the north end of the lake and started a fishing camp. He put in a road to the northeast end of the lake from the Johnstone Creek area. Later logging opened up access via the present route into the northwest corner of the lake. As part of his fishing camp, Martin built the two log cabins that are now part of the park maintenance facilities and maintained the camp for three or four years before selling it to Jack Boicy.

Tamarac Lodge.

Boicy operated the camp as Tamarac Lodge for at least a decade with various resident managers in charge. In the early 1970s, Jack was approached by a group that wanted to subdivide the property to build private homes or cottages. Feeling that the property should remain open to the public, he approached south Okanagan sportsmens' clubs and groups such as the Okanagan Similkameen Parks Society for support. With their combined efforts, the provincial government purchased the land in 1972 and began turning it into a park.

Conkle Lake Provincial Park campground is set on benchland in a tamarack (larch) and lodgepole pine forest on the northwest corner of the lake. The vehicle sites are neatly arranged to offer privacy and utility. Services are minimal with no showers, flush toilets or corner store to distract from the back-country camping experience. Make sure your food locker and fuel tank are both full before heading into the park. You may also want to plan your alternatives, should the park be full.

The beach, where tables and a boat launch are located to serve picnickers and fishermen, is only a short walk (or drive) from the campground. The sandy beach is a golden granite type of material with a fairly steep drop-off — good for swimming, but not ideal for non-swimmers or small children.

Fishing, according to the experts and the BC Ministry of Environment *Guide to Freshwater Fishing*, is for rainbow trout up to two kilograms. Tom

Evans has fished Conkle Lake since 1934. "We used to get a few big trout in those days." says Tom. "We could walk in there and spin cast off the shore or an old raft."

Waterfall trail.

Hikers will also find the area of interest. An easy trail winds back into the hills to the west of the campground where a beautiful multi-tiered waterfall is hidden. It's about a half hour walk, if you're not in any rush, and the best time to get sunlight on the falls is in mid-morning. A hiking trail is also being gradually developed around the lake.

With the park headquarters as kilometre 0.0, the backroad to the north offers two options. Keep left at the junction at km 1.1 and follow the narrow road northwest through an even narrower canyon between km 3.5 and 4.0. A junction at km 5.0, marked R200 or Ripperto Forest Service Road, is the start of a 52 kilometre shortcut to Okanagan Falls. If you continue straight ahead, you should have a relatively uneventful trip down to the West Kettle River and Highway 33 at Rhone, about 15 kilometres to the northeast.

Backroad to Okanagan Falls.

If the irresistible lure of the backcountry beckons, as it often does to us, you can swing west up Ripperto Creek and explore the maze of logging roads in the upland plateau. I certainly wouldn't guarantee that they will be passable when you choose to drive them, but we got through fine.

With the R200 sign as kilometre 0.0, we climbed steadily to the divide at km 6.3, keeping left at km 1.8 and right at a log landing at km 3.7. The divide, at about 1750 metres (5,740 feet), separates Ripperto Creek from the Kelly River drainage. With compasses at the ready, we switch-backed down to the Kelly River. After a leisurely lunch at an excellent Forest Service recreation site, we continued west over the marshy divide into the headwaters of Vaseux Creek.

The logging roads got progressively better as we drove westward on Road 200 to a junction near kilometre 36.0, (12K on the roadside markers). Here we decided to take the steep winding road down the edge of Shuttleworth Canyon, and around the Weyerhaeuser mill yard to Okanagan Falls and Highway 97.

If you have plenty of time, you can detour into Solco Lake "named after the South Okanagan Land Company," says Jack Coates. Or you can take the road to the right at the junction with the 12K marker and continue north on Okanagan Falls F.S. Road to Highway 33 near the Big White Ski Resort junction.(See *Okanagan Falls FS Road (R201)*, page 167, for details.)

If you're looking for a backcountry getaway and a place to beat the summer heat — consider Conkle Lake Provincial Park.

•••

49

Black Sage Road

By Murphy Shewchuk

Statistics: **For map, see page 180.**

Distance:	12.6 km, Oliver south to Road 22.
	8.0 km, Osoyoos north to Road 22.
Travel Time:	Approximately 15 minutes.
Condition:	Paved highway.
Season:	Year around.
Topo Maps:	Penticton, BC 82 E/SW (1:100,000).
Forest Maps:	Penticton Forest District Recreation Map.
Communities:	Oliver and Osoyoos.

The environments of the dry benchlands and the Okanagan River flood plain of the South Okanagan Valley are unique to British Columbia and Canada. These environments, in their natural state, support abundant and varied plant and animal life equally unique and valuable to man. The marshlands of the Okanagan River flood plain serve as one of the major migration resting areas and one of the few wintering areas for waterfowl in the interior of British Columbia.

Important bird migration route.
According to a BC Ministry of Environment report: "Up to one million ducks, one hundred thousand Canada Geese and thousands of other aquatic birds migrate annually through the Okanagan Valley. These birds attract, in turn, a variety of the often more spectacular raptorial birds such as hawks, falcons, eagles, vultures and owls."

Many other birds also use this area to nest and rear their young. And many species of dryland plants and animals, some of which are rare or endangered, are found here and not elsewhere in BC or Canada.

Man, unfortunately, has altered the natural state of the Okanagan environment to the detriment of the original inhabitants. The flood plain became the basis for extensive fruit farming and other agricultural pursuits. Then, when Nature persisted in its normal cycles, the Okanagan River was channeled to re-

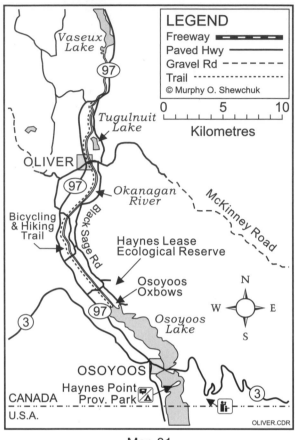

Map 31

Oliver - Osoyoos area.

duce flooding of the surrounding farmland. When most of the bottomland was taken up, agriculture, recreation and housing moved up to the benches, displacing the plants and animals that had adapted to the hot, dry environment.

Haynes Lease Ecological Reserve.

Efforts are, however, under way to preserve segments of the desert environment that have not already been totally altered. The Haynes Lease Ecological Reserve, butting on the northeast corner of Osoyoos Lake, is one example of several steps being taken in the area. The reserve contains three distinct land forms; the Okanagan River flood plain, gently sloping terraces above the flood plain, and the steep, southwestern slopes of Inkaneep (Throne) Mountain. The southwest facing slopes, well-drained soils and the rain shadow effect of the Cascade Mountains combine to make this area the most arid in Canada.

The three definable physical zones result in 13 identifiable plant communities varying from cattail wetlands to sumac thickets on the mountain face. In between grow scattered ponderosa pine, fields of antelope brush, sage and rabbitbush, and prickly-pear cactus, arrow-leaved balsamroot and bluebunch wheatgrass.

The list of species of birds, mammals and insects that survive (and even thrive) in this harsh environment is too long to present here, but a few are worth mentioning. Rare birds include the canyon wren, sage thrasher and burrowing owl. Rattlesnakes occur in rocky sites and, according to the Ecological Reserves Program report, "the western skink and short-horned lizard are expected to be present." The warm, weedy wetlands are home to largemouth and smallmouth bass and black crappies — fish not usually associated with BC.

International Bicycling and Hiking Trail.

Access to the area is easy. Road 22 leaves Highway 97 on the west side of the Okanagan Valley approximately 12.6 kilometres south of downtown Oliver or eight kilometres north of the junction of Highway 97 and 3 in Osoyoos. It crosses the valley floor and then a bridge over the flood control channel at km 1.1. Although there are gates on the channel dikes, the east dike is open to traffic. The dike road to the south ends at Osoyoos Lake, 1.8 kilometres from the bridge, with several opportunities to watch waterfowl or osprey, launch a car top boat or canoe in the flooded oxbows.

The west dike also serves as the base for an 18.4-kilometre-long bicycling and hiking trail that extends south to Osoyoos Lake from the McAlpine Bridge on Highway 97, north of Oliver. The northern half of the trail through Oliver is paved while the southern portion is gravel.

Osoyoos Oxbows.

Ducks Unlimited is involved with a program to re-water the Okanagan River oxbows that were left dry when the river was channeled in 1958. Working with the Ministry of Environment and other interested groups, DU built a weir and control valve that feeds water into 48 hectares (118 acres) of former marshland in what has become known as the Osoyoos Oxbows.

Black Sage Road.

Road 22 runs into Black Sage Road (71 Street) at km 1.6 near the historic Haynes Ranch House. This building dates back to the late 1800s, but time and vandals have taken their toll. Black Sage Road continues south for two kilometres to the Inkaneep Indian Reserve, and walk-through gates to the lower and upper sections of the ecological reserve. Vehicles aren't permitted and hikers should stay on the old roads to minimize damage to the fragile desert.

A signed road to the right, a few hundred metres to the north of the Haynes Ranch House on Black Sage Road, leads steeply up to a parking area and access to the upper section of the ecological reserve. Here you can walk south along an old road that takes you into the heart of the upper bench. Watch for cactus, grouse and pheasants underfoot and burrowing owls on nearby fence posts.

Black Sage Road continues north to Oliver along the east side of the valley, joining Camp McKinney Road at km 14.4 and rejoining Highway 97 at km 15.5. (See *Mount Baldy Loop* on page 170 for details.)

•••

50

Haynes Point Park

By Murphy Shewchuk

Statistics:	For map, see page 180.

Distance:	Three kilometres, junction of Hwy 3 & 97 to 32 Ave.
	1.5 km, east from Hwy 97 on 32 Ave.
Condition:	Paved access road. May be difficult to find.
Season:	Year around.
Topo Maps:	Penticton, BC 82 E/SW (1:100,000).
Forest Maps:	Penticton Forest District Recreation Map.
Communities:	Osoyoos and Oroville.

Haynes Point Provincial Park is located at the extreme southern end of the Canadian portion of the Okanagan Valley, approximately 2.5 kilometres southwest of the town of Osoyoos. Haynes Point Provincial Park was established in 1962 on 15 hectares (37 acres) of unique and interesting parkland — a narrow sandspit in Osoyoos Lake and an adjacent marsh.

Judge J.C. Haynes.

The park was named after Judge John Carmichael Haynes, a noted frontier jurist who brought law and order to the gold fields of Wildhorse Creek, near the present city of Cranbrook. The Haynes history in the Okanagan region goes back to the Rock Creek gold rush where, in 1860, John Carmichael Haynes was sent to assist the Gold Commissioner. Haynes was soon appointed Gold Commissioner as well as Customs Collector. His subsequent appointments included Member of the Legislative Council of BC and County Court Judge. Haynes acquired land at Osoyoos (then called Sooyoos) in 1866, and built a large home on the northeast side of the lake before his sudden death in 1888.

Hudson's Bay Company.

The region around Haynes Point Provincial Park is also steeped in history. North of the park, Highway 3 crosses a sandspit that was used by fur traders, explorers, miners, and First Nations people as a land bridge in their travels up and down the valley. The old Hudson's Bay Company Fur Brigade Trail passed through this very spot, nearly two centuries ago.

Okanagan desert.

Haynes Point Provincial Park is situated in an area which can boast of having Canada's only true desert. It receives less than 35 cm of rainfall per year, and enjoys long, sunny days and cool nights. The entire region is dominated by sagebrush, greasewood, prickly pear cactus and ponderosa pine. As one might expect, much of the wildlife is exotic and some species are found nowhere else in Canada. The short-horned lizard and the desert night snake, for instance, have only been reported a few times this century. These two reptiles share their desert home with many other unusual creatures, such as the secretive spadefoot toad and the burrowing owl.

The bird life is exceptional and varied, especially in the marshes. A visitor might see canyon wrens, white-throated swifts, or red-winged blackbirds, and for those with eyes keen enough to spot them, those specks circling high above the valley floor could just be turkey vultures.

Osoyoos Lake is reputed to be the warmest lake in Canada, and visitors to the park are likely to have excellent weather for swimming, boating, picnicking, and sun-tanning. Additional activities include nature study and fishing — there are rainbow trout and bass in the lake. Haynes Point Provincial Park has long been a popular destination for visitors to the Okanagan. As a result the park is part of the new BC Parks reservation system.

Orchards, vineyards and gardens.

The desert isn't all sagebrush and cactus. Some of the Okanagan's finest orchards, vineyards and gardens have been established where water can be pumped for irrigation. The Oliver-Osoyoos area has what is probably the highest number of fruit stands per kilometre of any area in Canada. From May to November, fresh fruit and vegetables are readily available direct from the producer almost anywhere along Highway 3 or Highway 97.

Osoyoos Historic Canal Walkway.

Water pumps have replaced the gravity-feed canal system that originally served the Okanagan orchards. On the western outskirts of Osoyoos, the bank of an abandoned canal has become an interpretive trail. The 3.5-kilometre-long canal walkway, bisected by Highway 3, separates the Okanagan desert from the green orchard.

•••

51

Pasayten Wilderness

By Murphy Shewchuk

Statistics:	For map, see page 185.

Distance:	21 km, Highway 3 to Pasayten River Bridge.
	35 km to end of road.
Travel Time:	One half to one hour.
Condition:	Gravel road. Some very rough sections.
Season:	May be closed in winter.
Topo Maps:	Princeton, BC 92 H/SE (1:100,000).
	Manning Park, BC 92 H/2 (1:50,000).
Forest Maps:	Merritt Forest District Recreation Map.
Communities:	Hope and Princeton.

The Pasayten River Forest Service Road heads east off the Hope-Princeton Highway (Highway 3) approximately 50 kilometres south of Princeton or two kilometres northeast of the Eastgate Esso station at the northeast entrance to Manning Park. With the junction at Highway 3 as your km 0 reference point, you will soon cross the Similkameen River and begin a switchback climb over the ridge separating the Similkameen from the north end of the Pasayten Canyon.

After about four or five kilometres, the road levels off and follows the Pasayten River canyon south (upstream). The road has been carved into the timber on the canyon wall, but there is a good viewpoint just past the 6K marker. At an elevation of about 1300 metres (4,265 feet) and high above the river, this first look south toward the Canada — U.S.A. boundary is quite spectacular. The sun glistens off exposed sections of the river. On the southern horizon 2207 metre (7,240 foot) Bunker Hill pokes up above the surrounding timber.

After a gradual descent along the sidehill, the road meets the Pasayten River near km 17. Although there are no facilities, there are several excellent places for self-contained camping between km 17 and km 21.

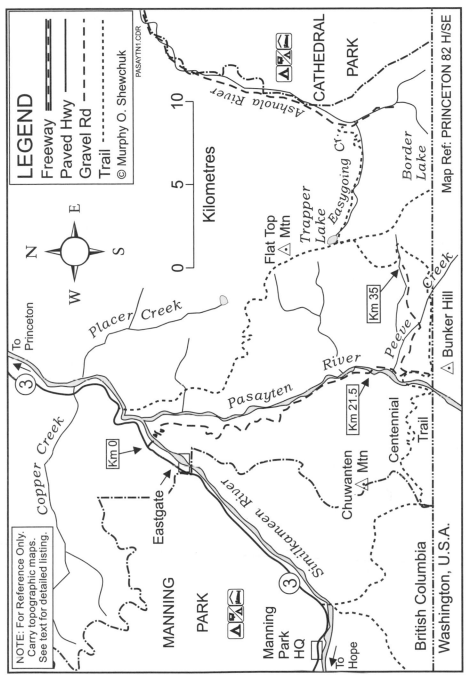

LEGEND

Freeway	═══════
Paved Hwy	─────
Gravel Rd	── ──
Trail	········

© Murphy O. Shewchuk

PASAYTN1.CDR

Kilometres

0   5   10

N E W S

Map Ref: PRINCETON 82 H/SE

NOTE: For Reference Only.
Carry topographic maps.
See text for detailed listing.

To Princeton

Placer Creek

Copper Creek

CATHEDRAL PARK

Ashnola River

Easygoing Cr

Border Lake

Trapper Lake

Flat Top △ Mtn

Km 35

Peeve Creek

△ Bunker Hill

Pasayten River

Km 21.5

Km 0

Eastgate

Chuwanten △ Mtn

Centennial Trail

Similkameen River

MANNING PARK

Manning Park HQ

To Hope

British Columbia
Washington, U.S.A.

Map 32
Pasayten Wilderness and Centennial Trail, Manning to Cathedral Parks.

185

Roads may be closed.

The Forest Road crosses the Pasayten River from the west to east side near km 21 where there is also a corral and loading chute. There is a sign nearby warning that "Roads in the area may be closed without further notice."

On our last visit the roads were not closed at this point. With no sign of heavy equipment standing by to leave us permanently stranded in the Pasayten, we continued south.

Our southward journey ended at a blocked road near km 23. The original road to the border and the access to the eastward section of the Centennial Trail continued south. Fortunately, a switchback turn led us up and east into an old burn and the Peeve Creek drainage. Although steep in a few sections and very rough in a few others, we followed the path of least resistance to a turn-around and trailhead of sorts near km 35.

Spectacular alpine meadows.

There were several vehicles parked there, and after a chat with a returning hunter, we tied on our hiking boots and scrambled up the tank-trapped fire break toward the distant alpine meadows. The elevation at the parking area was about 1875 metres and it took us about an hour to hike two kilometres to the flat-top ridge and meadows. Others who are not so easily distracted by birds, wildflowers, spectacular views and breathing could probably climb the 200 metre elevation in much less time.

The tank traps along the fire break were there to stop (slow down?) vehicular access to the fragile alpine. It was obvious that they were little more than a challenge for some ATV drivers. Our stay on the ridge was cut short by the waning sun and cool breezes blowing in from the north. We retraced our steps to our van and headed back down the road to the Pasayten River. We camped that night, planning to return to the alpine in the morning. The morning dawned grey — socked in with alternating rain and snow. Rather than risk life, limb and vehicle, we headed north to Highway 3 and Thanksgiving dinner at home.

Since that Thanksgiving, 1994, visit to the Pasayten Wilderness, we have done a bit of research and returned a number of times to hike various sections of the Centennial Trail.

Centennial Trail.

According to various reports, the Centennial Trail was created in 1966-67 as part of an effort to have a national trail from the Pacific to the Atlantic. It was to commemorate the 1866 amalgamation of Vancouver Island and mainland British Columbia as a Crown Colony; the 1867 Canadian Confederation; and the 1871 entry of British Columbia into Canada.

The original trail ran from Victoria to Nanaimo and across (by ferry, I presume) to Horseshoe Bay where it linked with the Skyline and Baden Powell

Trails. It then continued through Belcarra Park, Port Moody and up through the Fraser Valley to the Chilliwack River area. It was not until the Post Creek area off the Chilliwack River Road that it got into serious wilderness trekking. From the Chilliwack River to Manning Park, the original Centennial Trail is of dubious quality and has been obliterated by washouts, roads and logging in places.

Fig 49:
Pasayten alpine meadows, southeast of Trapper Lake, looking east to the peaks in Cathedral Park in early October. (Photo PRN-343 © Murphy Shewchuk.)

The section through Manning Park to Monument 83 on the Canada — U.S.A. boundary goes by a variety of different names, but is generally passable. Near Monument 83, the trail leaves Manning Park and enters the Merritt Forest District. The 11.5 kilometre descent to the Pasayten is relatively intact although the cable crossing at the Pasayten has been out for several years. (See the *Monument 83 to Pasayten River* section on page 189 for details.) A rough trail has been cut north to the Pasayten River Forest Service Road bridge near km 21 (see page 192). The trail then loops south to the boundary where it generally follows the boundary to the east end of the Say Fire burn before heading north to Trapper Lake. Unfortunately, the Say Fire (1984) and the earlier Bunkerhill Fire (1970) have both had a serious impact on parts of the trail. On the Canadian side of the border, salvage logging continues on or near the trail and it could be several years before the area sees serious revegetation.

Trapper Lake.

From Trapper Lake, the trail follows Easygoing Creek to the Ashnola River where it then links up with the Wall Creek Trail into Cathedral Park. Here again park status and budget have helped keep it well-marked and passable. To add to the confusion, trails from the Trapper Lake area also lead north to Similkameen Falls and south to Border Lake.

The section of the Centennial Trail from Monument 83 to the Ashnola River goes through public land under the supervision of the Merritt and Penticton Forest Districts. This section, generally known as the Pasayten Wilderness, has been the distant and forgotten cousin when it comes to its share of the Forest Service's meagre recreation budget.

Public interest has been here for nearly three decades. However, North Vancouver's veteran hiker, the late Bob Harris and groups such as the North Shore Hikers and the Back Country Horsemen do not appear to have been able to raise the route's "political profile" high enough to warrant massive infusions of cash. Instead, they have worked closely with other recreationists to gradually improve the trail system.

This is not to suggest that the route is impassable. Several years ago, Charlie Clapham, a Vancouver hiker, led a group of nine people on a series of hikes that covered the trail from Manning Park to Keremeos. Using four vehicles, they left two vehicles in Manning Park and moved the group and two vehicles ahead to the Pasayten. It is interesting to note that, travelling light, they were able to walk from the Pasayten River to the trailhead near Manning Park Lodge (an estimated 30 kilometres) in one day. After staying overnight in Keremeos, their second day of hiking took them from the Ashnola River up the Easygoing Creek trail to Trapper Lake and then down to their waiting vehicles at the Pasayten River — a distance, according to Charlie, of 26 to 27 kilometres. The hike through Cathedral Park was a little more complicated, but the details aren't essential to this chapter.

The Back Country Horsemen, with members throughout the province, have also been instrumental in maintaining the trail as well as an interest in it becoming part of the Trans Canada Trail system. The short season and long distance from communities has prompted the decision to move the Trans Canada Trail to the former KVR right-of-way. See the *Trans Canada Trail* section starting on page 68 for details.

While information on the Pasayten Wilderness and this part of the Centennial Trail is still limited, the work of Marg Anderson, Bob Harris, Jim McCrae and the various groups will serve as a foundation for a future detailed map/brochure. In the meantime, your best sources of information are the previously mentioned maps, personal contact with experienced hikers and horsemen and books such as this one.

•••

52

Centennial Trail: Monument 83 to Pasayten River

By Murphy Shewchuk

Statistics:	For maps, see pages 185 & 190.

Distance:	16 km, Highway 3 in Manning Park to Monument 83.
	11.5 km, Monument 83 to Pasayten River at Monument 85.
Travel Time:	One to two days.
Condition:	Variable. Some very rough sections with windfalls.
Season:	Summer - July through September, depending on seasonal
vagaries.	
Topo Maps:	Princeton, BC 92 H/SE (1:100,000).
	Manning Park, BC 92 H/2 (1:50,000).
Forest Maps:	Merritt Forest District Recreation Map.
Communities:	Hope and Princeton.

The Centennial Trail, as outlined in the *Pasayten Wilderness* chapter (see page 184) was the precursor to today's Trans Canada Trail. It was also an attempt to traverse British Columbia with a multi-purpose non-motorized travel route. Because of the short seasons at the higher elevations and significant distances between re-supply points, it did not attract significant numbers of hikers. The varying restrictions against horse traffic in the provincial parks also had a detrimental effect on rider usage.

Regardless of the traffic density, the Centennial Trail between Manning Park and Cathedral Park does offer some interesting challenges and excellent scenic and wildlife viewing opportunities in a near-wilderness setting. The section within Manning Park, from the Castle Creek — Monument 83 parking area on Highway 3 to Monument 83, is part of an old fire access road to the US Forest Service Fire Lookout Tower. The trail is 16 kilometres one way with an elevation change of 850 metres and a suggested hiking time of five hours. This portion of the trail is maintained by BC Parks and information on its current status should be available from the Manning Park District Office at (604) 824-2300 or the BC Parks Okanagan District office (see page 207).

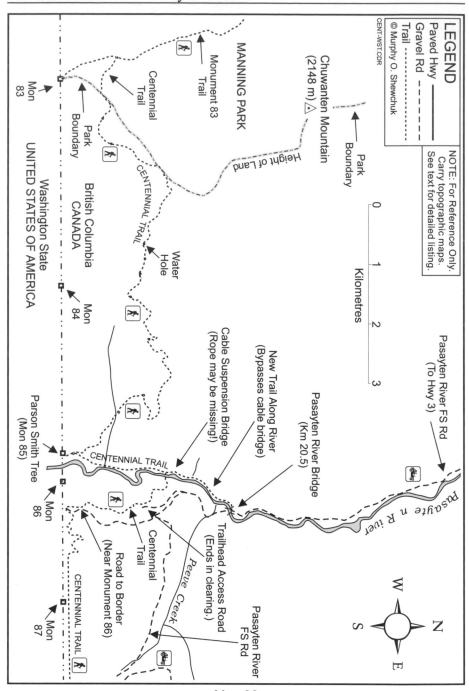

Map 33
Centennial Trail — Monument 83 to the Pasayten River.

Merritt Forest District.

Most of the trail from Monument 83 to the Pasayten River lies within the Merritt Forest District. With a small recreation staff and budget, trail maintenance has been largely left to volunteers such as the Back Country Horsemen and various hiking groups. The result is that you should expect to encounter windfalls and some trail degradation. It is generally wide enough for an experienced rider and horse, and should be passable for experienced mountain bicyclists. If you are travelling on horseback, a small chainsaw may prove to be an extremely valuable tool. Current information should be available from the Merritt Forest District office (see page 207).

The west-to-east (downhill) traverse of this route begins about 0.9 km northwest of Monument 83 — elevation 1981 metres (6,500 ft) — as a side trail off the old forest lookout road. In general, the first 1.5 km of the trail winds through a stand of old-growth timber.

Limited water.

The trail then generally climbs across a semi-open hillside through the upper reaches of an old burn. At approximately 2.6 km from the Monument 83 trail, the route begins a gradual descent toward the Pasayten River. For the next 2.4 km the trail winds through small timber at or near the summit of a rounded ridge. Approximately mid-point along this ridge is a clearing suitable for tent camping. A pit has been dug in a boggy spring to collect ground water — one of the few places along this section of the trail to refill your canteen. A water purifying system will be essential if you aren't going to boil the water.

After leaving the ridge, the trail descends through mixed timber, crossing two streams and several boggy hillsides. The streams were still flowing in a mid August trip through the area, but water purification will still be wise. The trail emerges from the pines onto an aspen covered slope near the Pasayten River — elevation 1190 metres (3,900 ft), approximately 11.5 km from Monument 83. Monument 85 and the International Boundary is about 200 metres to the south. There is a "Stop of Interest" shelter and information sign near Monument 85. It provides background details about the Parson Smith Tree - a tree on which a poem was carved in 1886. The remains of the tree have been removed to a museum in Washington State. See the *Parson Smith Tree Trail* section on page 192 for details.

The river marshes near Monument 85 are an excellent place for birdwatching. These same marshes also block horse and foot traffic from continuing east along the boundary. Instead, anyone continuing east on the Centennial Trail must detour north first. The remainder of the route north to the Pasayten River Bridge is described in the *Parson Smith Tree Trail* section.

•••

53

Centennial Trail: Parson Smith Tree Trail

By Murphy Shewchuk

| Statistics: | For maps, see pages 185, 190 and 193. |

Distance:	Approx. 3 km, Pasayten River Bridge to Monument 85.
Travel Time:	One to 1.5 hours each way.
Condition:	Variable. Some rough sections with occasional windfalls.
Season:	Summer - July through September.
Topo Maps:	Manning Park, BC 92 H/2 (1:50,000).
Forest Maps:	Merritt Forest District Recreation Map.
Communities:	Hope and Princeton.

Much of this trail is part of the Centennial Trail between Manning Park and Cathedral Park. However as the original Pasayten River cable crossing has succumbed to Nature and the trail has been extended north to the Pasayten River Forest Service bridge, I've chosen to write it up as a separate chapter. It also is an interesting day hike, lending itself to special consideration.

Access to the north end of the Parson Smith Tree Trail is from the Pasayten River Forest Service Road. This well-marked two-wheel-drive backroad leaves the Hope-Princeton Highway (Highway 3) approximately 50 km south of Princeton (two kilometres north of Eastgate). See the *Pasayten Wilderness* section on page 184 for more information.

Parking is available in a clearing on the west side of the Forest Service road immediately north of the Pasayten River bridge, approximately 20.5 km from Highway 3. There were no trailhead markers or other signs in place when we last visited the area.

Scramble and ramble.

Parson Smith Tree Trail begins at the southwest corner of the parking clearing, and after a short scramble up and around several large boulders, proceeds southward, paralleling the Pasayten River upstream. The first 1.25 km of the trail was been recently cut through a stand of small timber. It is narrow in sec-

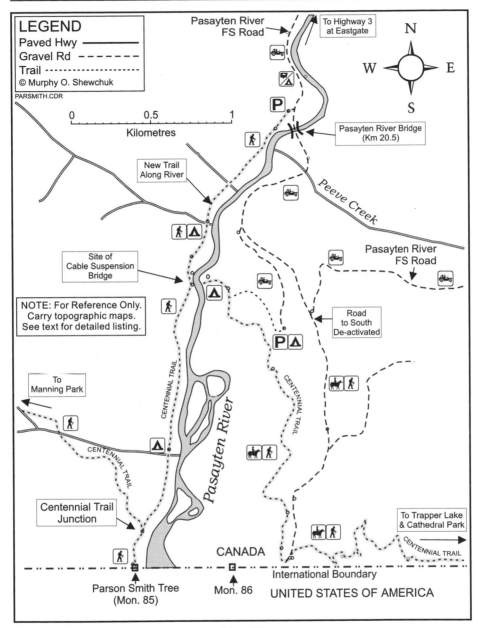

LEGEND

Paved Hwy ———
Gravel Rd – – – – –
Trail ·················

© Murphy O. Shewchuk

PARSMITH.CDR

0   0.5   1

Kilometres

Pasayten River
FS Road

To Highway 3
at Eastgate

N
W   E
S

Pasayten River Bridge
(Km 20.5)

New Trail
Along River

Peeve Creek

Pasayten River
FS Road

Site of
Cable Suspension
Bridge

NOTE: For Reference Only.
Carry topographic maps.
See text for detailed listing.

Road
to South
De-activated

To
Manning Park

CENTENNIAL TRAIL

CENTENNIAL TRAIL

Pasayten River

CENTENNIAL TRAIL

Centennial Trail
Junction

To Trapper Lake
& Cathedral Park

CENTENNIAL TRAIL

CANADA

International Boundary

Parson Smith Tree
(Mon. 85)

Mon. 86

UNITED STATES OF AMERICA

Map 34
Upper Pasayten River and the Centennial Trail.

tions and could be difficult for a horse and rider, particularly until widened and the occasional windfall has been removed.

The trail generally follows the hillside or narrow benches well away from the river. However, it descends to the river edge at a creek crossing approximately 0.8 km from the parking area. This location could be an excellent spot for a walk-in wilderness campsite.

This new section of trail joins the older BC Centennial Trail at the former cable crossing, approximately 1.25 km south of the Forest Service bridge. The former cable bridge across the Pasayten River was reduced to one weathered fibre rope when we last visited and that was not likely to survive another winter. The remainder of the trail to Monument 85 is much older and wider. There are several locations that are suitable for wilderness camping, including another side stream approximately 1 km south of the cable crossing.

The junction of the Centennial Trail to Monument 83 and Manning Park may be difficult to find. However, after you check out the "Stop of Interest" shelter and sign near Monument 85 on the International Boundary, you can back-track downstream about 100 to 200 metres and you should see it angling up the hillside to the west.

Fig 50:
Murphy at Monument 85.
(Photo PRN-412 © Murphy Shewchuk.)

Parson Smith Tree.

The information sign provides details about the Parson Smith Tree — a tree on which a poem was carved in 1886. The remains of the tree have been removed to a museum in Washington State.

A magazine article entitled "The Parson Smith Tree" by Joan Burton published in the October, 1986 edition of *Northwest Living* tells the story of "Parson" Smith. While we don't have space to reprint the article here, a few details may help satisfy the curious hiker.

> *I've roamed in many foreign parts my boys*
> *And many lands have seen.*
> *But Columbia is my idol yet*
> *Of all lands she is queen.*
> > *Parson Smith, June 1886.*

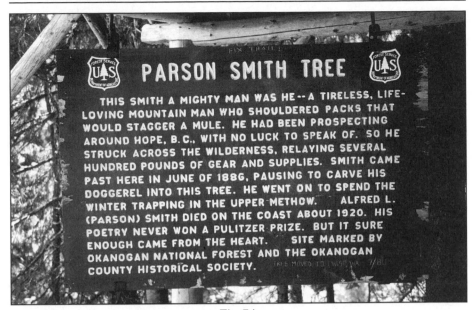

PARSON SMITH TREE

THIS SMITH A MIGHTY MAN WAS HE -- A TIRELESS, LIFE-
LOVING MOUNTAIN MAN WHO SHOULDERED PACKS THAT
WOULD STAGGER A MULE. HE HAD BEEN PROSPECTING
AROUND HOPE, B.C., WITH NO LUCK TO SPEAK OF. SO HE
STRUCK ACROSS THE WILDERNESS, RELAYING SEVERAL
HUNDRED POUNDS OF GEAR AND SUPPLIES. SMITH CAME
PAST HERE IN JUNE OF 1886, PAUSING TO CARVE HIS
DOGGEREL INTO THIS TREE. HE WENT ON TO SPEND THE
WINTER TRAPPING IN THE UPPER METHOW. ALFRED L.
(PARSON) SMITH DIED ON THE COAST ABOUT 1920. HIS
POETRY NEVER WON A PULITZER PRIZE. BUT IT SURE
ENOUGH CAME FROM THE HEART. SITE MARKED BY
OKANOGAN NATIONAL FOREST AND THE OKANOGAN
COUNTY HISTORICAL SOCIETY.

Fig 51:
Sign at the Canada-USA Boundary. (Photo PRN-414 © Murphy Shewchuk.)

"The poem, a tribute to Columbia, which is now the state of Washington, was carved on a tree trunk near the Canadian border, more than 50 miles from the closest American wagon road." writes Joan Burton.

"Although the author/artist has become a legend, not much is known about him." One story "tells that 'Parson' Alfred L. Smith was prospecting for white quartz with a partner near the Pasayten River in June 1886. The partner went back to Canada with an injury and Smith remained in camp to wait for his return...

"In his leisure Smith carefully skinned off the outer bark of a lodgepole pine... Then he began carving, designing a unique artistic spacing for the words of his poem. The partner never returned and Smith [returned]... to the trapper's camp at Winthrop."

The tree was discovered in 1908 by crews clearing the survey lines for the international boundary. Various attempts were made to preserve it in place. However in July, 1980 it was removed from the banks of the Pasayten, chemically treated and placed in an airtight case. It can now be seen at the Early Winters Visitor Center on the North Cascades Highway 20, located 29 kilometres (18 miles) east of Washington Pass.

While you won't find the Parson Smith Tree here, you may discover that the river marshes near Monument 85 are an excellent place for birdwatching.

•••

54

Centennial Trail: Pasayten River Bridge to Ashnola River

By Murphy Shewchuk

Statistics: **For maps, see pages 185, 193, 198 and 201.**

Distance: Approx. 26 km, Pasayten River Bridge to Ashnola River.
Travel Time: One day minimum.
Condition: Variable. Some rough sections with occasional windfalls.
Season: Summer - July through September.
Topo Maps: Manning Park, BC 92 H/2 (1:50,000).
                 Ashnola River, BC 92 H/1 (1:50,000).
Forest Maps: Merritt Forest District Recreation Map.
                 Penticton Forest District Recreation Map.
Communities: Hope, Princeton and Keremeos.

As it is with the Monument 83 to Pasayten River section and the Parson Smith Tree Trail, much of this trail is part of the Centennial Trail between Manning Park and Cathedral Park. Some sections, such as the route from the Pasayten Bridge to Monument 86, the trail from the Say Fire to Trapper Lake, or the trail from the Easygoing Creek Road to Trapper Lake, can be interesting day hikes. Hiking the complete trail from the Pasayten River to the Ashnola will require advance planning and a considerable degree of fitness.

Pasayten Bridge to Monument 86.

Access to the north end of the trail from the Pasayten Bridge to Monument 86 is from the Pasayten River Forest Service Road. This well-marked two-wheel-drive backroad leaves the Hope-Princeton Highway (Highway 3) approximately 50 km south of Princeton (two kilometres north of Eastgate). See the *Pasayten Wilderness* section on page 184 for more information.

Parking is available in a clearing on the west side of the Forest Service road immediately north of the Pasayten River bridge, approximately 20.5 km from

Highway 3. There were no trailhead markers or other signs in place during the summer and fall of 1996. Parking is also available at the old trailhead clearing approximately 1.7 km south of the bridge, on the benchland between the Forest Service road and the Pasayten River.

The original Centennial Trail crossed the Pasayten River at the cable crossing approximately 1.2 km south of the present forest road bridge. It then wound through a grove of timber mixed with boggy section for about 0.5 km before beginning a steady climb southeast to the US Border and the junction with the old fire access road. An old trail winds down to the river from the old trailhead clearing. Efforts have also been made to cut a new trail directly south of the clearing in order to link up with the original Centennial Trail while avoiding the boggy section near the river cable crossing.

In general, the 2.1 km trail to the border winds through a stand of old-growth timber. It is narrow in a few sections, but should not be difficult for an experienced horse and rider. There are a few boggy sections where the trail crosses creeks or springs and a few areas where windfall roots have torn up the trail.

The trail reaches the border clearing and then swings east and up a short incline to the old fire road, which also ends near the north edge of the border clearing. When we last visited, there was a picnic table at the end of the road. British Columbia Centennial Trail signs marked both the eastward continuation of the trail along the border and the northwest route back to the cable crossing.

Switchback Climb.

From the end of the old fire road, the Centennial Trail climbs eastward away from the Pasayten River. It generally follows the boundary, sometimes swinging north a few hundred metres to ease the grade and avoid the very steep sections. We have climbed east from the end of the fire road to the summit, passing through a mixture of old growth and the younger trees that have filled in the Bunkerhill burn. We have not gone all the way through on this section, but usually reliable sources suggest that the trail continues east for a total of six kilometres before swinging north up a fork of Peeve Creek.

Say Fire to Trapper Lake.

The Centennial Trail then crosses the remnants of the Say Fire and the salvage operation before continuing north to Trapper Lake. The trail through the burn can be confusing because of the network of roads and cattle trails AND a marsh that is situated in the middle of the valley. The trail generally continues northeast to ford a creek just upstream of the grass marsh. It then swings west along the hillside and an old logging road for about a kilometre before disappearing into the timber 20 to 30 metres east of a creek flowing out of the north.

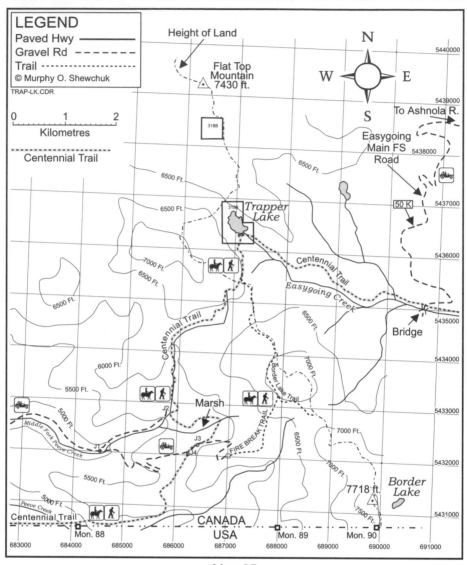

Map 35
Centennial Trail. Monument 88 - Trapper Lake - Easygoing Creek area.

Access to the south end of the Trapper Lake Trail is also available from the Pasayten River Forest Service Road approximately 9.1 kilometres east of the Pasayten River bridge — J1 on the map on page 198. The main road follows the valley bottom at this point and a side road angles to the northeast. When we last visited the area, this side road had been partially de-activated and was barely passable with a four-wheel-drive vehicle. From J1 it is about 1.6 kilometres to the trailhead (J2 on the map) where the creek crossing had been completely excavated. As mentioned above, the trail started into the trees 20 to 30 metres east of the creek. Parking was also available at an old log landing at the junction (J1).

The Trapper Lake Trail climbs steadily north through old growth timber with several creek crossings and mixed boggy sections for the first 1.5 kilometres. It then continues climbing on a drier semi-open hillside for about 1.9 kilometres before reaching the height of land at an elevation of about 1980 metres (6500 ft).

There is a four-way junction a short distance north of the height of land. The trail to the north (straight ahead) leads about one kilometre to Trapper Lake. The final 0.5 km to the lake winds through a sub-alpine marshy area that will put most hiking boots to the test.

In general, the 4.5 kilometre trail is narrow in a few sections, but should not be difficult for an experienced horse and rider. There are a few boggy sections, where the trail crosses creeks or springs, that should be approached with caution.

Trapper Lake to the Ashnola River.

The Centennial Trail continues southeast of Trapper Lake. After crossing the creek a few times in the first kilometre, the trail follows the north side of Easygoing Creek for about 3 kilometres to where the trail crosses Easygoing Main Forest Road. This can be a suitable pick-up point for through hikers or an excellent parking and/or wilderness camping location for day hikers interested in exploring the Trapper Lake and Border Lake area. See the map on page 201 for an overview of the Keremeos — Cathedral Park — Trapper Lake area.

East of the road crossing, the Centennial Trail follows Easygoing Creek downstream for about a kilometre before beginning a zig-zag descent northeast to the Ashnola River near the 40K marker on Ashnola Road. The trail crosses Easygoing Main F.S. Road about 1.5 kilometres from the Ashnola Road — if you hike or ride down the trail from Trapper Lake, look for the continuation of the trail about 100 metres north of where it emerges from the trees onto Easygoing Main Road.

Wall Creek Bridge.

A new footbridge was built across the Ashnola River late in 1998 to access the Wall Creek Trail, a continuation of the Centennial Trail into Cathedral Park. It is located about two kilometres north of the junction of Easygoing Main and the Ashnola Road, near the 38K point on the Ashnola Road.

•••

55

Ashnola Road

By Murphy Shewchuk

Statistics:	For map, see page 201.

Distance:	25 km, Keremeos to Cathedral Base Camp.
	73 km, Keremeos to Easygoing Creek bridge.
Travel Time:	Two to three hours.
Condition:	Paved , then gravel.
Season:	Best in dry weather. May be closed in winter.
Topo Maps:	Keremeos, BC 82 E/4 (1:50,000).
	Ashnola River, BC 92 H/1 (1:50,000).
Forest Map:	Penticton Forest District Recreation Map.
Communities:	Keremeos.

Ashnola Road, although often associated with Cathedral Park, also provides access to a number of BC Forest Service recreation sites. The northeast end of the road is marked by a Cathedral Lakes Lodge sign near Highway 3, a few kilometres west of downtown Keremeos. After passing through the "Red Bridge" and following the south side of the Similkameen River westward for about eight kilometres, the road swings south and up the Ashnola valley. The pavement ends about 10 kilometres from Highway 3.

Forest Road.

The end of the pavement and 0K of the Forest Service Road coincide with the foot of the Ashnola Canyon. A kilometre later, the road crosses over to the west side of the river and begins a steady climb upstream. There are several designated Forest Service recreation sites and numerous unorganized sites along the river, some with toilet facilities and many without.

Cathedral Provincial Park.

The main entrance signpost for Cathedral Park is on the right side of the road near km 19. The Cathedral Lakes Lodge base camp and parking area is across the Ashnola River at km 22.2. See the *Cathedral Provincial Park* section on page 203 for more information. For those interested in hiking up to the Ca-

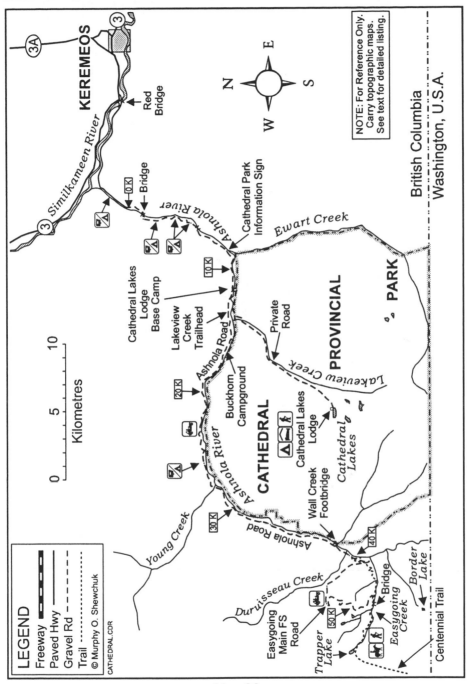

Map 36
Ashnola Road and Cathedral Provincial Park area, southwest of Keremeos.

thedral Lakes area, the Lakeview Creek Trailhead and campground is another 1.6 kilometres farther up Ashnola Road. Buckhorn Campground is located alongside the river at km 26.7.

The road swings west near the Cathedral Park entrance signs and follows the river upstream in a gradual arc before heading in a southerly direction near the 30K marker. There are a number of "dispersed use" camping areas between the road and the river. Self-contained "pack it in - pack it out" camping is the rule in these camping areas as they are not maintained by the Forest Service.

Motorized Recreation Regulated Area.

A map and information sign near km 43 explains the restrictions imposed in the "Placer Mountain to Border Lake Motorized Recreation Regulated Area". In general, all motorized recreation vehicles except snowmobiles must keep to the designated routes in order to help protect sensitive alpine meadows, grass-lands and wildlife habitat. Additional information is available from the Penticton Forest District at (250) 490-2200 or 1-800-661-4099.

Wall Creek Bridge.

A new footbridge has been built across the Ashnola River near Wall Creek at km 49.1. It will serve as a much-needed crossing for hikers interested in us-ing the Centennial Trail or the Wall Creek Trail. The main road forks near the 40K marker (km 50.9) with the old road continuing along the valley floor for another half kilometre. There is another rudimentary campsite near the fork, this one has signs of frequent horse traffic.

The Centennial Trail also joins the Ashnola Road at the junction. The trail can be followed southwest through the trees for about one kilometre before it crosses Easygoing Main F.S. Road. At last check, the crossing was not well marked. Look for the continuation of the trail 50 to 100 metres south (down the road) from where you first climb up onto the road. See the *Centennial Trail: Pasayten River Bridge to Ashnola River* section on page 196 for more details.

Easygoing Main F.S. Road.

From the junction near the 40K marker, the Forest Road climbs southwest and then northwest up Duruisseau Creek before swinging west and then south. If you keep left at the major junctions, you should climb up to the plateau and reach Easygoing Creek approximately 12.8 kilometres from the Easygoing Main / Ashnola Road junction. There are a number of steep, narrow sections on this route that can make it tricky in wet weather so use extreme caution.

There is ample room to park at near Easygoing Creek bridge and explore the high country. The Centennial Trail leads west about 4.5 kilometres to Trapper Lake. If time permits, you can also explore the trail to Border Lake.

•••

56

Cathedral Provincial Park

By Murphy Shewchuk

Statistics:	For map, see page 201.

Distance:	25 km, Keremeos to Cathedral Base Camp.
	15 km, Base Camp to Cathedral Lakes Lodge.
Travel Time:	Two to three hours, Keremeos to Lodge.
Elevation gain:	1585 metres, Keremeos to Cathedral Lakes Lodge.
Condition:	Paved , then gravel. Private access to Lodge.
Season:	Best in dry weather. May be closed in winter.
Topo Maps:	Keremeos, BC 82 E/4 (1:50,000).
	Ashnola River, BC 92 H/1 (1:50,000).
Forest Map:	Penticton Forest District Recreation Map.
Communities:	Keremeos and Princeton.

British Columbia's mountain roads can put anyone's resources to the test, whether they be mental, physical or vehicular. Steep grades, sharp turns, narrow bridges, muddy ruts and windfalls can take the fun out of heading into the back country. Those same conditions can change your family sedan to a creaky, muddy mess or worse in a matter of a few kilometres. For some of us, the choice is to buy a four-wheel-drive vehicle, stock it up with spare parts, maps and emergency supplies and then boldly set out in search of back country roads to explore.

Cathedral Lakes Lodge.

Cathedral Lakes Lodge, in Cathedral Provincial Park, offers a second choice. For a fee, they will take you into the heart of one of BC's finest wilderness areas. The round trip fee applies only if you are camping at the park wilderness campsites. If you are staying at Cathedral Lakes Lodge, transportation is included in the accommodation fee. It is worth noting that the road is restricted to park use permit holders and advance reservations are normally required, so plan ahead.

Cathedral Lakes wilderness, in the Okanagan Range of the Cascade Mountains south of Keremeos, has drawn lovers of nature for nearly a century. Before the road, hikers and horsemen followed difficult trails through narrow mountain valleys and along windswept ridges to reach the heart of what is now Cathedral Provincial Park.

Fig 52:
Golden Mantled Squirrel at Quiniscoe Lake.
(Photo CAP-142 © Murphy Shewchuk.)

The rough trails didn't deter them from returning to this hidden paradise which features a cluster of half a dozen clear cool lakes, at over 2000 metres (6,500 feet) above sea level, surrounded by picturesque ridges and alpine peaks that reach up to 2628 metres (8,622 feet). The present road and excellent trail system opened up the Cathedrals to a much broader range of visitors. Today seniors and youngsters can also reach the lodge or park campgrounds in the Quiniscoe Lake area where the options are many and all quite spectacular.

Well-marked trails.

"Trails are well-marked so that even a novice hiker can reach these places without any danger," says Chess Lyons, the man who, nearly half a century ago, recommended that the park be created. "Whether it is a pleasant forest walk around the lakes or a climb to spectacular vistas and geological wonders, Cathedral Park has it all in a remarkably convenient area for the novice as well as the professional mountaineer."

Wildlife and wildflowers also make the park worth exploring. Chess Lyons' book, *Trees, Shrubs and Flowers to know in British Columbia*, has been the BC naturalist's Bible for 40 years and his suggestions about the local plant life are worth noting.

"Cathedral Park is in the dry interior where the weather is dependable. Towards the end of July and into the first week in August there is a very fine wildflower display. Meadows and swales are bright with lupine, Indian paintbrush, wood betony and veronica. Shrubby cinquefoil, a plant with flowers that look like buttercups, grows in dense masses on some of the slopes.

"White heather and red heather come into bloom just as the peak of the flowers is passing. On the higher elevations all of the plants are adapted to harsh weather and press close to the ground. Many have small hairy leaves to resist water evaporation. Willow grows only an inch or two high, yet in the spring it flaunts pussy willows that rival those growing on large shrubs."

High mountain lakes.

According to local historians, Indians who lived along the Similkameen and Ashnola Rivers knew of these high mountain lakes long before the arrival of the fur traders. They came here in summer to trap hoary marmots, from which they made valuable blankets. An International Boundary Survey recorded these magnificent mountains and sparkling lakes for the first time in 1860. Cathedral Mountain, from which the area gets its name, was named in 1901 by Carl and George Smith because it looked "something like a big church."

Cathedral Lakes Lodge and the provincial park owe their humble beginnings and preservation to two men with foresight and determination. Herb Clark of Keremeos fell in love with the land as a young man of 19. He then went to work in the mines to save money to purchase his dream. In 1934, with about $500 saved, he purchased two parcels of land from the British Columbia government. One parcel was located on Quiniscoe Lake and the other between Glacier and Pyramid Lakes. Next he established a horseback guiding service.

Chess Lyons, then head of British Columbia's three-man Parks Branch, first visited the area about five years after Herb Clark bought his land: "Jim McKeen (Mt. McKeen), a schoolboy friend, swears I was in there in 1939, but I can't remember," writes Chess Lyons in a November, 1991 letter. "I did go in with Joe Harris Herb's partner in 1941, had a good look around and recommended it for a provincial park. However, the Forest Service thought there was timberland involved and put a hold on it for many years.

"About 1944, Herb and I rode in, climbed about everything in sight, then made a packhorse trip into the back country. I took 16 mm color film and much of it was used in various films I put together.

"Then Ruth Kirk and I did another trip and made a short film for CBC's Klahanie. The Gehringers were building the lodge at that time."

Herb Clark, with partners Tom Fleet and Karl and Helmut Gehringer, formed Cathedral Lakes Resort Ltd. in 1964. Work on a private road was completed in 1965 and construction was started on the present buildings.

Park established in 1968.

Cathedral Provincial Park was officially established in 1968, nearly 30 years after Chess Lyons made his recommendations. According to Lyons, "Geologically, the park is fascinating and presents many facets. Except for the highest peaks, glaciers of the last ice age have rounded the mountain slopes. As the glaciers receded, the ice on the northern slopes lingered and created large bowls called cirques. This was done by a long process of water melting and

Fig 53:
Giant's Cleft. © Murphy Shewchuk

then freezing in the rock beneath, breaking them apart. The volcanic nature of some of the mountains is demonstrated in the Devil's Fenceposts which are symmetrical columns now twisted and bent but resembling a huge piling of wood. In Stone City (or Hamburger City) there are most unusual formations of rocks shaped into massive discs. They are considered so unusual that a geologist did his Master's thesis on them. At the Giant Cleft you will find a split in the rock face of the mountain caused by some tremendous forces of the past. Geologists believe the impressive cleft was caused by the erosion of an intrusion of softer rock. Smokey the Bear is another impressive rock formation close by. In silhouette, it appears as a gigantic replica of the forest-fire-fighting ursine complete with his forest ranger hat. It's a picture you can't duplicate."

Cathedral Provincial Park is indeed a picture you can't duplicate. It is a unique piece of British Columbia that offers those unable to spend a day of hard slogging the opportunity to explore this wilderness on the same footing as those better able to surmount the challenge of getting there. Once at camp, whether the lodge or the nearby park campgrounds, the irresistible draw of the Giant's Cleft, alpine wildflowers and turquoise lakes beckons everyone. Go prepared to enjoy Nature at her finest and toughest. Don't forget your boots, warm clothing, slicker and water bottle. Above all, don't forget your film.

•••

57
Information Sources

Apex Mountain Resort
PO Box 1060,
Penticton BC, Canada V2A 7N7
Tel: 1 800 387 2739
Fax: (250) 292 8622
Snow phone: (250) 492 2880

Back Country Horsemen
c/o Jim McCrae,
494 - 256 St.,
Aldergrove, BC V4W 2H8
Tel: 604 856-5477

BC Parks
Okanagan District,
PO Box 399,
Summerland, BC V0H 1Z0
Tel: (250) 494-6500

BC Parks
West Kootenay District,
RR 3, 4750 Highway 3A,
Nelson, BC V1L 5P6

Beaver Lake Mountain Resort
6350 Beaver Lake Road,
Winfield, BC V4V 1T5
Tel: (250) 762-2225

Big White Ski Resort,
P.O. Box 2039 Stn. R.,
Kelowna, BC V1X 4K5
Tel: (250) 765-3101
Fax: (250) 765-8200
www.bigwhite.com

Cathedral Lakes Lodge
Site 4, Comp 8
Slocan Park, BC V0G 2E0
Tel: (250) 226-7560
Fax: (250) 354-0230

Reservations 1-888-255-4453

Central Okanagan Regional District
1450 KLO Road
Kelowna, BC
Tel: (250) 763-4918

Chute Lake Resort
RR1, Site 16, Comp 16,
Naramata, BC V0H 1N0
Tel: (250) 493-3535
Fax: (250) 496-4017
E-Mail: chutelake@vip.net

Hatheume Lake Resort
PO Box 490,
Peachland, BC V0H 1X0
Tel: (250) 767-2642

Kelowna Visitor Info Centre
544 Harvey Avenue,
Kelowna, BC V1Y 6C9
Tel. (250) 861-1515
Fax: (250) 861-3624

Merritt Forest District,
PO Box 4400,
Merritt, BC V1K 1B8
Tel: (250) 378-8400
Fax: (250) 378-8481
Toll Free 1-800-665-1511

Mount Baldy Ski Area,
c/o Borderline Ski Club,
PO Box 1528,
Oliver, BC V0H 1T0
Tel: (250) 498-2262

Nickel Plate Cross Country Ski Club
PO Box 27,
Penticton, BC V2A 6J9.

North Okanagan Cross-Country Ski
Club,
PO Box 1543,
Vernon, BC V1T 8C2

O'Keefe Ranch
PO Box 955, Highway 97,
Vernon, BC V1T 6M8
Tel: (250) 542-7868

Oliver Visitor Info Centre
36205 - 93rd Street
PO Box 460,
Oliver, BC V0H 1T0
Tel: (250) 498-6321
Fax: (250) 498-3156

Osoyoos Business and Community
Development Centre
PO Box 500
Osoyoos, BC V0H 1V0
Tel: (250) 495-3366

Osoyoos Visitor Info Centre
PO Box 227,
Osoyoos, BC V0H 1V0
Tel: (250) 495-7142
Fax: (250) 495-6161
Toll Free 1-888-676-9667

Pacific Agri-Food Research Centre
4200 Highway 97
Summerland, BC V0H 1Z0
Tel: (250) 494-7711

Penticton Forest District
102 Industrial Place
Penticton, BC V2A 7C8
Tel: (250) 490-2200
1-800-661-4099

Salmon Arm Forest District
PO Box 100, Stn Main
Salmon Arm, BC V1E 4S4
Tel: (250) 833-3400

Silver Star Mountain Resort,
PO Box 2,

Silver Star Mountain, BC V0E 1G0
Tel: (250) 542-0224

Summerland Visitor Info Centre
15600 Highway 97
Box 1075,
Summerland, BC V0H 1Z0
Tel: (250) 494-2686
Fax: (250) 494-4039

Thompson Okanagan Tourism Associa-
tion,
1332 Water Street,
Kelowna, B.C, V1Y 9P4
Tel: (250) 860-5999
Fax: (250) 860-9993

Trans Canada Trail Project
c/o Bill Archibald,
24208 - 102nd Ave.,
Maple Ridge, BC V2W 1J1
Tel: (604) 463-9586

Vernon Forest District
2501 - 14th Avenue
Vernon, BC V1T 8Z1
Tel: (250) 558-1700

Vernon Tourism
PO Box 520,
6326 Highway 97 North,
Vernon, BC V1T 6M4
Tel: (250) 542-1415
Fax: (250) 542-3256
Reservations only: 1-800-665-0795
E-Mail: <verntour@junction.net>

Western Canada Wilderness Committee
Kelowna Branch
Box 28082
East Kelowna, BC V1W 4A6
Tel: (250) 765-5883

Weyerhaeuser Canada Ltd.
Maple St.
Okanagan Falls, BC V0H 1R0
Tel: (250) 497-8211

58
Bibliography

Barlee, N.L. *Gold Creeks and Ghost Towns*. Hancock House Publishers Ltd., Surrey, BC 1988.

Burbridge, Joan. *Wildflowers of the Southern Interior of British Columbia and adjacent parts of Washington, Idaho and Montana*. University of British Columbia Press, Vancouver, BC 1989.

Christie, Jack. *Inside Out British Columbia*. Raincoast Books, Vancouver, BC 1998.

Falk, Les. *Hiking Trails in the Okanagan*. Mosaic Enterprises Limited, Kelowna, BC 1982.

Hatton, William J. *Bridesville Country: A Brief History*. Oliver Printing, Oliver, BC 1981.

Hayman, Bob. *RMH - Memoirs of Bob Hayman*. Gordon Hayman, Peachland, BC 1991.

Hill, Beth. *Exploring the Kettle Valley Railway*. Polestar Press, Winlaw, BC 1989.

Langford, Dan & Sandra. *Cycling the Kettle Valley Railway*. Rocky Mountain Books, Calgary, AB 1997.

Lyons, C.P. *Trees, Shrubs and Flowers to know in British Columbia*. Toronto, ON. 1952.

McLean, Stan. *The History of the O'Keefe Ranch*. Stan McLean, Vernon, BC 1984.

McNeil, Holly and Dona Sturmanis. *Okanagan Secrets & Surprises*. Okanagan Editions, Winfield, BC 1995.

Nanton, Isabel and Mary Simpson. *Adventuring in British Columbia*. Douglas & McIntyre, Vancouver, BC 1996.

Neering, Rosemary. *A Traveller's Guide to Historic British Columbia.* Whitecap Books, Vancouver, BC 1993.

Peachey, Gordon. *The Okanagan.* Gordon Peachey, Kelowna, BC 1984.

Peachland Memories, Volume One. Published by the Peachland Historical Society, Box 244, Peachland, BC, V0H 1X0 1983.

Peachland Memories, Volume Two. Published by the Peachland Historical Society, Box 244, Peachland, BC, V0H 1X0 1983.

Read, Stanley E. *A Place Called Pennask.* Mitchell Press, Vancouver, BC 1977.

Sanford, Barrie. *McCulloch's Wonder: The Story of the Kettle Valley Railway* Whitecap Books, North Vancouver, BC 1977.

Shewchuk, Murphy O. *Backroads Explorer Vol. 2 Similkameen & South Okanagan.* Hancock House Publishers Ltd. Surrey, BC 1988.

Shewchuk, Murphy O. *Coquihalla Country: An Outdoor Recreation Guide.* Sonotek Publishing Ltd. Merritt, BC 1990 (revised 1998).

Shewchuk, Murphy O. *Exploring the Nicola Valley.* Douglas & McIntyre, Vancouver, BC 1981.

Shewchuk, Murphy O. *Fur, Gold & Opals.* Hancock House Publishers Ltd. Surrey, BC 1975.

Stewart, Dave. *Okanagan Back Roads: Volume 2 North Okanagan - Shuswap.* Saltaire Publishing Ltd. Sidney, BC 1975.

Surtees,Ursula. *Kelowna: The Orchard City.* An Illustrated History. (includes Partners in Progress by Mark Zuehlke). Windsor Publications, Ltd. 1989.

Vernon Outdoors Club. *Hiking Trails.* Vernon Outdoors Club, Vernon, BC 1989

Woolliams, Nina G. *Cattle Ranch: The Story of the Douglas Lake Cattle Company.* Douglas & McIntyre, Vancouver, BC 1979.

•••

59
Index

60
About The Authors

Fig 54:
Judie Steeves

Judie Steeves

Judie Steeves has been both writing about and enjoying the outdoors for most of her life. Although she was born on British Columbia's coast, her family moved inland to Penticton in 1952, where she grew up. As a youngster she loved fishing with her Dad on Okanagan Lake and dozens of small lakes hidden in the hills around the Okanagan Valley. With her Mom she learned to identify and appreciate the native wildflowers, bushes and trees that dot the hillsides and adorn the shores of the Okanagan.

She began camping as a girl through the Guiding movement. She then honed her outdoors skills as an adult exploring the wild nooks and crannies of this province with her husband Dennis Vergnano and their two daughters, Gillian and Emily.

Her writing career began at the Penticton Herald in 1967, proofreading copy and writing teen news, then continued under Nick Russell in Vancouver City College's journalism program, from which she graduated in 1970.

She later worked as editor of the weekly Delta Optimist, and as a reporter for the now-defunct daily Columbian Newspaper in New Westminster.

After several years in public relations at Lower Mainland colleges and UBC, she moved with her young family to the Cariboo where they lived in the wilderness. While there she worked with the BC CattleBelles to produce a cookbook called Beef Recipe Round-up.

She returned to the Okanagan in 1986. Judie has been a reporter at the Kelowna Capital News since 1991, starting her weekly outdoors column "Trail Mix" in 1993.

In 1998 she was presented with the BC environment minister's award, and she has received several awards from the BC and Yukon Community Newspapers' Association for her writing.

•••